Digital Video Essentials
Apple Final Cut Pro 6

LISA RYSINGER

DELMAR
CENGAGE Learning

Australia • Brazil • Japan • Korea • Mexico • Singapore • Spain • United Kingdom • United States

**Digital Video Essentials:
Apple Final Cut Pro 6**
Lisa Rysinger

Vice President, Career and Professional
Editorial: Dave Garza

Director of Learning Solutions: Sandy Clark

Acquisitions Editor: James Gish

Managing Editor: Larry Main

Product Manager: Nicole Calisi

Editorial Assistant: Sarah Timm

Vice President, Career and Professional
Marketing: Jennifer McAvey

Marketing Director: Debbie Yarnell

Marketing Manager: Erin Brennan

Marketing Coordinator: Jonathan Sheehan

Production Director: Wendy Troeger

Production Manager: Stacy Masucci

Senior Content Project Manager:
Kathryn B. Kucharek

Cover Designer:
Bruce Bond

Senior Art Director: Joy Kocsis

Technology Project Manager:
Christopher Catalina

Production Technology Analyst:
Thomas Stover

Library of Congress Control Number: 1401877915

ISBN-13: 978-1-4018-7791-0

ISBN-10: 1-4018-7791-5

Delmar
5 Maxwell Drive
Clifton Park, NY 12065-2919
USA

Cengage Learning products are represented in Canada by Nelson Education, Ltd.

For your lifelong learning solutions, visit **delmar.cengage.com**

Visit our corporate website at **cengage.com**.

Notice to the Reader
Publisher does not warrant or guarantee any of the products described herein or perform any independent analysis in connection with any of the product information contained herein. Publisher does not assume, and expressly disclaims, any obligation to obtain and include information other than that provided to it by the manufacturer. The reader is expressly warned to consider and adopt all safety precautions that might be indicated by the activities described herein and to avoid all potential hazards. By following the instructions contained herein, the reader willingly assumes all risks in connection with such instructions. The publisher makes no representations or warranties of any kind, including but not limited to, the warranties of fitness for particular purpose or merchantability, nor are any such representations implied with respect to the material set forth herein, and the publisher takes no responsibility with respect to such material. The publisher shall not be liable for any special, consequential, or exemplary damages resulting, in whole or part, from the readers' use of, or reliance upon, this material.

Printed in Canada
1 2 3 4 5 XX 12 11 10 09 08

Table of Contents

Preface

About This Text

Digital Video Essentials: Apple Final Cut Pro 6 is a concise, step-by-step guide to editing with the industry's program of choice, Apple's award-winning Final Cut Pro. Essential to both the digital video novice and the professional, this comprehensive book covers the important features that editors need to get up and running quickly. By using a clear, straightforward approach, supported with full-color visuals, *Digital Video Essentials: Apple Final Cut Pro 6* guides editors through the software's features and teaches them how to manage this powerful program. It also features Noise Industries's FxFactory Pro, the new effects suite that will revolutionize how editors create with Final Cut Studio. Complete with a DVD packed with resources, tutorials, a trial version of FxFactory, special offers, and more, *Digital Video Essentials: Apple Final Cut Pro 6* is the essential DV book for the essential DV program.

Textbook Organization

Chapter 1: Digital Video Fundamentals

Chapter 1 provides an overview of digital video, explaining its terminology, concepts, and techniques. It discusses the history and evolution of digital video, as well as how digital video is used today in broadcast television, filmmaking, multimedia, and the Internet.

Chapter 2: Digital Video and Apple Inc.

Chapter 2 discusses Apple's contributions to the field of digital video and provides an overview of Apple's entire digital video product line. It will also examine the features of Final Cut Pro and how it is used professionally in the industry.

Chapter 3: Getting Started with Final Cut Pro

Chapter 3 provides an introduction to Final Cut Pro. The workspace will be examined, including the Browser, Viewer, Canvas, and Timeline windows. Audio and video settings, user preferences, and system settings will be discussed. Chapter 3 will also examine how to import audio, video, and still images into Final Cut Pro. Projects, sequences, bins, media files, and clips will also be addressed.

Chapter 4: Capturing Video

Chapter 4 discusses scratch disks, device control software, how to calculate hard disk space, and how to connect FireWire devices, such as video cameras and decks. The Log and Capture window will be examined. Setting in and out points and capturing clips will be demonstrated. Batch capturing and capturing entire tapes will also be discussed.

Chapter 5: Basic Editing Techniques

Chapter 5 examines basic editing techniques in Final Cut Pro, like adding clips to the sequence, changing a clip's in and out points, and cutting a clip using the Razor Blade tool. Navigating the sequence, linking and unlinking clips, working with multiple tracks, using markers, creating a freeze frame, and changing a clip's speed will also be demonstrated.

Chapter 6: Creating Video Transitions

Chapter 6 examines how to create video transitions in Final Cut Pro. The different categories of transitions, such as Dissolves, Wipes, and Irises, will be discussed. Adding, adjusting, and rendering transitions will be demonstrated. Third-party transitions from Noise Industries will also be showcased.

Chapter 7: Using Layers and Transparency

Chapter 7 examines the techniques for working with layers in Final Cut Pro. Alpha channels, mattes, masks, transparency, and composite modes will be discussed. Working with layered Photoshop files will also be addressed.

Chapter 8: Adding Motion

Chapter 8 discusses techniques for creating motion in Final Cut Pro. Applying motion to still images using keyframes will be demonstrated. Working with multiple video tracks will be examined. Topics include rotation, scale, center, anchor point, cropping, distortion, and motion blur.

Chapter 9: Creating Effects Using Video Filters

Chapter 9 examines techniques for creating effects in Final Cut Pro. Applying and controlling video filters will be demonstrated. The different filter categories such as Blurs, Color Correction, and Stylize will be discussed. Third-party transitions from Noise Industries will also be showcased. Apple's professional color grading and finishing application Color will be discussed.

Chapter 10: Creating Titles and Graphics

Chapter 10 discusses how to create titles and graphics in Final Cut Pro. Basic principles such as action and title safe areas, broadcast safe colors, and using sans-serif fonts will be addressed. Final Cut Pro's text generators and third-party text generators will be demonstrated. LiveType and Motion will be examined.

Chapter 11: Working with Audio and Music

Chapter 11 examines how to work with audio in Final Cut Pro. The Voice Over Tool, audio transitions, audio filters, and levels will be demonstrated. Soundtrack Pro will be discussed.

Chapter 12: Rendering and Exporting

Chapter 12 discusses how to render and export video in Final Cut Pro. Supported video and formats and compression options will be examined. Exporting using QuickTime Conversion will be demonstrated. Compressor and DVD Studio Pro will be examined. Backing up and archiving finished work will also be addressed.

Glossary

This book has a comprehensive glossary of terminology, which includes traditional video, computer, and digital video terms.

DVD

This book features a DVD, which includes resources, tutorials, a trial version of FxFactory, product information, special offers, and more! Take a closer look at how Noise Industries is harnessing the power of Apple's hardware and software to expand the effects capabilities of Final Cut Pro. Learn troubleshooting techniques for Final Cut Studio. Discover resources for digital video related books, magazines, websites, mailing lists, groups and organizations, developers, educational classes, seminars, and workshops.

Features

The following list provides some of the salient features of the text and DVD:

- *Objectives clearly state the learning goals of each chapter.*
- *Color photographs and illustrations supplement the text throughout.*
- *Review questions and exercises reinforce the material presented in each chapter.*
- *Industry professionals discuss in exclusive interviews how they use Final Cut Pro.*
- *Other applications in Final Cut Studio are examined in the Spotlight segments.*
- *FxFactory Pro, a revolutionary visual effects suite created by Noise Industries for Final Cut Studio, is showcased.*
- *Industry terms are bolded throughout the text as they are introduced and listed in the Glossary for easy reference.*
- *A DVD, which includes resources, tutorials, a trial version of FxFactory, product information, special offers and more, is included.*

How to Use This Text

The following features can be found throughout this book:

Objectives

Objectives start off each chapter. They describe the competencies that readers should achieve upon understanding the chapter material.

OBJECTIVES

Understand scratch disks and device control

Learn how to connect a capture device

Examine the Log and Capture window

Learn how to log footage by setting in and out points

Learn how to capture individual clips, batch capture multiple clips, capture video without using timecode, and capture entire tapes

---

Notes and Tips

Notes and Tips provide special hints, practical techniques, and information to readers.

TIP ✪ *You can also hit the Space Bar on your keyboard to start or stop playing a clip.*

 VTR stands for videotape recorder—a video camera or deck with timecode.

Sidebars

Sidebars appear throughout the text, offering additional valuable information on specific topics.

Digital Video Discs, DVDs

*A **DVD**, or **digital video disc** (sometimes called digital versatile disc), is a storage medium that will hold gigabytes of information on a single disc. It has enough space to include an entire feature-length film with superior picture quality and sound, not to mention lots of extra footage! The first generation of DVDs can store between 4.7 GB and 8.5 GB per disc; however, the next generation of high-definition DVDs can hold between 15 GB and 50 GB per disc.*

DVDs are available in a variety of formats, many of which can be played on both a computer and a standalone DVD player. Current DVD formats include DVD-R, DVD-RW, DVD+R, DVD+RW, DVD-RAM, HD-DVD, and Blu-ray DVD.

Spotlights

Special Spotlight segments are featured throughout the text and include interviews featuring successful industry professionals using Final Cut Pro, Noise Industries's FxFactory Pro, a revolutionary visual effects suite for Final Cut Studio, and other Final Cut Studio applications like LiveType, Motion, SoundTrack Pro, Color, Compressor, and DVD Studio Pro.

SPOTLIGHT

FIG-03-20 Jeff Greenberg is the president of the Philadelphia Final Cut Pro Users Group and the principal instructor for Future Media Concepts.

Jeff Greenberg

OCCUPATIONS: principal instructor, Future Media Concepts; president, Philadelphia Final Cut Pro User's Group; Freelance Colorist, Consultant, Editor

JOB DESCRIPTIONS: As the principal instructor of the nation's largest media training group, I teach intensive classes (two to three 8-hour days) and speak at national conferences, such as NAB. I primarily teach high-end editing software to professionals in the field, helping them become better at their jobs. As the

Keyboard Shortcuts

Keyboard Shortcuts are listed at the end of each chapter, when needed, to provide readers with quick and easy access to new material as it is learned.

 KEYBOARD SHORTCUTS

Final Cut Pro > Audio/Video Settings	*Option-Command-Q*
File > New Project	*Shift-Command-N*
File > Save Project As	*Shift-Command-S*
Final Cut Pro > User Preferences	*Option-Q*
Sequence > Settings	*Command-0 (zero)*
Final Cut Pro > System Settings	*Shift-Q*
View > Clip in Editor	*Option-Return*
Final Cut Pro > Easy Setup	*Control-Q*
Sequence > Render All > Both	*Option-R*
Sequence > Render Selection > Both	*Command-R*
Window > Arrange > Standard	*Control-U*
File > New Bin	*Command-B*
File > New Sequence	*Command-N*
File > Import > Files	*Command-I*

Review Questions and Exercises

Review Questions and Exercises are located at the end of each chapter and allow readers to assess their understanding of the text. Exercises are intended to reinforce chapter material through practical application.

 REWIND

1. What is QuickTime, and how has it advanced digital video technology?
2. What is FireWire, and how has it impacted digital video?
3. What is the SuperDrive, and how has it influenced DVD authoring?
4. How is Final Cut Pro used professionally?
5. What are Apple's consumer DV products?
6. What is Compressor?
7. What is Motion?
8. What is Soundtrack Pro?
9. What is DVD Studio Pro?
10. What is Color?

 TAKE TWO

1. Visit Apple's website at www.apple.com/quicktime. Study and describe the many ways QuickTime can be used. Be sure to look at the QuickTime tutorials.
2. Search Apple's website for interviews with industry professionals using Final Cut Pro for film and broadcast television.
3. Visit Apple's website at www.apple.com/retail. Locate the website of an Apple retail store near you. Check their calendar of events for DV-related workshops and seminars. Or visit www.apple.com/usergroups to find a users' group meeting in your area.

Author Lisa Rysinger and her Rhodesian Ridgeback, Zulu.

About the Author

Lisa Rysinger is the owner of VIDE Productions, Inc., a digital video production company that produces everything from corporate training videos to television commercials, as well as multimedia and DVDs. Ms. Rysinger has taught digital video at the college level for over five years. She has a bachelor's degree in Radio, Television, and Film and a master's degree in Writing from Rowan University where she graduated with honors. Ms. Rysinger recently founded the South Jersey Digital Video Users Group. Her other affiliations include the Philadelphia Final Cut Pro Users Group, the Macintosh Users Group of Southern New Jersey, and the South Jersey Apple Users Group. In addition to this text, Ms. Rysinger is the author of *Exploring Digital Video,* which is currently in its second edition. Her upcoming titles include *Digital Video Essentials: Adobe After Effects* and *Digital Video Essentials: DVD Authoring.* She also serves as a digital video consultant and conducts group lectures and seminars. Ms. Rysinger has been featured in numerous interviews, including articles in the *New York Times* and the *Philadelphia Inquirer.*

The Learning Package

This instructor's CD was developed to assist instructors in planning and implementing their instructional programs. It includes PowerPoint presentation slides, answers to the questions in the text, course syllabi, exams, and more.
ISBN- 1401877923

Acknowledgments

I'd like to thank the following people at Delmar Cengage Learning for their unwavering support and expertise: Jim Gish, Senior Acquisitions Editor; Nicole Calisi, Product Manager; Kathryn Kucharek, Senior Content Product Manager; Sarah Timm, Editorial Assistant; Sandy Clark, Director of Learning Solutions; Larry Main, Managing Editor; Stacy Masucci, Production Manager; Andi Majot, Content Project Manager; and everyone else at Delmar Cengage in production, marketing, and sales for all your hard work. Special thanks to John Bryan for serving as my technical editor and Mardelle Kunz, the world's greatest copyeditor! I'd also like to thank the following professionals for taking the time out of their busy schedules to participate in the Spotlight segments: Gabriele de Simone, Noise Industries; John Bryan, Independent Video Producer; Jeff Greenberg, President, Philadelphia Final Cut Pro Users Group; and Tiffani Sherman, Video Producer, Multijurisdictional Counterdrug Task Force Training Program at St. Petersburg College. Finally, special thanks to my family and friends for your continued motivation and support.

Questions and Feedback

Delmar Cengage Learning and the author welcome your questions and feedback. If you have suggestions that you think others would benefit from, please let us know and we will try to include them in the next edition.

To send us your questions and/or feedback, you can contact the publisher at:

Delmar Cengage Learning
Executive Woods
5 Maxwell Drive
Clifton Park, NY 12065
Attn: Media Arts and Design Team
800-998-7498

Or the author at:
DVessentials@vide.com

Dedication

This book is dedicated to digital video editors everywhere—keep shaping reality until it's perfect!

CHAPTER **1**

Digital Video Fundamentals

OBJECTIVES

Learn how digital video differs from analog video

Understand the principles and technologies used in digital video editing

Discover what factors influence file size in digital video

Learn the conventions used to create digital video for broadcast, multimedia, and the Internet

Find out how digital video has influenced television and filmmaking

DIGITAL VIDEO TECHNOLOGY is hot right now. In addition to the DVD craze, everybody wants to learn how to connect their digital camcorder to their computer and edit video. But not so long ago, this concept was a revolutionary one. Video and computers used to be two very distinct technologies. When the television and the computer were each created, no one anticipated they would one day merge. But that is in fact what did happen. Slowly each field began to overlap a little more. Now you can surf the Internet on your TV, or use a computerized **digital video recorder (DVR)** to record hours and hours of programming without videotape. Video has evolved into digital video, or DV. But in order to truly grasp digital video, we must first understand traditional video technology.

FIG-01-01 Digital video editing has never been easier on the Macintosh. This laptop computer communicates directly with this Sony digital video camera using Apple's FireWire technology.

Traditional Analog Video vs. Digital Video

Traditional video uses an **analog** signal, which is an electrical signal that fluctuates exactly like the original signal it is mimicking. **Digital video, or DV,** converts the analog signal into binary form, which is represented by a series of zeros and ones. Think of the analog video signal as a language, like English, and the digital video signal as Spanish. Traditionally, video cameras were only analog, and therefore only spoke English. In order to be able to communicate with the computer, which only spoke Spanish, a video card had to be used to convert the analog signal into a digital signal, or English into Spanish. Today's video cameras are digital and no longer require a video card to act as a translator.

Analog videotape has been around for quite some time. Even though the analog broadcast signal will be completely replaced by the digital broadcast signal in 2009, millions of people have been using analog video equipment for years, and it will take some time before analog videotape is phased out completely. Analog videotape formats, such as Betacam SP, are still being used in the professional arena, and many consumers still use VHS tapes. Therefore, you can expect to see both the analog and the digital videotape formats coexist in the foreseeable future, even though digital is now the preferred format.

The Video Signal

To edit digital video successfully, it is important to understand the technical aspects of video. The video signal itself is broken down into two parts: chrominance and luminance. **Chrominance** is the color portion of the video signal. Red, green, and blue, or **RGB,** are the three additive primary colors used to construct a video image. All the other colors are created from these three. Print media, on the other hand, uses **CMYK:** cyan, magenta, yellow, and black. **Luminance** is the black-and-white portion of the video signal, or its lightness and darkness values.

A **component** video signal is a broadcast-quality signal, in which the red, green, blue, and luminance portions are kept separate. An **S-video** signal separates the chrominance and luminance portions. In a **composite** video signal, the chrominance and luminance portions are blended together.

A component video signal is the highest-quality video signal because it has the least amount of interference. It is used professionally. However, digital television sets, DVD players, and DVRs are now bringing the component video signal to high-end consumers. S-video is used at the prosumer level. Newer video cameras, VCRs, and television sets offer S-video. The composite video signal is the lowest-quality video signal because it has the most interference. Most older consumer TVs, VCRs, and video cameras only have a composite signal.

TIP ✪ *Prosumer* *is a cross between professional and consumer. Some high-end consumer camcorders would be considered prosumer because they offer more features than typical consumer cameras, but not as many features as professional cameras.*

THE VIDEO SIGNAL

CONSUMER	PROSUMER	PROFESSIONAL
Composite	S-Video	Component
1 cable	1 cable	4 cables
Chrominance & Luminance are blended	Chrominance & Luminance kept separate	Chrominance (3) Red Green Blue
		Luminance (1)

The NTSC Video Standard

When a video signal is broadcast in the United States, it must adhere to a set of standards that was set forth by the **NTSC (National Television Standards Committee).** While the NTSC video standard is prevalent in North America, it is not the only video standard used worldwide. Other countries throughout the world use **PAL (Phase Alternate Line)** or **SECAM (Systeme Electronique Pour Couleur Avec Memoire).** PAL is used in the United Kingdom, Western Europe, and Africa. SECAM is used in France, Russia, and Eastern Europe.

The NTSC video standard requires that the video signal be broadcast at 525 horizontal lines of resolution and at 30 (29.97) **frames per second,** or **fps.** Video, like motion picture film, is really a set of still images recorded and played back in rapid succession. In video, there are 30 frames, or still images, in one second. Motion picture film runs at 24 fps.

The NTSC video standard has 525 horizontal lines of resolution. The video image is reproduced on the TV screen by scanning these lines of resolution in two separate passes. Each pass is referred to as a **field.** The odd lines are scanned first, and the even lines are scanned second. These two fields combine to form one **frame** of video. The method of combining two fields to form a frame is called **interlaced** video. Hence, the television set is interlaced. The computer monitor, on the other hand, is **noninterlaced,** or **progressive.** The computer monitor draws all its lines of resolution in a single pass. Then it goes blank for a fraction of a second before it draws the next frame.

A computer monitor uses **pixels,** or a series of small blocks, to draw a video image. A standard analog video image is 640 pixels wide by 480 pixels high. This width to height proportion of the video frame is called an **aspect ratio.** The current NTSC video standard has a 4:3 aspect ratio. Think of the television set as a rectangle that is four units wide and three units high. It doesn't matter if it's a 13-inch TV or 27-inch TV; the aspect ratio is still 4:3.

 The current NTSC standard will be phased out by 2009 in favor of a new digital standard.

FIG-01-02

Aspect Ratio

Standard Television 4:3

(4 units wide)

1	2	3	4
2			
3			

(3 units high)

Linear Editing vs. Nonlinear Editing

Traditional video editing is called **linear editing.** In linear editing, the video program is edited consecutively from beginning to end. One or more video decks—the source decks—play the original videotape from the video camera, and a second video deck—the record deck—records the selected shots onto the master, or edited, videotape. **Nonlinear editing,** on the other hand, is nonconsecutive in nature. The differences between linear editing and nonlinear editing can be clearly illustrated by using the analogy of an audio cassette tape and an audio compact disc, or CD.

An audio cassette tape is linear. To get to the fifth song on an audio cassette tape, you have to fast-forward through songs one, two, three, and four. An audio CD is nonlinear. Theoretically, it takes the same amount of time to get to the fifth song as it does to the first, the second, the third, or the tenth.

Nonlinear, or digital video, editing has several distinct advantages over linear editing. It is faster. Changes are easier to make. Therefore, editors have more creative freedom arranging their shots. They can easily change the editing order of their shots to see which arrangement they like best.

Another advantage of digital video is that it does not suffer from generation loss because the video signal is binary. **Generation loss** is the degradation of image quality caused by the duplication of an analog videotape. If you take a VHS tape and make a copy of it and then make a copy of your copy, the third generation tape has an inferior picture quality when compared with the first generation tape. Conversely, with digital video you can copy a digital video file over and over again, and the last image will be identical in quality to the first one.

Analog videotape is also prone to drop out. **Drop out** occurs when video information is missing on the tape, which in turn causes a white streak to appear. While digital video still records a digital signal onto tape, the digital format is more durable.

Advantages of Digital Video Editing

- *Editing is faster*
- *Changes are easier to make*
- *Allows more creative freedom*
- *Doesn't suffer generation loss*
- *Less prone to drop out*

Digital Video, DV

Digital video was revolutionized on the Macintosh computer platform with the advent of QuickTime, a type of software compression that shrinks the size of digital video files. Avid Technology was the company that pioneered the digital video,

FIG-01-03 Today's DV software makes video editing easier than ever before. Changes can be made with just a click of the mouse.

or nonlinear editing system, and it still has a strong presence in the digital video industry today. This new style of editing video on the computer was called nonlinear editing in the professional arena. When it originated in the consumer realm it was known as **desktop video.** As the computer technology continued to evolve, the gap between nonlinear editing and desktop video began to decrease. The term digital video was coined. Today, professional editing systems have become quite affordable, and many freelancers have entered the digital video market.

The Principle of Random Access

The founding principle of digital video technology is called random access (not to be confused with RAM, random-access memory). The principle of **random access** states that it takes the same amount of time to get to any one point. In linear editing, shot A is followed by shot B, which is followed by shot C, etc. Any changes to the consecutive order of the edited shots are time consuming and difficult to make. However, in nonlinear editing, because of the principle of random access, shots A, B, and C can be rearranged quickly and easily with the click of a mouse.

FireWire

Digital video technology really started to take off when Apple Computer invented **FireWire,** or **IEEE 1394,** a protocol that allows digital video cameras and computers to transmit digital video signals back and forth. FireWire replaced the need for the traditional video card to digitize video, or convert the analog signal into binary form.

FireWire is Apple Computer's trade name for the interface IEEE 1394. It is an international standard that allows high-speed connections and transfer rates between a computer and peripherals.

 *IEEE stands for the **Institute of Electrical and Electronics Engineers.***

Because digital video cameras already record the video signal in digital form, there is no need to translate it "from English into Spanish." The digital signal is

FIG·01·04 The four-pin end of this FireWire cable connects to a digital video camera, while the six-pin end plugs into the computer.

then transferred from the digital video camera into the computer via FireWire. All the major electronics manufacturers, like Sony and Panasonic, adopted FireWire technology. Today, FireWire comes standard with every model of Macintosh computer and is an option on many PCs.

Digital Video Cameras and Tape Formats

So, just how is an image actually recorded on a video camera? Video cameras use a **CCD,** or **charge-coupled device,** which is a computer chip that converts the optical image into electrical impulses. The number and size of the CCDs directly correlate to image quality. Most consumer videotape formats have one CCD, or computer chip, that processes the three primary colors of the video signal. Three-CCD, or three-chip, cameras have one chip for the color red, one chip for the color green, and one chip for the color blue. Prosumer and professional cameras usually have three CCDs. The size and type of chips account for the differences in price and quality. The bigger the CCD is, the higher the resolution and the more expensive the camera will be.

FIG-01-05 This prosumer digital video camera by Sony uses three CCDs.

Because the consumer digital video format offers high picture quality at a fraction of the cost of similar analog cameras, it is no surprise that the digital video standard has been so widely embraced. Mini-DV and Digital-8 are both consumer digital videotape formats. In the prosumer realm, Sony's DVCAM and Panasonic's DVCPRO are both popular digital videotape formats. They have superior resolution when compared to consumer digital video. The professional digital video cameras use larger and more expensive CCDs, and are, therefore, quite costly. Sony's Betacam SX, JVC's Digital-S, and Panasonic's DVCPRO 50 are all professional digital videotape formats.

DIGITAL VIDEOTAPE FORMATS

CONSUMER	PROSUMER	PROFESSIONAL
Mini-DV	DVCAM	Betacam SX
Digital-8	DVCPRO	Digital-S
		DVCPRO 50

Timecode

*Most digital video cameras can read and write **timecode**, which is an electrical signal that assigns a numerical address to every frame of the videotape. Timecode is measured in and displayed as Hours: Minutes: Seconds: Frames. Higher-end models offer selectable functions that give the users options to control how the timecode is recorded.*

*There are two types of timecode in digital video editing: drop frame and nondrop frame. **Drop-frame timecode** is 29.97 frames per second, and the numbers are separated using semicolons (00;00;00;00). **Nondrop-frame timecode** is 30 frames per second, and it uses all colons to separate the numbers (00:00:00:00). Final Cut Pro displays drop-frame timecode differently from other programs; it only uses the semicolon to separate the seconds and frames (00:00:00;00).*

Digital Video Cards

Capturing video is a lot easier today than it used to be, due to the creation of FireWire (IEEE 1394). However, the advent of FireWire did not lead to the extinction of the traditional **digital video card,** which translated the analog video signal into digital form, rather it led to its evolution. There is a new generation of video cards that do more than just convert the analog signal into a digital one. These new video cards, with both analog and digital video support, offer multiple layers of real-time video editing. **Real-time** means that special effects created in popular video editing software programs, such as basic transitions, motion, and transparency, no longer have to be rendered before they can be previewed on the computer screen.

 Apple's Final Cut Pro supports numerous real-time filters and effects by utilizing RT Extreme, a technology that takes advantage of Apple's hardware and operating system.

A **render** is the process the computer takes to carry out a particular set of instructions or tasks. The term render is commonly used to refer to the high-end calculations required to edit digital video or create 3D animation. Typically, in digital video editing, special effects like transitions, filters, motion, and transparency require time to render.

A **transition** is a special effect, such as a dissolve or wipe, which appears while you are transitioning from one video clip to another. A **filter** manipulates the video's individual pixels, usually by altering its color. **Motion** can be applied to a video image, a photograph, a title, or a still image or graphic. Motion can zoom in and out, pan left and right, and rotate. **Transparency** shows several images at the same time by using different techniques to combine multiple layers into a single layer of video. These effects can be programmed in popular video editing software, may or may not

FIG-01-06 In digital video editing, most special effects like transitions, filters, motion, and transparency require time to render.

be previewed in real-time, and typically require additional time to render before the movie can be outputted.

Many of these video cards also support a second computer monitor and an NTSC video monitor for previewing and playing the video. Without a video card, a FireWire camera must be attached to the computer while editing in order to view the video in its actual resolution. Many professional digital video editors will purchase one of these new video cards because the added features will save time and money. The next generation of video cards can range in price from hundreds of dollars to thousands of dollars. Manufacturers of popular video cards for the Macintosh include Avid, AJA Video Systems, and Black Magic Design.

Digital Video Standard

Digital video technology is revolutionizing the industry. Originally, a consortium of ten prominent electronics companies came together to develop the digital video standard: Sony, Panasonic, JVC, Hitachi, Sanyo, Sharp, Mitsubishi, Toshiba, Philips, and Thompson.

They set forth the standard for two types of digital video: SD, standard definition, and HD, high definition (HDTV). The standard DV cassette has 482 horizontal lines of resolution and can record for up to 270 minutes. It uses a digital component signal that is comparable to Betacam SP. Standard DV uses a 5:1 data compression ratio and a type of MPEG 2 video codec.

 Codec is short for Compression/Decompression.

Digital Video Discs, DVDs

*A **DVD**, or **digital video disc** (sometimes called digital versatile disc), is a storage medium that will hold gigabytes of information on a single disc. It has enough space to include an entire feature-length film with superior picture quality and sound, not to mention lots of extra footage! The first generation of DVDs can store between 4.7 GB and 8.5 GB per disc; however, the next generation of high-definition DVDs can hold between 15 GB and 50 GB per disc.*

DVDs are available in a variety of formats, many of which can be played on both a computer and a standalone DVD player. Current DVD formats include DVD-R, DVD-RW, DVD+R, DVD+RW, DVD-RAM, HD-DVD, and Blu-ray DVD.

FIG-01-07 This first-generation DVD-R disc works with Apple's SuperDrive and has a capacity of 4.7 GB.

Compression and Sampling

Whether you are using FireWire or one of the newer generations of video cards, the digital video files are compressed using a codec. A **codec** is a mathematical algorithm used to decrease the file size of a video image. Because digital video files are so large, they need to be compressed to make them more manageable.

Typically, a high-quality, five-minute digital video clip, compressed using the **DV-NTSC** codec, will occupy over one gigabyte of hard drive space. There are many different types of codecs; *MPEG* and *Cinepak* are two popular ones. Cinepak was often used for CD-ROMs, while MPEG is used for DVDs.

When the digital video signal is recorded, the video information is sampled and compressed. Again, there are two parts of a video signal: the chrominance, or color portion, and the luminance, or black-and-white portion. There are two primary methods for sampling the data: digital component 4:2:2 and digital component 4:1:1.

Luminance and Color Difference Components (Y, R-Y, B-Y)

The luminance portion of the video signal is designated by the letter Y. The chrominance portion of the video signal is divided into two parts: the CR component R-Y and the CB component B-Y. These sampling methods yield a total bit rate, which is measured in megabits per second, Mb/s.

DIGITAL COMPONENT 4:2:2

Pixels $\times$ Lines $\times$ FPS $\times$ 8 = Total Bit Rate

Y Luminance: $720 \times 482 \times 30 \times 8 = 83$ Mb/s
CR Component: $360 \times 482 \times 30 \times 8 = 41.5$ Mb/s
CB Component: $360 \times 482 \times 30 \times 8 = 41.5$ Mb/s

Total Bit Rate = 166 Mb/s

DIGITAL COMPONENT 4:1:1

Pixels $\times$ Lines $\times$ FPS $\times$ 8 = Total Bit Rate

Y Luminance: $720 \times 482 \times 30 \times 8 = 83$ Mb/s
CR Component: $180 \times 482 \times 30 \times 8 = 20.75$ Mb/s
CB Component: $180 \times 482 \times 30 \times 8 = 20.75$ Mb/s

Total Bit Rate = 124.5 Mb/s

File Size

Every pixel in a frame of digital video contains information. In a standard 720×480 frame, there are over 300,000 pixels. Keep in mind that there are 30 (29.97) frames in a single second of video. It is easy to understand why the file sizes in digital video are so huge, running hundreds of megabytes, even gigabytes, depending upon the length and quality of the video clip. Compared to the size of a word processing document, digital video files are enormous. Editing digital video is one of the most taxing things you can do on a computer. Huge amounts of information must be processed, and large files are created and moved regularly.

There are three primary factors that determine file size in digital video: resolution, frame rate, and color depth. **Resolution** is the size of the video frame, which is measured in pixels. **Frame rate** is the number of frames that are displayed in one second of video, which is measured in frames per second (fps). Finally, **color depth** is the number of colors represented in a video image, which is measured in bits. Audio is also relevant to the size of a digital video file; however, it is much smaller in comparison to the video portion. Nevertheless, it becomes an issue when smaller file sizes are imperative.

Digital Video Conventions

There are typical conventions for creating digital video for broadcast, multimedia, and the Internet. Most digital video programs come with presets that automatically determine the appropriate video and audio settings for each project. However, these settings can be customized if need be. Therefore, it is important to understand what the typical conventions are and how to manipulate them with regard to file size.

Standard Broadcast and Prosumer

There are two primary resolutions in use today for standard broadcast digital video. The resolution for video that was originally shot on an analog video camera is 640 × 480 pixels. The resolution for video that was originally shot on a digital video camera is 720 × 480 pixels. Both resolutions are also referred to as **full-screen video.**

The frame rate for standard broadcast digital video is 30 (29.97) frames per second. This is also referred to as **full-motion video.** Video for broadcast television must have 32-bit color depth. Waveform monitors and vectorscopes are professional test equipment used to measure the quality of video signals. If you were creating a commercial for television, this equipment would be used to test the video signal before it was broadcast.

 *A **waveform monitor** measures the luminance portion of the video signal, and a **vectorscope** measures the chrominance portion of the video signal.*

Full-screen, full-motion video that is not intended for broadcast is typically 24-bit color. This is often the standard for industrial or prosumer digital video. Typically, standard broadcast and prosumer quality audio is either 48 kHz (digital) or 44 kHz (analog), 16-bit stereo.

	STANDARD BROADCAST	PROSUMER
Video		
Resolution	720 × 480 pixels (digital) 640 × 480 (analog) 72 dpi	720 × 480 pixels (digital) 640 × 480 (analog) 72 dpi
Frame Rate	30 (29.97) fps	30 (29.97) fps
Color Depth	32-bit	24-bit
Audio		
Sample Rate	48 kHz (digital) 44 kHz (analog)	48 kHz (digital) 44 kHz (analog)
Sample Size	16-bit	16-bit
Channels	2, Stereo	2, Stereo

Multimedia

The standards for multimedia are far more flexible than they are for broadcast. It depends entirely upon the device playing the video, be it a hard drive, CD drive, iPod, cell phone, or other device. The most conventional multimedia option is for video playback on the computer.

Computers with faster processors, faster drives, and a lot of RAM will play larger digital video files more smoothly than slower, older systems. Typically, digital video to be played on the average computer is often created as quarter-screen video, although many newer systems are capable of playing back full-screen video. The resolution for quarter-screen video is usually either 320 × 240 pixels (analog) or 360 × 240 pixels (digital).

The frame rate for multimedia is often 15 frames per second. However, this may be increased to 30 frames per second if the computer system the digital video will be played upon is fast enough. It is less taxing to increase the frame rate to full motion than it is to increase the resolution to full screen, so that is usually increased first. Color depth for multimedia is usually 16-bit, but it can sometimes be increased to 24-bit. Color depth can be adjusted by using the quality slider when compressing digital video. Multimedia audio is typically 48 kHz or 32 kHz (digital), or 44 kHz or 22 kHz (analog), 16-bit stereo.

MULTIMEDIA (COMPUTER)	
Video	
Resolution	360 × 240 pixels (digital) 320 × 240 pixels (analog) 72 dpi
Frame Rate	15 fps or 30 fps
Color Depth	16-bit or 24-bit
Audio	
Sample Rate	32 kHz or 48 kHz (digital) 22 kHz or 44 kHz (analog)
Sample Size	16-bit
Channels	2, Stereo

The Internet

Because some people still connect to the Internet via phone lines, using large digital video files on the Internet is not always a viable option. There are two basic methods for transmitting video over the Internet: downloadable video or streaming video.

With **downloadable video,** a copy of the entire digital video movie is downloaded to the user's computer. Files are larger and this option takes longer to download, but one advantage is that the user has a copy of the digital video movie. The movie file remains on the user's computer until it is deleted. Some downloadable video can be configured to start playing while the actual download is still taking place. This is called a **fast-start** or a **progressive download.**

A second alternative is to stream the video over the Internet. **Streaming video** temporarily loads the video onto the user's computer, frame by frame, while it plays. Files are smaller and this option is faster, but the digital video file is not actually downloaded onto the computer's hard drive and cannot be saved and played back. The quality of streaming video is usually lower than downloadable video.

Typical video resolutions for the Internet are varied. They can be as small as 160 × 120 pixels (analog) or as large as 400 × 300 pixels, as long as the original aspect ratio of the video is preserved. Frame rate is often 10 frames per second and color depth can be as low as 8-bit. Audio for the Internet can be as low as 8 kHz, 8-bit mono, but can also be as high as 48 kHz (digital), 16-bit stereo, especially if audio quality is a priority.

	INTERNET (LOW BANDWIDTH)	INTERNET (HIGH BANDWIDTH)
Video		
Resolution	180 × 120 pixels (digital) 160 × 120 pixels (analog) 72 dpi	360 × 240 pixels (digital) 320 × 240 pixels (analog) 72 dpi
Frame Rate	6, 8, or 10 fps	15 or 30 fps
Color Depth	8-bit	16-bit
Audio		
Sample Rate	8, 11, or 16 kHz	22, 32, 44, or 48 kHz
Sample Size	8-bit	16-bit
Channels	1, Mono	2, Stereo

Digital Television, DTV

Digital television (DTV) is a new broadcasting standard that encompasses digital standard-definition television (SDTV) and high-definition television (HDTV). The **Federal Communications Commission (FCC)** is the government body responsible for making the laws regarding television broadcasts. They have mandated that the analog video signal will be completely phased out by 2009 and replaced with DTV.

Standard-definition television (SDTV) is the new broadcast digital signal that will replace the traditional analog NTSC video standard. It will be available in either standard 4:3 or widescreen 16:9 aspect ratio, but not high definition.

High-definition television (HDTV) is the digital television video standard that offers high-resolution video and surround-sound audio. The aspect ratio for high-definition television is 16:9. It can be one of two resolutions: 1280 × 720 pixels (progressive) or 1920 × 1080 pixels (interlaced). Because of the increased aspect ratio, HDTV has a superior picture quality, emulating motion picture film. HDTV is quickly gaining in popularity. Many television stations, including the major networks, are broadcasting portions of their prime time programming in HDTV. CBS was the first network to begin broadcasting a daytime soap opera, *The Young and the Restless*, in HDTV. Home Box Office, HBO, now offers a high-definition channel HBO, which airs the same programming twenty-four hours a day as regular HBO. Other premium channels have followed suit. Recently, HDTV sets have dropped substantially in price and are becoming more and more affordable.

 Some channels now offering HD programming include ABC, CBS, Cinemax, Discovery, ESPN, FOX, HBO, National Geographic, NBC, Showtime, Starz, TNT, WB, and WHYY.

Aspect Ratio

FIG-01-08

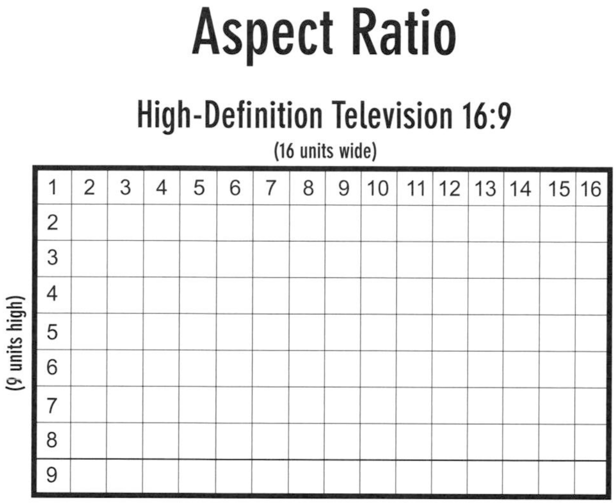

High-Definition Television 16:9

(16 units wide)

High-Definition Video, HDV

*Another exciting development regarding HDTV technology is the creation of a new prosumer format called **high-definition video**, or **HDV**. The HDV specification uses MPEG-2 encoding to record 16:9 high-definition video onto a standard Mini-DV tape and then stream it across standard FireWire (IEEE 1394) interfaces. This technology, dubbed "HD for the masses," opens the door to prosumers by allowing them to create high-definition video for under $4,000.*

In May 2003, JVC was the first manufacturer to offer HDV technology with the GR-HD1 video camera. It records 720 progressive at a resolution of 1280 x 720 pixels at 30 full frames per second. Sony soon followed in November 2004 with the HDR-FX1 video camera. Sony's camera uses a different HD recording mode, which is also approved under the HDV specification. The HDR-FX1 records 1080 interlaced at a resolution of 1440 x 1080 pixels at 60 half frames per second. Sony is also offering DV-HDV videotape for improved performance with the HDR-FX1.

➤ *The HDV specification supports MPEG-2 compressed video at one of two possible resolutions; 720p (1280 x 720 progressive) has a data rate of approximately 19 Mbps, and 1080i (1440 x 1080 interlaced) has a data rate of approximately 25 Mbps. Note that 1080i for HDTV is actually 1920 x 1080 pixels.*

FIRST-GENERATION HDV CAMERA SPECIFICATIONS

CAMERA	JVC GR-HD1	SONY HDR-FX1
Recording Mode	720p	1080i
Resolution	1280 × 720 pixels	1440 × 1080 pixels
Frame Rate	30 progressive	60 interlaced
CCDs	1 @ 1.18 MP each	3 @ 1 MP each
Optical Zoom	10×	12×
Light Sensitivity	35 Lux	3 Lux

Digital Filmmaking

Another venue that can be attributed to the recent advances in digital video technology is **digital filmmaking.** Many budding filmmakers are turning to digital video to make their film aspirations a reality; it has become a cost-effective alternative to those with a story to tell.

Typically, filmmakers shoot digital video, edit it on the computer, and then pay to have their movies transferred to either 16 mm or 35 mm film. New models of digital video cameras, which shoot at *either* 30 fps or 24 fps, are aimed specifically at digital filmmakers. Digital video cameras are much more affordable to shoot with, compared to the high costs of shooting, developing, and editing film.

> Star Wars: *Episode II* Attack of the Clones *was the first major motion picture to remain digital from beginning to end. It was shot on special high-definition cameras, edited digitally at Industrial Light and Magic, and shown in select theaters outfitted with new digital projectors.*

Shooting HDTV, editing it on the computer, and later transferring it to film is currently a good way to rival film's quality. And, as the technology continues to evolve, it will become even more affordable.

FIG-01-09 Digital filmmaking cameras give independent filmmakers an inexpensive alternative to shooting on film.

Summary

Computer technology has revolutionized the way we edit video. Digital video has made video editing faster, easier, and superior in every way. But more importantly, it has opened the door to a whole new generation of video editors. Virtually anyone can pick up a digital video camera, connect it to a home computer, and start editing video. However, the difference between an amateur digital video editor and a professional one is still distinct; experimenting with the technology is fun, but truly grasping it requires dedication, perseverance, and hard work.

 **REWIND**

1. Define digital video.
2. What is the difference between linear editing and nonlinear editing?
3. What is the principle of random access?

4. Name three advantages of digital video editing.
5. What is FireWire (IEEE 1394), and why is it important?
6. Explain the difference between composite and component video signals.
7. What is the NTSC video standard?
8. What is the difference between interlaced and noninterlaced?
9. What three factors influence file size in digital video?
10. What are the conventions for creating digital video for broadcast? For multimedia? For the Internet?

TAKE TWO

1. Make flash cards to help yourself learn new terminology. Write any terms you are not familiar with on the front of 3 × 5 index cards and their definitions on the back. Then quiz yourself until you are familiar with all the terminology. Separate any terms that you are having trouble remembering into a pile and spend some extra time focusing specifically on those terms.
2. Make two columns on a piece of paper, one for digital video and one for analog video. Write down everything you learned from this chapter. Compare and contrast their similarities and differences.
3. Make three columns on a piece of paper: one for broadcast, one for multimedia, and one for the Internet. Then number one to three under each column. Determine the three factors that determine file size in digital video. Using these factors, list the conventions for broadcast, multimedia, and the Internet. Be specific!

CHAPTER 2

Digital Video and Apple Inc.

FROM THE MAC'S breakout in 1984, epitomized by the famous commercial rallying against Big Brother, to the sheer power of today's Mac Pro and the sleek design of the 30-inch Cinema display, Apple has always been on the cutting edge of computer technology. Along the way, Apple has also innovated and defined numerous advances in digital video technology, including QuickTime and FireWire.

Today, Apple offers a complete digital video product line, from its iLife applications like iMovie and iDVD, which are geared to consumers, to its award-winning Final Cut Pro, which is embraced by industry professionals everywhere.

Apple's Advances in Digital Video Technology

While the speed of Apple's processors, coupled with the optimized power of Final Cut Pro, is a digital video editor's dream, DV on the Mac had a much more modest beginning. It began in 1991 with **QuickTime,** Apple's enabling software that allows other applications to handle multimedia files.

QuickTime

First there was QuickTime. Long before Apple had its own DV applications, it created QuickTime, the technology that allowed other software programs to work with video, audio, and animation files. It was the foundation for digital video on the Mac. All the early digital video editing applications utilized QuickTime's multimedia architecture, including Avid's Media Composer and Adobe Premiere.

FIG-02-01

Over the years, QuickTime has evolved from an enabling technology to multiple, full-blown multimedia applications. QuickTime Pro is a media authoring program that can edit movies, create slide shows, convert over a dozen file formats, and prepare video for the Internet, a mobile phone, or an iPod—all for just $29.99. QuickTime Player is a free application that plays video, audio, QuickTimeVR, and graphics files. QuickTime Streaming Server is a free, open source application that delivers real-time or on-demand media over the Internet. Finally, QuickTime Broadcaster is a program used for broadcasting live events.

FIG-02-02 With QuickTime Pro, editors can add special effects to their movies.

Whether it was NASA using QuickTime VR technology to showcase the Pathfinder's first panoramas of Mars over the Internet, or Grandma editing movies of the grandkids, complete with snazzy filters and effects, QuickTime has become synonymous with digital video on the Mac. Today, there are hundreds of millions of computer users around the world using QuickTime on both their Macs and their PCs.

FireWire (IEEE 1394)

Then there was FireWire. Apple invented FireWire, and in 1995, the Institute of Electrical and Electronics Engineers defined it as IEEE 1394. FireWire is a high-speed, cross-platform protocol that can move large amounts of data between computers and peripheral devices. The first standard had transfer rates up to 400 megabits per second; today FireWire is in its second generation, doubling that rate to 800 megabits per second. Major manufacturers employ FireWire in their multimedia devices, including digital video cameras and decks, digital video recorders, even music systems and cable set-top boxes. Today, FireWire is integrated into every model of Macintosh computer.

 Sony calls its IEEE 1394 interface i.LINK.

FireWire revolutionized digital video editing by replacing the need for the digital video card to convert analog video. Instead, digital video cameras equipped with FireWire could transfer DV directly to the computer, and vice versa. In fact, FireWire technology became so important to the industry, it received a Primetime Emmy Engineering Award in 2001 from the National Academy of Television Arts and Sciences.

FIG-02-03 This first-generation FireWire cable has a transfer rate of up to 400 megabits per second.

 In 2004, at NAB (National Association of Broadcasters) in Las Vegas, Apple and Panasonic announced the world's first direct digital transfer of 100 Mbps DV-HD (high-definition video) over FireWire.

The SuperDrive

And then there was the SuperDrive. In 2001, Apple began shipping the **SuperDrive,** a combination CD-RW/DVD-R drive that could read and write both CDs and DVDs. In fact, DVDs burned on the SuperDrive could be played back on most consumer DVD players.

Unveiled at the 2001 Macworld Expo in San Francisco, the SuperDrive made its debut alongside the free consumer DVD authoring program, iDVD, and the professional DVD authoring program, DVD Studio Pro. For the first time, both consumers and professionals could cost-effectively create professional-looking DVDs on the Mac.

➡ *Today's 16x SuperDrive supports CD-R, CD-RW, DVD-R, DVD+R, DVD-RW, DVD+RW, and DVD+R DL discs.*

FIG-02-04 Apple unveiled the first SuperDrive in January 2001 at the Macworld Expo in San Francisco; it now ships standard or as an option throughout Apple's entire computer lineup.

The iPod

In 2001, Apple released the first iPod, which went on to become the fastest selling music player in history. Together, the iPod and iTunes, which is Apple's online music store, transformed the music industry. But it didn't stop there. The iPod evolved to eventually play photos and video, too. Today hundreds of television shows and movies are available to purchase from the iTunes store and can be played on video iPods.

FIG-02-05 The iPod evolved to play photographs and video, in addition to music. *Image courtesy of Maria Arguello, Apple User Group Regional Liaison for the Northeast United States and Bill Achuff, Achuff Photography.*

Apple TV

After selling millions of downloads of movies and TV shows through the iTunes store, Apple capitalized on that success by creating Apple TV in 2007—a device that allows users to wirelessly watch all their iTunes content on their widescreen televisions. Viewers can sit back and browse through their entire digital media collection on their TV sets with just a click of the Apple Remote.

The iPhone

Apple broke new ground again in 2007 by introducing the iPhone—a revolutionary new mobile phone that is also a widescreen video iPod and has full web browsing and e-mailing capabilities. It supports 640 × 480 pixel video at 30 frames per second with 48 kHz stereo audio. From QuickTime to the iPhone, Apple continues to lead the digital video revolution.

Apple's Digital Video Programs

Despite QuickTime's creation in 1991, it wasn't until 1999 that Apple officially launched its very own digital video product line. Digital video editing programs iMovie and Final Cut Pro were released in 1999, courting both consumers and professionals respectively. DVD authoring applications iDVD and DVD Studio Pro followed shortly thereafter, in 2001. Final Cut Express was released in 2003, as a midrange alternative to the award-winning Final Cut Pro. Then Apple unveiled Motion in 2004, its state-of-the-art, real-time motion graphics application. In 2005, the first version of Final Cut Studio shipped, bundling Apple's professional applications at a substantially discounted price. And in 2007, Apple unveiled Color, its new professional color grading and finishing application.

FIG-02-06

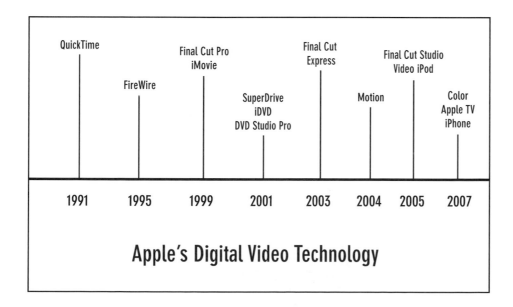

Apple's Digital Video Technology

iMovie HD

FIG-02-07

iMovie introduced the average Mac user to digital video. Beloved by students, parents, and DV hobbyists, iMovie blasted out of the gate in 1999 and has shown no signs of slowing down. In fact, it is as popular today as ever. And **iMovie HD** now supports HDV.

iMovie is digital video editing made simple. To get started, all you need is iMovie, a Mac, and a digital video camera with FireWire. iMovie's trademark is its simplicity—simply use FireWire to connect your DV camera to your Mac and start editing. It truly is plug and play. Most Mac users can get up and running in iMovie with little effort.

FIG-02-08 With its simplicity, iMovie has turned many Mac users into digital video editors, including students, teachers, small business owners, even grandparents.

iDVD

FIG-02-09

When it was released in 2001, **iDVD** became the perfect companion to iMovie. What better way for amateur moviemakers to showcase their work than on DVD, the most popular consumer electronics product of all time? Bundled free with every SuperDrive, iDVD immediately became a powerful application by providing the average computer user with the ability to easily create professional-looking DVDs that will play in most consumer DVD players.

FIG-02-10 iDVD debuted alongside Apple's SuperDrive in 2001 as an simpler alternative to DVD Studio Pro. The ability to select from professional-looking themes and iDVD's drag-and-drop simplicity helped revolutionize DVD authoring.

Final Cut Express HD

FIG-02-11

With iMovie on the consumer end and Final Cut Pro on the professional end, Apple did not have a midrange digital video editing program until it introduced Final Cut Express in 2003. Targeted primarily at prosumers, **Final Cut Express HD** uses the same interface as its award-winning counterpart Final Cut Pro and offers many high-end features at the midrange price of $299. Voted the "Best Editing Value" by *Videomaker* magazine, Final Cut Express is now garnering its own share of the spotlight.

FIG-02-12 Final Cut Express offers more professional features than iMovie and is aimed at advanced digital video hobbyists.

Final Cut Studio

FIG-02-13 Final Cut Studio 2 includes Final Cut Pro 6, Soundtrack Pro 2, Compressor 3, DVD Studio Pro 4, Motion 3, and Color.

Final Cut Studio offers users all the professional digital video editing applications bundled together at a discounted price. When it was first released in 2005, you could still purchase Final Cut Pro independently from Final Cut Studio, but that is no longer the case. Now in its second version, **Final Cut Studio** includes Final Cut Pro 6, Soundtrack Pro 2, Compressor 3, DVD Studio Pro 4, Motion 3, and Color. Apple's Final

Cut Studio 2 retails for $1,299; upgrades can be purchased from previous versions of Final Cut Pro for $699 or from Final Cut Studio for $499. More information and resources can be found on Apple's website at www.apple.com/finalcutstudio.

Final Cut Pro

FIG-02-14

Industry professionals are using Final Cut Pro more and more every day. From broadcast news and promotional segments to television shows like *The Closer,* editors love **Final Cut Pro** as a fast, high-performance, and affordable real-time DV editing solution. Final Cut Pro has made inroads in the film community as well, with independent films like *Napoleon Dynamite* and Hollywood blockbusters like *Cold Mountain.*

Likewise, freelance editors and small production companies also rely on Final Cut Pro as a cost-effective and competitive nonlinear editing solution. Larger post-production houses use Final Cut Pro to create everything from music videos to infomercials, while videographers use it to create corporate and industrial videos with

FIG-02-15 Apple's Final Cut Pro is widely used and respected throughout the industry.

high-quality content under strict budgetary constraints. Even event videographers use Final Cut Pro to create wedding and special event videos, taking advantage of the same high-end features to give their businesses the competitive edge. Regardless of the market, Final Cut Pro has found its place among industry pros demanding high-end, cutting-edge technology at a price they can afford.

 Now, in addition to an Emmy, Apple's digital video editing program Final Cut Pro has won numerous awards, including recent recognition from the National Association of Broadcasters, DV *Magazine, Computer Graphics World, and EMedia.*

Broad Format Support

One reason Final Cut Pro is such a powerful program is because of its ability to create high-quality video in a variety of formats. Because Final Cut Pro is designed around a resolution-independent architecture, it can easily work in either standard-definition (SD) or high-definition (HD) digital video for both NTSC and PAL. It supports a variety of frame rates and resolutions, including 1080i, 1080p, and 720p HD video.

*Final Cut Pro uses broadcast-quality codecs, supporting 8-bit and 10-bit uncompressed video for both standard-definition and high-definition. With version 6, Apple introduced **ProRes 422**, a new format that offers uncompressed HD quality at SD file sizes. And with the new open format Timeline, you can mix and match source material from different formats and even different frame rates.*

FIG-02-16 Using Final Cut Pro, you can export your video using dozens of different codecs.

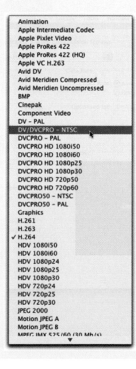

Real-Time Effects

*Final Cut Pro is powered by RT Extreme with Dynamic RT, so you can have real-time performance for DV, SD, HDV, and HD video. Apple's **RT Extreme** technology harnesses the power of the Mac OS and its hardware to preview more than 150 effects in real-time for both SD and HD. RT Extreme also supports multiple streams of video simultaneously. **Dynamic RT** automatically analyzes your system and adjusts your video's quality and frame rate as it plays. And with Apple's new **FxPlug** standard, third-party developers can create hundreds of real-time, hardware accelerated plug-ins for Final Cut Pro.*

FIG-02-17 Thanks to Apple's FxPlug standard, third-party developers can offer additional filters like these supplied by Noise Industries.

LiveType

FIG-02-18

*In addition to its high-end editing features, Final Cut Pro also includes **LiveType**, which creates professional-quality titles and graphics. LiveType features **LiveFonts,** which are 32-bit animated fonts that make use of color and motion. It also comes with **FontMaker,** a utility to create your own animated fonts.*

You can save valuable time by applying customizable motion behaviors such as fades, zooms, and rotations to regular fonts. LiveType also gives you keyframe and timing controls for even greater flexibility. Hundreds of royalty-free textures and graphics can be integrated into LiveType animations, providing endless possibilities. And with LiveType, you can individually manipulate each character of the text, rather than being forced to work with entire blocks of text.

Finally, LiveType is compatible with all QuickTime supported file formats. It supports different resolutions and frame rates, including SD, HD, NTSC, and PAL. LiveType also works with both TrueType and PostScript fonts.

FIG-02-19 LiveType comes with Final Cut Pro and is used to create animated text and motion graphics.

Cinema Tools

FIG-02-20

*Furthering Final Cut Pro's versatility is the ability to manage film projects; Apple's **Cinema Tools** software tracks the relationship between the original film footage and its respective digital files, allowing frame-accurate, 24-fps editing. It also generates the necessary lists that are required by negative cutters. Editors using Cinema Tools can easily manage projects shot on 16mm or 35mm film, or HD.*

FIG-02-21 Cinema Tools is software included with Final Cut Pro to assist in managing film projects.

Final Cut Pro's versatility and professional high-end features are why editors in video, film, and television all use Apple's Final Cut Pro. Its competitive price and powerful design make it one of the leading nonlinear editing programs in the industry.

 **SPOTLIGHT**

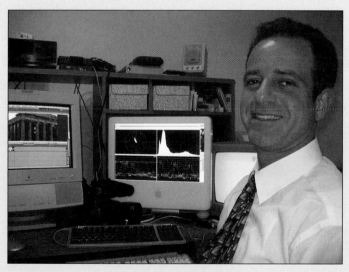

FIG-02-22 John Bryan is an Independent Video Producer in the Delaware Valley.

John R. Bryan

USER GROUP AFFILIATIONS: South Jersey Apple User Group, Philadelphia Final Cut Pro User Group, South Jersey Digital Video Users Group

OCCUPATIONS: Teacher, Independent Video Producer, Still Photographer, Webmaster

NUMBER OF YEARS USING MACS: Ten

NUMBER OF YEARS CREATING DV: Eight

DV PROGRAMS USED: Final Cut Studio, Adobe Premiere, Final Cut Express, iMovie

DIGITAL VIDEO CAMERAS: Sony PD-170, Canon ZR45
MACS YOU CURRENTLY OWN: iMac Intel Core Duo, PowerBook G4 1 GHz with SuperDrive
FAVORITE DV WEBSITE: www.DV.com
FAVORITE MAC WEBSITE: *Wired:* Cult of Mac Blog, www.cultofmac.com
AVERAGE NUMBER OF HOURS YOU USE MACS PER DAY: Twelve

1. As an independent video producer, what type of projects do you edit with Final Cut Pro?

Over the years, I've mainly kept busy by shooting, editing, and producing wedding videos. Increasingly, I'm developing video in other areas, such as creating videos for a local performance artist and creating motion titles and graphics for a local television program. I've also just completed a video in the documentary style for a local chapter of a national philanthropic organization.

2. Why did you select Final Cut Pro over other digital video applications?

I first got interested in digital video by fiddling around with iMovie, which came free with my Macintosh computer. Because I thought it was so cool to be able to do video on the computer, I decided to take some courses in digital video at a local community college. Formally trained using Adobe Premiere, I migrated to Final Cut Pro due to the powerful creative features included, such as LiveType for titling. I also found that Final Cut Pro was fairly simple to use and was tightly integrated with Apple's other fantastic tools, such as Soundtrack and Motion.

3. What are your three favorite features or tools in Final Cut Pro, and why are they your favorites?

One of my favorite features of Final Cut Pro is "nested sequences." I use them all the time to manage scenes and workflow and to cut down on rendering time. I also like Final Cut Pro's color correction tools. I've been able to rescue many a clip with them. Being able to export sequences as reference movies for editing in Apple's other excellent editing applications is also a favorite feature of the program I value. It saves lots of time.

4. How do you use LiveType? What are your impressions of it?

LiveType is a fantastic program that enables you to create sophisticated, broadcast-quality, animated or static titles for your videos. The program includes some really dynamite animated templates, which are easily and endlessly customizable. Whenever I create a title sequence I'm particularly impressed with, I save it as a template so I'll have easy access to it to use as a starting point in a future project. LiveType allows you to keyframe every character of a title for unlimited possibilities. I can't say enough how much I love this program.

5. How do you use Soundtrack? What are your impressions of it?

I've actually been using Soundtrack longer than I've been using Final Cut Pro. I originally started using Soundtrack when it was a standalone program after I saw a demo of it on the Internet. I couldn't believe how easy it was to create your own music! I like how Soundtrack allows you to synch your score perfectly with your video. It comes with some really great loops and sound effects, and it's easy to create your own loops as well. Soundtrack also does a good job at removing audio noise from your video.

6. What other digital video programs do you use and why?

I use iMovie and iDVD quite frequently for my home movies for times when I want to get video quickly off the tape and onto DVD to share with family and friends. I use Motion a lot in my professional work. It's fantastic for easily creating movie-quality motion graphics.

7. If you could change three things about Final Cut Pro, what would they be and why?

I'm pretty satisfied with Final Cut Pro as it is, though if they could come up with a way to make it easier to log and capture footage I'd be happy, as I find logging and capturing a boring and tedious process. Also, I find it sometimes tricky to drag clips onto the Timeline from the Browser. If you're not careful, it's easy to overwrite clips and/or split up clips instead of merely inserting a clip on the Timeline. Another area where improvement could be made is to make it easier to work with chapter markers.

8. What advice would you give an editor who is new to FCP?

I'd say just have fun with the program. The best way to learn anything new, especially in the creative field, is to play. When I began learning Final Cut, I went out on a nature walk with my video camera, shot about twenty minutes of footage, and brought it in to Final Cut Pro and just had fun with it by trying out everything Final Cut offers.

Soundtrack Pro

FIG-02-23

Music is an important element in digital video editing. **Soundtrack Pro** is Apple's standalone music creation program designed to allow editors to score their own video projects. Hundreds of royalty-free audio loops and sound effects can be quickly and easily combined to create original, high-quality, professional soundtracks.

Video can be imported into Soundtrack, providing a visual cue in the scoring process. Other features include the ability to search for music files according to instrument, genre, or mood, and the ability to stretch and resize tracks to match a program's length. You can even import other AIFF, WAV, and Acid loops into Soundtrack; third-party audio loop CDs can also be purchased.

FIG-02-24 Soundtrack Pro is bundled with Final Cut Studio for the creation of musical scores.

Compressor

FIG-02-25

Also included in the software bundled with Final Cut Studio is Apple's professional encoding program, **Compressor.** Whether you plan to distribute media on DVD, iPod, Apple TV, mobile phones, or stream it over the Internet, Compressor supports various formats, including MPEG-2 and H.264. You can automate batch encoding in Compressor by dragging and dropping files and assigning presets. You can also convert standards back and forth between NTSC and PAL. You can even use the included Qmaster application to distribute your encoding across a network of Macs.

 Compressor also creates files for next generation HD-DVD and Blu-ray discs.

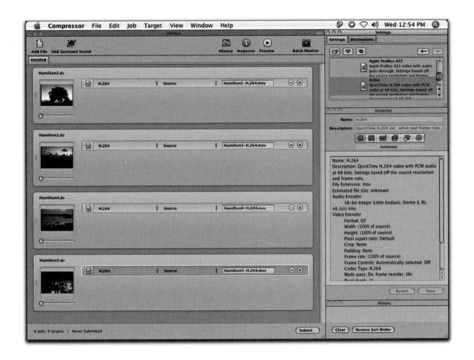

FIG-02-26 Compressor, Apple's professional batch encoding software that is included with Final Cut Studio, offers presets for various industry-standard encoding formats.

DVD Studio Pro

FIG-02-27

When Apple unveiled **DVD Studio Pro** in 2001 and announced that it would be sold for under $1,000, a new era in DVD authoring began. DVD Studio Pro and the SuperDrive set a new standard, putting the industry on notice by making professional DVD authoring on the Mac very affordable.

Today DVD Studio Pro 4 comes bundled with Final Cut Studio 2. You can now burn discs in various formats, including DVD-R, single and dual-layer DVD+R, DVD-RW, DVD+RW, and DVD RAM. DVD Studio Pro 4 also creates disc images for commercial replication for both the traditional red laser and new blue laser formats. Features also include copy protection flags and region encoding.

FIG-02-28 DVD
Studio Pro is used to
author professional
DVDs for business and
entertainment.

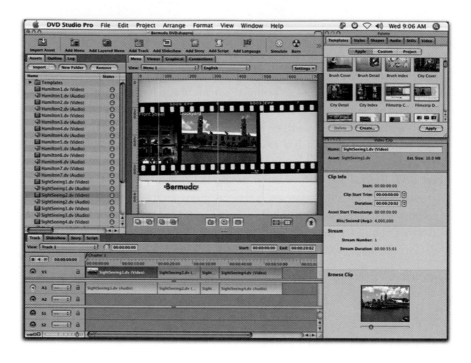

Motion

FIG-02-29

Apple released **Motion** in 2004, its first real-time 3D motion graphics design
program. Motion offers high-performance animation with its intuitive real-time
design environment. Motion 3 includes more than 150 hardware accelerated filters

and effects. It also uses the FxPlug standard, so you can purchase additional effects from third-party developers.

Color

FIG-02-31

In 2007, Apple introduced **Color,** its professional color grading and finishing application. Color creates primary and secondary color grade adjustments for SD, HD, and 2K projects, while letting you preview the results in real-time. You can use Color to create a signature look for a single project or apply that look to multiple projects. It includes more than thirty-five professional effects and more than twenty custom looks. Color also supports third-party plug-ins.

FIG-02-32 Color is Apple's new color grading and finishing program.

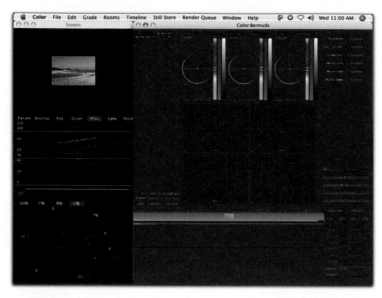

Summary

Regardless of whether you are a digital video hobbyist, a professional, or a student, editing digital video on the Mac has never been more exciting. With integrated technologies like QuickTime, FireWire, and the SuperDrive, digital video enthusiasts have a clear advantage on the Mac. And Apple continues to lead the industry, embracing newer technologies like high-definition video and the Internet, and creating innovative new devices like Apple TV, video iPods, and the iPhone. Combine those technologies with Apple's powerful Final Cut Studio applications, and DV on the Mac becomes an unbeatable combination.

 REWIND

1. What is QuickTime, and how has it advanced digital video technology?
2. What is FireWire, and how has it impacted digital video?
3. What is the SuperDrive, and how has it influenced DVD authoring?
4. How is Final Cut Pro used professionally?
5. What are Apple's consumer DV products?
6. What is Compressor?
7. What is Motion?
8. What is Soundtrack Pro?
9. What is DVD Studio Pro?
10. What is Color?

 TAKE TWO

1. Visit Apple's website at www.apple.com/quicktime. Study and describe the many ways QuickTime can be used. Be sure to look at the QuickTime tutorials.
2. Search Apple's website for interviews with industry professionals using Final Cut Pro for film and broadcast television.
3. Visit Apple's website at www.apple.com/retail. Locate the website of an Apple retail store near you. Check their calendar of events for DV-related workshops and seminars. Or visit www.apple.com/usergroups to find a users' group meeting in your area.

CHAPTER 3

Getting Started with Final Cut Pro

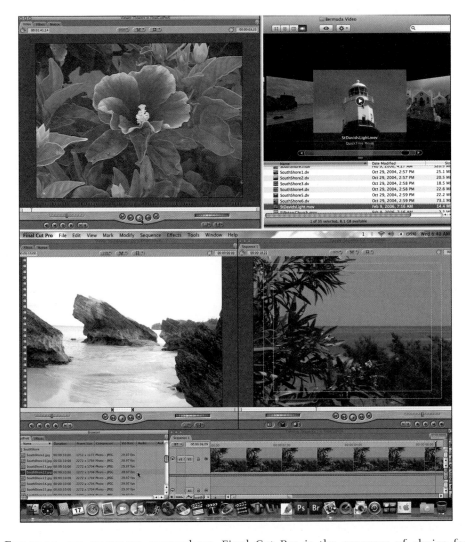

FAVORED BY EDITORS everywhere, Final Cut Pro is the program of choice for professional video editing. Because the program is so powerful, mastering it may seem a bit daunting at first; however, spending the time to become properly acclimated with the interface now will pay dividends later. Understanding Final

Cut Pro's settings and learning how to customize its preferences to best suit your particular editing needs will help you get the most out of this program.

Getting Started

When you launch Final Cut Pro, the External A/V dialog box will appear by default if you do not have a FireWire device, such as a video camera or deck, connected. You will be prompted to check your connections or to continue. Click Continue if you would like to launch Final Cut Pro without a video camera or deck connected. You can always launch Final Cut Pro now, and connect a FireWire device later. If you would like to connect a video camera now, plug the four-pin end of the FireWire cable into the camera and the six-pin end of the FireWire cable into the computer. Then power on the camera and put it into VTR or VCR mode before clicking the Check Again button.

FIG-03-01 If you do not have a video camera or deck connected properly, Final Cut Pro will automatically prompt you to check your connections by default.

TIP ✪ *You can disable the External A/V dialog box by checking the "Do not warn again" option in the lower left corner. You can also select Final Cut Pro > Audio/Video Settings, or press Option-Command-Q on the keyboard. Then check the "Do not show External A/V Device Warning when device not found on launch" option in the A/V Devices tab.*

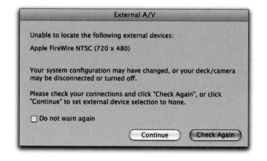

*After you install Final Cut Pro, you will be prompted the first time to select an Easy Setup and set your scratch disk. These settings can be changed later and will be addressed in detail, but you may wish to select a common setup now, such as DV-NTSC, and set your internal hard drive as your scratch disk. An **Easy Setup** is a preconfigured group of settings that allows Final Cut Pro to work with a specific video format. A **scratch disk** is a hard drive that has been designated by a particular software program to store the files created by that program.*

Creating a Project

If this is the first time you launched Final Cut Pro, an untitled project will appear; otherwise, the last project you opened will automatically load by default. If you want to create a new project, select File > New Project from the menu bar, or press Shift-Command-N on the keyboard.

After creating a new project, you can name it and designate a place to save it by selecting File > Save Project As, or by pressing Shift-Command-S. A dialog box will appear so you can choose a name and place to save it on your hard drive.

FIG-03-02 In this example, the file is named SampleProject and is saved in the Final Cut Pro Documents folder, within the user's Documents folder.

 The extension for a Final Cut Pro project file is .fcp.

Organization is especially important when editing digital video. A **project file,** like one created by Final Cut Pro, is typically a small file that acts as a pointer to its source material. **Source files** used in an editing project, such as video, audio, and graphics files, take up large amounts of hard disk space. The project file works in conjunction with the source material in order to preserve hard disk space; it does not replace the need for the original files by incorporating them into itself. If a source file is moved, renamed, or deleted, the project file will notice it is missing. If the source file is not relinked with the project file, the material will be missing from the project.

Therefore, it is especially important to keep track of all the files used in a digital video editing project. Developing and maintaining an organized system is the best way to avoid confusion and mistakes. Digital video editors will often set up hard drives to be used expressly for storing their digital video files. By default, Final Cut Pro stores its files within a series of folders in the user's Documents folder.

TIP ✪ *Name your files distinctly so you can differentiate one project's files from another's. Also try to store all the files for a project in the same place. Avoid using multiple hard drives, folders, and subfolders for the same project. Be consistent and pay attention to where the files are being stored.*

Customizing Preferences and Settings

Final Cut Pro gives the user flexibility and control over how the software operates. You can customize the program's User Preferences, System Settings, and Audio/ Video Settings. **User Preferences** are controls that allow you to customize how Final Cut Pro's features operate. The User Preferences dialog box has six tabs: General, Editing, Labels, Timeline Options, Render Control, and Audio Outputs. To modify the User Preferences, select Final Cut Pro > User Preferences, or press Option-Q.

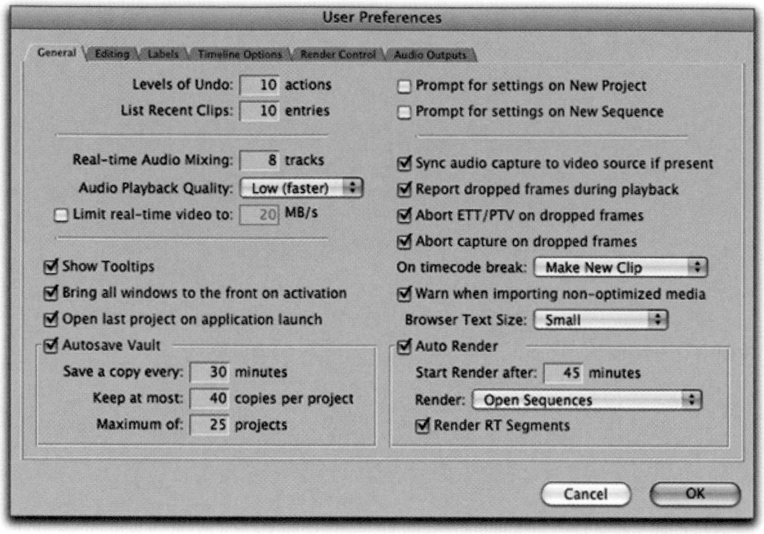

FIG-03-03 In the General tab, you can control how Final Cut Pro launches and creates new projects and sequences. You can customize such features as the levels of undo, settings for a new project, and abort capture on dropped frames.

FIG-03-04 In the Editing tab, you can customize many editing features of Final Cut Pro, such as the duration of still images and dynamic trimming.

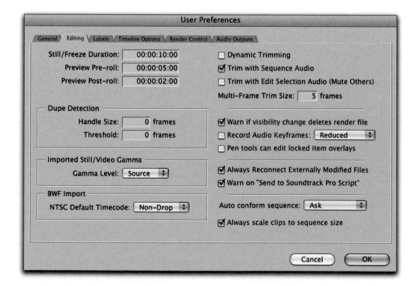

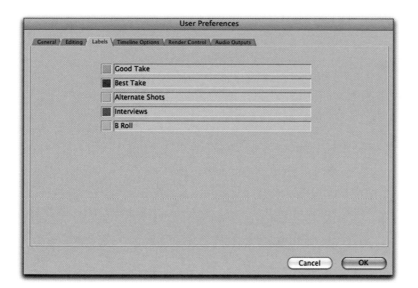

FIG-03-05 In the Labels tab, you can assign custom names, such as Interviews and B-roll, to label colors. Once you customize a label name, it automatically changes in every Final Cut Pro project.

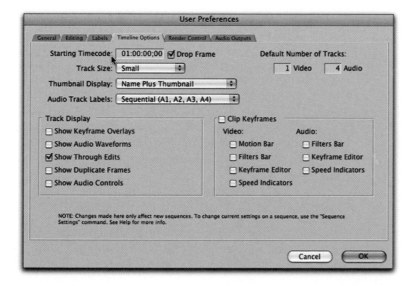

FIG-03-06 In the Timeline Options tab, you can change the way you use the timeline and view sequences by changing options like the starting timecode and the default number of video and audio tracks.

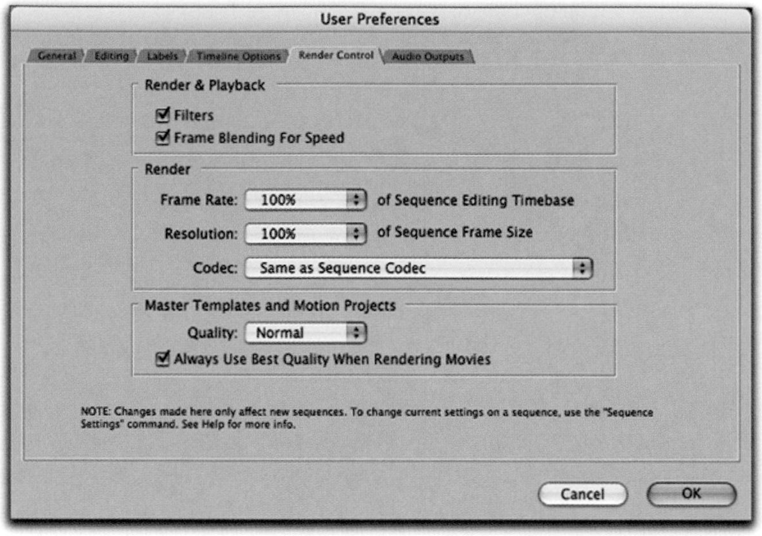

FIG-03-07 In the Render Control tab, you can control the render quality of the new sequences you create in settings such as the default frame rate and resolution.

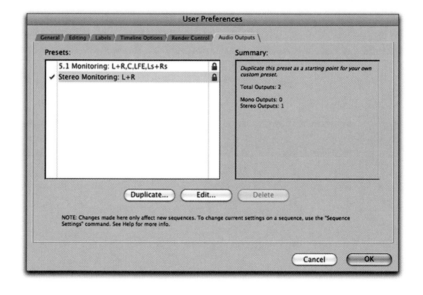

FIG-03-08 In the Audio Outputs tab, Stereo Monitoring is the preset for new sequences in this example.

TIP ✪ *User Preferences controls the preferences for new sequences only. For existing sequences that you wish to modify, select Sequence > Settings, or press Command-0 (zero). Be sure to make the sequence active first, or the Settings menu option will be grayed out. You can make the sequence active by either double-clicking on its icon in the Project tab of the Browser, or by clicking once on its tab in the Timeline.*

In the program's **System Settings,** you can control scratch disks, memory, and other options relating to how your computer is set up to work with Final Cut Pro. There are six tabs in the System Settings dialog box: Scratch Disks, Search Folders, Memory & Cache, Playback Control, External Editors, and Effect Handling. To change the default system settings, select Final Cut Pro > System Settings, or press Shift-Q.

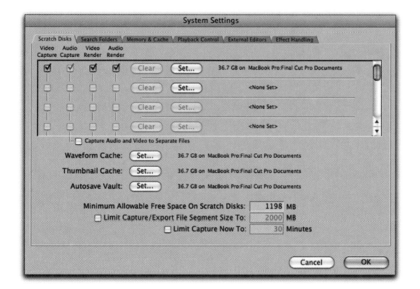

FIG-03-09 In the Scratch Disks tab, you can set multiple hard drives as scratch disks, selecting where to store the audio and video files that Final Cut Pro creates.

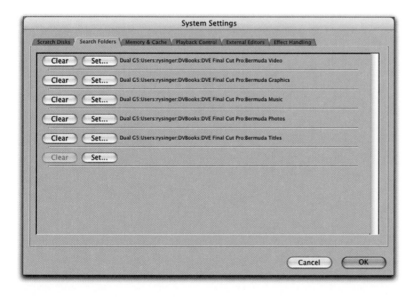

FIG-03-10 In the Search Folders tab, you can designate which folders Final Cut Pro will automatically search in for media files to reconnect with.

FIG-03-11 In the Memory & Cache tab, you can customize how much RAM Final Cut Pro uses to maximize its performance.

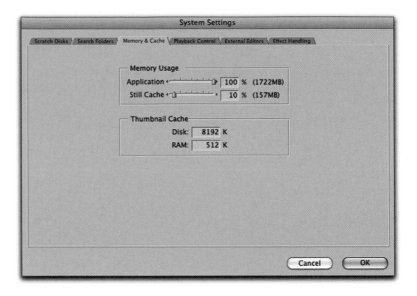

FIG-03-12 In the Playback Control tab, you can adjust the video quality and frame rate for video playback for all open projects and sequences.

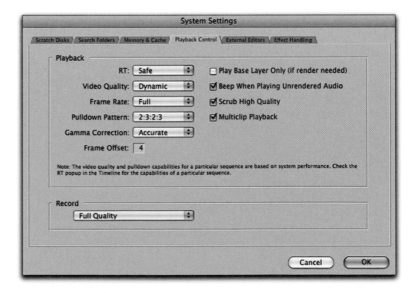

FIG-03-13 In the External Editors tab, you can designate other applications, such as Adobe Photoshop, to open specific media files. Select the media file in the Browser or Timeline, and select View > Clip in Editor, or press Option-Return; the file can be modified and saved in the external application, and Final Cut Pro will automatically reconnect to the updated media file.

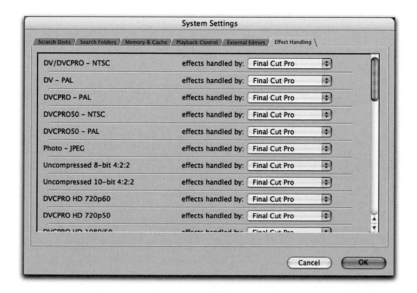

FIG-03-14 In the Effect Handling tab, you can assign either Final Cut Pro or a third-party video effects accelerator card to process effects.

You can customize Final Cut Pro to work with specific video formats and equipment in the **Audio/Video Settings.** There are five tabs in the Audio/Video Settings dialog box: Summary, Sequence Presets, Capture Presets, Device Control Presets, and A/V Devices. To modify the default Audio/Video Settings, select Final Cut Pro > Audio/Video Settings, or press Option-Command-Q.

FIG-03-15 In the Summary tab, the selected A/V devices, sequence settings, capture settings, and device control settings are summarized.

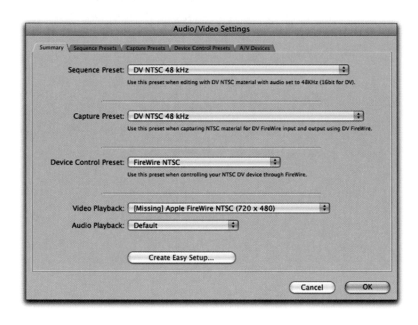

TIP ✪ *To make quick changes to your editing configuration in Final Cut Pro, select Final Cut Pro > Easy Setup, or press Control-Q. Then choose the desired preset for your video format from the pop-up menu.*

FIG-03-16 In the Sequence Presets tab, you can select the video and audio formats for a sequence, such as frame rate and codec, to be used during editing. You can modify a sequence's settings at any time by selecting Sequence > Settings, or pressing Command-0 (zero). Again, be sure to make the sequence active first or the Settings menu option will be grayed out. You can make the sequence active by either double-clicking on its icon in the Project tab of the Browser, or by clicking once on its tab in the Timeline window.

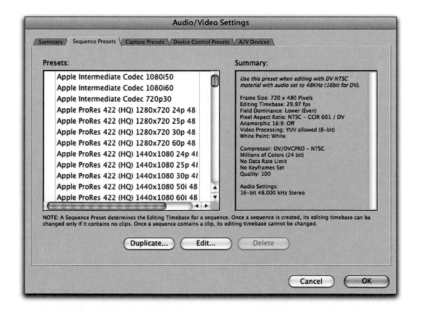

> *If your sequence settings and your media don't match, you'll need to convert the media to match your sequence before you can play it back in real-time. First select the Timeline window to make it active; otherwise the Render options will be grayed out. Then select Sequence > Render All > Both, or press Option-R, to render all the media in the Timeline. You can also choose to render only the clips marked on the Timeline with the red line by selecting them and choosing Sequence > Render Selection > Both, or pressing Command-R. (Choosing Both renders both the video and audio portions of the media.)*

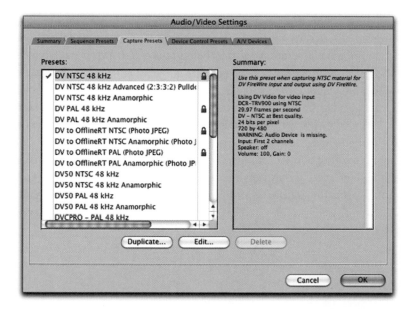

FIG-03-17 In the Capture Presets tab, you can select the appropriate resolution, frame rate, codec, and audio settings to capture your media to disk. Typically, your capture presets should match the format of your source footage.

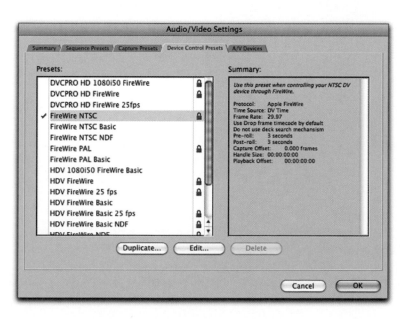

FIG-03-18 In the Device Control Presets tab, you can select the settings for the appropriate video/audio device, such as a camcorder or video deck, to communicate with Final Cut Pro. This will allow you to capture video to and output video from your computer.

FIG-03-19 In the A/V Devices tab, you can select the desired settings for Playback Output and/or Edit to Tape/Print to Video.

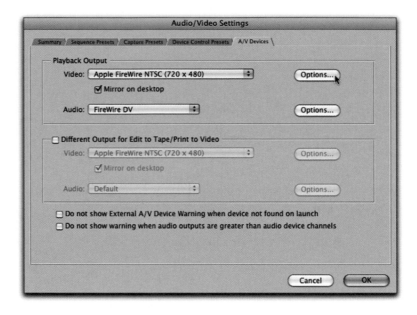

SPOTLIGHT

FIG-03-20 Jeff Greenberg is the president of the Philadelphia Final Cut Pro Users Group and the principal instructor for Future Media Concepts.

Jeff Greenberg

OCCUPATIONS: principal instructor, Future Media Concepts; president, Philadelphia Final Cut Pro User's Group; Freelance Colorist, Consultant, Editor
JOB DESCRIPTIONS: As the principal instructor of the nation's largest media training group, I teach intensive classes (two to three 8-hour days) and speak at national conferences, such as NAB. I primarily teach high-end editing software to professionals in the field, helping them become better at their jobs. As the

president of the PhilaFCPUG, I organize and present meetings involved with Apple's pro technology, all out of a sense of professional community. Oh, yeah, and I edit (film, video, commercials, and documentaries), as well as specialize in finishing.

DEGREES/CERTIFICATIONS: Film/Video (Communications) at Penn State University, cum Laude, Phi Beta Kappa; Apple Certified Repair, Certified Trainer: *Apple:* Final Cut Pro, Advanced Final Cut Pro, Motion, DVD Studio Pro, Soundtrack Pro; *Avid:* 101, 110, 201, 210, 239, 305 (Introduction to advanced editing and effects); *Avid DS:* 101, 201, 301 (Introduction to advanced editing and effects); *Boris:* Boris Red; *Adobe:* Photoshop and After Effects

PROFESSIONAL AFFILIATIONS: International Television Association, ITVA; Philadelphia Independent Film and Video Association, PIFVA

NUMBER OF YEARS IN FIELD: Ten

NUMBER OF YEARS USING MACS: Twenty plus

MACS CURRENTLY USED AT WORK: Six offices, five dual G5/MacPros per office

MAC PROGRAMS CURRENTLY USED AT WORK: Final Cut Pro, DVD Studio Pro, Motion, Keynote, iLife, and a couple I can't mention.

AVERAGE NUMBER OF HOURS YOU USE MACS PER DAY: Eight to ten

WEBSITES: www.fmctraining.com; www.finalcutpronews.com; www.philafcpug.org

1. What are the advantages of joining a group like the Philadelphia Final Cut Pro Users Group?

Our group is a loosely organized set of editors who solely use Apple's pro applications. Everyone has a strength in a network. You never know who is going to be the lynchpin in solving your next "whatever"—for a job, technical glitch, solution, or to help you find a shooter. That's what these sorts of groups are for.

2. How long have you been using Final Cut Pro?

Since version 1.0, so I think that's 1999? I wish I could say I had played with it when it was a Macromedia product.

3. What are Final Cut Pro's three greatest strengths?

Intuitive. There's more than one way to do most tasks. Pick whatever feels natural to start with . . . graduate to picking methods that permit you to do your work fastest.

Depth. It is not just a DV application. Learn it today at an affordable format (DV). Later, start working in standard-definition (SD). When the time comes that you have a chance to work in high-definition, Final Cut Pro is the same interface!

Compositing. It is easy to do effects that are fairly complex. The ability to build many layers quickly is reminiscent of the ease in Photoshop.

Can I add a fourth? The programmers really seem to listen to what the editors want/need.

And a fifth? The full suite, FCS2 (updated in 2007) brings a full-featured color correction application called Color.

4. What are Final Cut Pro's three greatest weaknesses?

Its media management is messy. Wait, that's not exactly true. It's okay. It's just less intuitive than it can be/should be. Part of that, I'm sure, is chained to the flexibility of QuickTime and being able to have footage anywhere.

Visual interface. There are some parts of it that really bother me. The font is often too small in many of the windows on larger displays. I hear this complaint from other editors all the time. It's just too grey-on-grey, as well (which is excellent for color correction, but frustrating during the offline edit). I'm not advocating the idea of having a candy-coated interface; it's just sometimes a very slight luminance change that tells you that you're using a specific window or that a button is on/off.

Nonmodality. I like FCP's interface—the idea of being able to do anything, anytime (nonmodal)—but it's a bit frustrating in long form. It's easy to accidentally grab something (an edge of a clip, a transition) and accidentally adjust it without being able to see it because you're looking at over a hundred edits.

Fourth, as an instructor, I see people *all the time* learn one way of editing (or doing something) and never progress beyond that, unless they spend time taking a class. The same strength of intuitive ability hampers people in the long term, because they don't develop the less-intuitive skills that make or break editors.

5. What is your favorite feature or tool of Final Cut Pro?

It's compositing—how easy it is to add elements to a complex stack of clips or text. In other systems, I do quite a bit of mousing, whereas in FCP, I'm doing it with one key. Building complex moments in the Timeline is really easy. An immediate second feature is the integration with other applications, like Photoshop, LiveType, Motion, and Soundtrack.

6. If you could change one thing about Final Cut Pro, what would it be?

Flat out: media management. I'd either have some smart wizards or revamp the mapping of media the way Avid does.

7. How does Final Cut Pro compare with other professional DV editing applications?

It's got huge acceptance; it's been used for several feature films and television shows! Since Apple controls both the hardware and software, it often seems to be ahead of other applications by months or quarters. I've tried lower-end applications; they're not bad, but they don't understand the tools you need for editing. While, yes, I'm happy that DV and software like FCP (and others) has made editing democratic . . . often in other software, programmers don't always understand why certain features should be implemented (or protected).

8. How popular is Final Cut Pro among professional digital video editors?

In the professional arena three years ago, it was all Avid. Today? Most editors need to know both Avid and Final Cut Pro. Apple has set a price point that absolutely forces competition.

9. What advice could you offer to someone new to Final Cut Pro?

It's a tough industry. Please don't pick this up if you think you're going to make millions of dollars. Right now, I see the industry as having a revolution similar to what the publishing industry had in the 1980s. iMovie makes the basic stuff really easy. Be patient with yourself. If you're new to video editing, it's not word processing. Editing isn't effects; it's not cool titles (although those things help the overall look). Editing is deciding where a cut goes and what motivates it. It's a very aesthetic art. In most cases, editing should be invisible. Of course, I'll suggest that you take an Apple authorized class to learn most efficiently, but I will say that my viewpoint is biased in that regard. The other big thing is people think that learning an application makes them competent. All the time I ask people how long it took them to become good at something they're good at (could be their job, a musical instrument, or a hobby). And I point out that very similarly, they'll need just as much devotion and time to become gifted with this toolset.

The Final Cut Pro Workspace

In addition to customizing how Final Cut Pro operates, you can also control how it looks. The Final Cut Pro editing interface is comprised of a series of windows that can be arranged in various layouts to suit your personal editing preferences. You can choose from one of five preset layouts or create a custom layout or layouts of your own. Select Window > Arrange > Standard, or press Control-U, to choose the Standard window layout for Final Cut Pro. In addition to the Standard layout, other preset layouts include Audio Mixing, Color Correction, Multiple Edits, and Two Up. If you have a dual screen configuration, Final Cut Pro will give you different layout options.

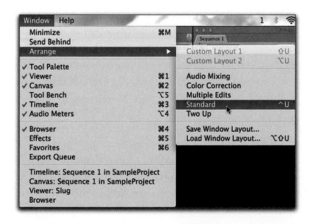

FIG-03-21 Select Window > Arrange > Standard, or press Control-U, to choose the Standard window layout for Final Cut Pro.

FIG-03-22 This is the Standard window layout for Final Cut Pro, which is the default window layout.

FIG-03-23 This is the Two Up window layout for Final Cut Pro. To select it, choose Window > Arrange > Two Up.

TIP *To create a custom window layout, first resize and arrange the windows into the layout you prefer. Then select Window > Arrange > Save Window Layout. Name your layout style uniquely, and it will automatically appear in the list. You can save multiple custom layouts if you so choose.*

Because of the multiple windows utilized by digital video programs, many editors choose to work with two computer monitors to more easily manage these windows. A screen size of at least 17 inches or greater is recommended for editing digital video, and two monitors are preferred.

Professional editors often edit with a video deck connected to their computer and use an NTSC video monitor to accurately preview their work. The computer

> *screen actually has a greater color depth than a television set, so the colors chosen on a computer monitor are not the actual colors that will be broadcast on a television. Using an NTSC video monitor allows the editor to see what the finished product will actually look like during the editing phase.*

No matter which digital video program you choose to edit with, the window layout is essentially the same. There is a project window for storing and organizing all of your media; Final Cut Pro calls this the Browser. There is a timeline for arranging your clips and placing your transitions; Final Cut Pro calls this the Timeline window. Finally, there is a window to preview your work; Final Cut Pro has two windows that work in tandem, the Viewer and the Canvas.

FIG·03·24 In Final Cut Pro, editors store the project's media in the Browser window, view the clips in the Viewer window, construct the edit in the Timeline window, and view the edited sequence in the Canvas window. The Tool palette and Audio Meters are also visible in the Standard layout.

> *To move any window's location, drag it by its title bar. You can resize the Browser and Canvas windows by dragging the lower right corner. You can also use the scroll bars to view different areas of the window at one time. You can resize the Viewer and Canvas windows by positioning the cursor along the sides, then clicking and dragging. You can also use this technique to resize the dividing line between the audio and video tracks in the Timeline window. To return to the default window sizes, select Window > Arrange > Standard, or press Control-U.*

The Browser

You prepare to edit by storing all of your **media,** such as video, audio, photographs, still graphics, and motion graphics files, in the Project tab of the Browser. An audio, video, or graphic file is also called a **clip** in Final Cut Pro. The **Browser** allows you to

TIP✪ *To select multiple items in the Browser at one time, hold down the Command key while you click on the desired items' icons. They need not be in order, and you can deselect any item by clicking on its icon a second time.*

organize your media and determine information, such as file type, duration, frame size, and more. To aid in organization, media files can also be stored within an individual folder called a **bin** in Final Cut Pro.

You can view the files in the Browser in either Column view, as text, or in Icon view, as images. Column, or list, view provides more technical information, while Icon view provides a visual cue. To switch from Column view, the default, to Icon view, click on the Browser window to make it active. Then select View > Browser > Items as Medium Icons. You also have the option of viewing small or large icons.

FIG-03-25 Column view provides more detailed information about the media files, such as their duration, frame size, compressor, frame rate, and audio.

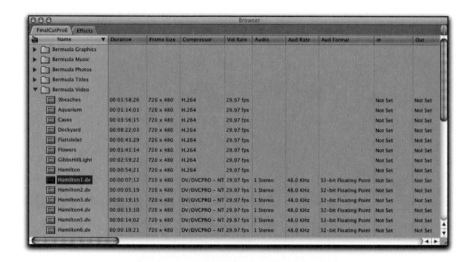

FIG-03-26 In Icon view, you need to double-click on a bin to view its items.

While it is often easier to organize your media into folders before you import the files into Final Cut Pro, you may decide you need to add additional folders, or bins, once you are working in the project. To create a bin in Final Cut Pro, position your cursor within the Project tab of the Browser where you would like the bin to be created and click. For instance, you may want to create one bin inside another. Then select File > New Bin, or press Command-B.

To view the contents of a bin in Column view, click on the triangle to the left of the bin name. To hide its contents, click the triangle a second time. In Icon view, double-click on a bin to open it and view its contents.

In Column view, to arrange the items in the Project tab alphabetically, click on the Name bar at the top of the window. If the triangle to the right is facing down, the items are listed in descending order. If the triangle is facing up, the items are listed in ascending order. Click the triangle a second time to change to its order back again. You can also modify the view of the items of the Project tab by selecting another category, such as duration or frame size, to reorder them. Simply click on the name of the desired category at the top of the window, and click its triangle to change between descending and ascending order.

Sequences are also stored in the Browser. A **sequence** is a series of edited media clips within a project. You can have multiple sequences in the same project. Sequences are listed in the Project tab of the Browser, along with the media files. By default, Final Cut Pro automatically creates Sequence 1 when a new project is opened. To create additional sequences, select File > New Sequence, or press Command-N.

In addition to the Project tab, the Effects tab is also located in the Browser. Click on the Effects tab to make it active. Video and audio transitions and filters can be accessed from the Effects tab. Video generators, such as bars and tone, mattes, shapes, and titles, are also located here. Any installed third-party filters, transitions, and generators can be accessed here as well.

TIP ☼ *You can rename a bin or sequence at any time by clicking the file once to highlight it. Then click a second time to highlight its name. In order to prevent confusion, it is a good idea NOT to rename your media files or folders once they have been imported into the project.*

FIG-03-27 Click on the Effects tab to make it active. Nested in a series of bins are multiple categories of video and audio transitions, filters, and generators. Third-party plug-ins are also installed here.

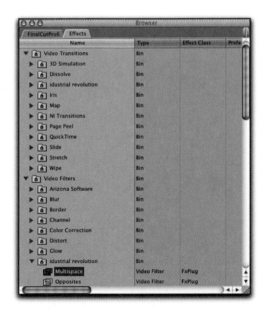

The Viewer

The **Viewer** acts as a staging area for individual clips. You can play the source clips and watch them in the Video tab of the Viewer. Keep in mind that the Viewer window is used for working with your source material, whereas the Canvas window is used for viewing your edited material. You can also adjust the settings of filters and motion in the Viewer for clips on the timeline. First double-click on the clip in the Timeline window. Then click on either the Filters or Motion tab in the Viewer to access its respective settings. You can also adjust the audio and transition settings for clips on the timeline in this same manner. You must double-click on the clip in the Timeline window first, however, or the settings you are viewing may be for the wrong clip.

FIG-03-28 Source clips are played in the Video tab of the Viewer window.

FIG-03-29 To adjust the filter settings of a clip, first double-click on the clip in the Timeline window and then click on the Filters tab in the Viewer window.

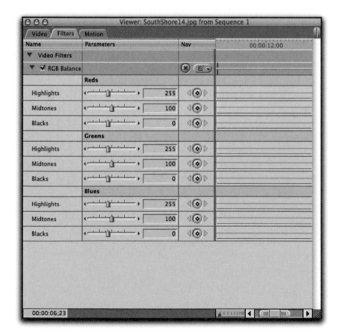

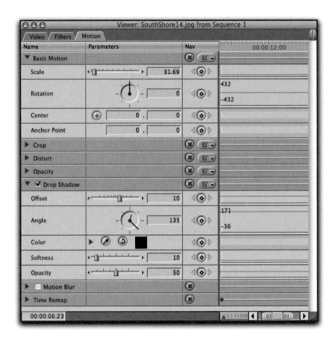

FIG-03-30 To adjust the motion settings of a clip, first double-click on the clip in the Timeline window and then click on the Motion tab in the Viewer window.

FIG-03-31 To adjust the transition settings of a clip, first double-click on the clip in the Timeline window and then click on the Transitions tab in the Viewer window.

FIG-03-32 To adjust the audio settings of a clip, first double-click on the clip in the Timeline window and then click on the Audio tab in the Viewer window.

The Timeline

While individual clips are prepared in the Viewer, they are actually placed on the **timeline** in chronological order to construct the edit. Final Cut Pro lets you further divide the timeline into a series of sequences.

The Timeline window displays both video and audio tracks. Typically, one video clip will have two corresponding audio tracks, for the left and right channels of the stereo sound. Final Cut Pro is capable of displaying up to 99 video and 99 audio tracks per sequence.

FIG-03-33 In this example, two video tracks are displayed using the Filmstrip view, and the audio waveforms are visible. These options take longer for the screen to redraw when navigating the Timeline, but provide the editor with more visual information.

Like the Browser window, the Timeline window also gives you options for how it displays clips. These settings can be customized by selecting Sequence > Settings, or by pressing Command-0 (zero). Again, be sure to make the sequence active first or the Settings menu option will be grayed out. You can make the sequence active by either double-clicking on its icon in the Project tab of the Browser, or by clicking once on its tab in the Timeline window.

You can choose to edit by viewing the file by Name, viewing it visually using the Filmstrip view, or by a combination of the two, Name Plus Thumbnail. Other options include the size of the tracks themselves, and whether or not to display the audio waveforms.

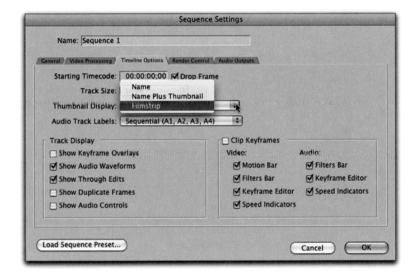

FIG-03-34 You can change the track display in the Timeline window to view either Name, Filmstrip, or Name Plus Thumbnail view.

The Canvas

As you arrange your clips on the timeline, you can view the progress of your edit by playing the sequence in the **Canvas** window. Although the Canvas window looks similar to the Viewer, it has a different function. The Viewer works with individual source clips, while the Canvas works with the edited sequence. In addition to viewing edited sequences, you can also perform different styles of edits directly in the Canvas window itself.

FIG-03-35 Sequence 1 plays in the Canvas window, as do all edited sequences from the timeline.

FIG-03-36 You can also perform different editing styles, such as Fit to Fill, from the Canvas window.

The Tool Palette

Final Cut Pro has a series of tools located in the Tool palette to help you edit more quickly. There is a series of selection tools for selecting clips and a Razor Blade tool for dividing the clips into segments. There is also a series of track tools to select audio and video tracks. The edit tools perform common edits, such as slip, slide, ripple, and roll. The view tools help you zoom in and out and move across the timeline. There are even pen tools, and tools to help you crop and distort images.

FIG-03-37 You can access additional tools in the Tool palette by clicking and holding any of the tool icons that show triangles. This will reveal the pop-up selectors. Drag across until you reach your selection, and then release the mouse.

The Audio Meters

Another window visible in the Standard layout is the floating Audio Meters window. The floating Audio Meters window uses a stereo display to show the output levels of the audio that is playing from either the Viewer or the Timeline window.

FIG-03-38 You can monitor a clip's audio levels as it plays by viewing them in the Audio Meters window.

Importing Media

In addition to capturing video from tape, you can also import existing digital video clips into Final Cut Pro, as well as audio, photographs, still graphics, and motion graphics. Final Cut Pro is compatible with a variety of media formats, including QuickTime and AVIs, AIFF and WAVE files, and PSD and JPEG files, among others.

 Encapsulate PostScript files (EPS), like those generated in Adobe Illustrator, are vector-based graphics and cannot be imported into Final Cut Pro!

FIG-03-39 You can import the following video and motion graphics files: QuickTime Movie, AVI, and Macromedia Flash (the video portion only).

FIG-03-40 You can import the following audio formats: AIFF/AIFC, Sound Designer II, System 7 Sound, AU, and WAVE.

FIG-03-41 You can import the following still graphics files: BMP, FlashPix, GIF, JPEG/JFIF, MacPaint, Photoshop (layered), PICS, PICT, PNG, QuickTime Image, SGI, TGA, and TIFF. You can also import a numbered series of still frames.

You can import media into Final Cut Pro by importing individual files, or by importing a folder and its contents. Select File > Import > Files, or press Command-I, to import one or more files at a time. Hold down the Command key to make multiple selections. Select File > Import > Folder to import a folder and all of its contents into Final Cut Pro; any subfolders and their contents will also be imported.

FIG-03-42 To import a folder and its contents into Final Cut Pro, select File > Import > Folder.

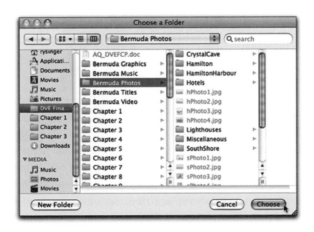

FIG-03-43 The Choose a Folder dialog box will open. Select the folder you wish to import, and click Choose.

FIG-03-44 The folder and all of its items will import automatically; any subfolders and their contents will also be imported. You can view the imported folder items in the Project tab of the Browser window.

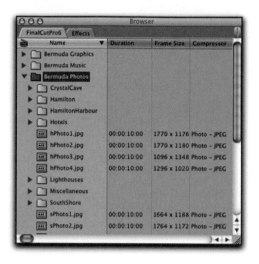

Summary

Because Final Cut Pro incorporates such powerful editing features, you need to practice working with the interface to become comfortable. After you have spent time customizing your settings and your workspace, you will not only enjoy editing more, but you will also optimize your workflow.

KEYBOARD SHORTCUTS		
Final Cut Pro > Audio/Video Settings	*Option-Command-Q*
File > New Project	*Shift-Command-N*
File > Save Project As	*Shift-Command-S*
Final Cut Pro > User Preferences	*Option-Q*
Sequence > Settings	*Command-0 (zero)*
Final Cut Pro > System Settings	*Shift-Q*
View > Clip in Editor	*Option-Return*
Final Cut Pro > Easy Setup	*Control-Q*
Sequence > Render All > Both	*Option-R*
Sequence > Render Selection > Both	*Command-R*
Window > Arrange > Standard	*Control-U*
File > New Bin	*Command-B*
File > New Sequence	*Command-N*
File > Import > Files	*Command-I*

REWIND

1. What is a project file and its relationship to source files?
2. Name the three categories of settings and preferences you can access to customize Final Cut Pro.
3. What is the function of the Browser window?
4. What is the function of the Timeline window?
5. What is the function of the Viewer window?

6. What is the function of the Canvas window?
7. What is a clip?
8. What is a bin?
9. What is a sequence?
10. What types of files can you import into Final Cut Pro?

 **TAKE TWO**

1. Create a New Project in Final Cut Pro. Name it uniquely, and save it in your user's Final Cut Pro Documents folder, or in another specified location.
2. Select the appropriate User Preferences, System Settings, and Audio/Video Settings. Customize your workspace by selecting your desired window layout.
3. Organize any existing media files for your project into folders on your hard drive. Then import them into the project and save it.

CHAPTER 4

Capturing Video

AFTER YOU ARE familiar with the Final Cut Pro interface, understand how to customize its preferences and settings, and know how to create a project and to import footage, you are ready to begin the video capture process. There are several methods for capturing video using Final Cut Pro's Log and Capture window.

You can capture a single clip at a time, batch capture multiple clips at once, capture video without using timecode, or capture an entire tape at one time.

Preparing to Capture Video

Logging and capturing video is an important stage in the editing process. It can be tedious and time consuming, and is often the task digital video editors like least. Nevertheless, before you can edit your video footage, you must first get it into the computer. It is a critical part of the process; however, before you begin capturing, you need to learn how to set your scratch disks, connect your capture device, and understand how to log your footage.

Setting Scratch Disks

A scratch disk is a hard drive that has been designated in advance by a particular software program to store specific files that the application will create. By default, Final Cut Pro uses the hard disk on which the application is installed to store captured video, audio, and render files. However, you can change the default scratch disk and add additional scratch disks up to a total of twelve. When selecting a hard drive to become a scratch disk, keep in mind that the drive needs to be fast enough to not drop frames and have enough free space to hold large video files.

> *Dropped frames occur when a hard drive can't keep up with the amount of information that is coming through at any given moment. Dropped frames can cause playback to appear stuttered and are unacceptable in professional digital video editing. There are several options that can be set regarding dropped frames in the General tab of the User Preferences. You can have Final Cut Pro alert you if there were dropped frames during capture, or even have it abort the capture process if dropped frames occur. You can also tell Final Cut Pro to abort the outputting process if any dropped frames occur during playback. (Final Cut Pro uses the abbreviations ETT for Export To Tape and PTV for Print To Video.) Dropped frames can be caused by a variety of reasons, such as issues with the hard drive or software conflicts. To troubleshoot dropped frame problems with Final Cut Pro, visit Apple's website at www.apple.com/support/finalcutpro for the latest information.*

TIP ✪ *Visit Apple's website at www.apple.com/support/finalcutpro for more information about compatible capture devices.*

Connecting a Capture Device

In addition to setting your scratch disks, you also need to connect a capture device, such as a FireWire video camera or video deck, before you can begin the capture process. Final Cut Pro has software built in to control a variety of capture devices.

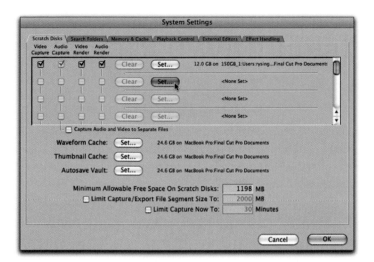

FIG-04-01 To set scratch disks in Final Cut Pro, select Final Cut Pro > System Settings, or press Shift-Q. Designate a new scratch disk by clicking the Set button.

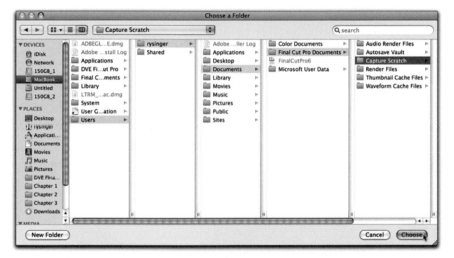

FIG-04-02 In this example, the internal hard disk is selected as the new scratch disk; the files are going to be stored in the Capture Scratch folder in the User's Final Cut Pro Documents folder.

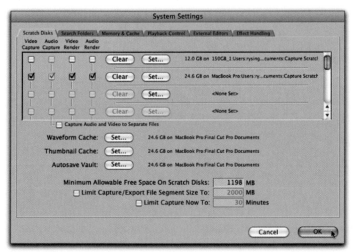

FIG-04-03 Once the new scratch disk has been added, you can uncheck the four Capture and Render boxes on the old scratch disk. Clicking the Clear button will remove the hard drive from the list entirely.

FIG-04-04 To connect a FireWire video camera, plug the four-pin end of the FireWire cable into the DV IN/OUT port on the camera.

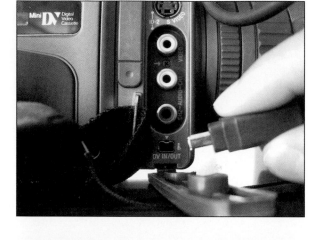

FIG-04-05 Then plug the six-pin end of the FireWire cable into the FireWire port of your Macintosh computer.

> *Device control* is a software feature or plug-in that allows an editing program to communicate with video devices, such as cameras and decks. Device control can be built into the digital video program itself, like it is with Final Cut Pro, or it can be third-party software that works with the editing program as a plug-in. Device control uses timecode to remotely operate the video source. You can press a button on the computer to play, pause, stop, rewind, and fast-forward. You can even tell the computer to go directly to a single frame of video using its numerical timecode address.

Logging Clips

When you use a capture device with timecode, you have the ability to log your video clips by setting in and out points. An **in point** is the numerical timecode address that marks the exact video frame where capture is to begin. Likewise, an **out point** is a numerical timecode address that marks the exact video frame where capture is to end.

> ### Advantages of Logging Clips
> ◆ *File space can be saved by recording only the footage you plan to use.*
> ◆ *Notes describing the footage can be added to help during the editing process.*
> ◆ *Familiarizing yourself with the footage can alert you to potential problems and help you make important editing choices.*
> ◆ *Keeping a printed list of the logged clips can help you later to re-create a project if the captured clips are accidentally modified or deleted.*

Log and Capture Window

The Log and Capture window in Final Cut Pro allows you to remotely control your capture device. You will use it to screen and log your footage. In addition to a preview area, there are tabs for Logging, Clip Settings, and Capture Settings.

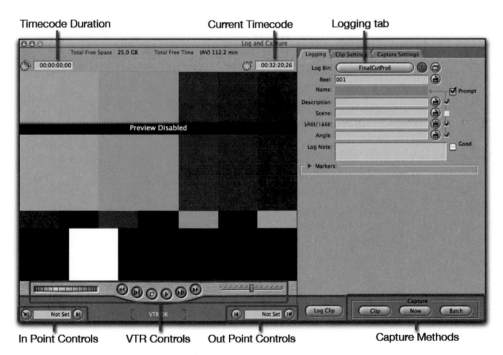

Timecode Duration   Current Timecode   Logging tab

In Point Controls   VTR Controls   Out Point Controls   Capture Methods

FIG-04-06 Use the Log and Capture window to control your capture device, and log and capture your clips by setting in and out points.

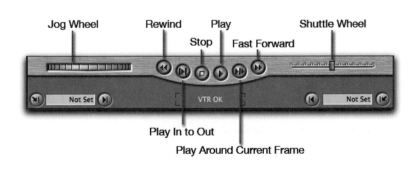

Jog Wheel   Rewind   Play   Shuttle Wheel

Stop   Fast Forward

Play In to Out

Play Around Current Frame

FIG-04-07 Use the controls to rewind, stop, play, and fast-forward. The shuttle wheel allows you to advance quickly while previewing your footage. The jog wheel allows you to move forward or backward frame by frame.

FIG-04-08 Use the controls at the bottom of the preview area to set the in and out points of a clip.

Logging Tab

The Logging tab allows you to enter additional information about the clip. In addition to naming the clip, you can enter which reel, or tape, it came from, as well as assigning scene, shot, and take numbers. You can also add comments describing the clip, and mark the clip as Good. You can later use the Good designation to search for clips in the Column view of the Browser window.

FIG-04-09 Assign additional information about a clip in the Logging tab of the Log and Capture window.

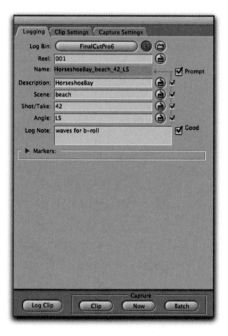

Clip Settings Tab

The Clip Settings tab allows you to monitor and/or adjust the video and audio levels of a clip before it is captured. FireWire video cannot be adjusted; however, if you have a third-party video capture card installed, you may have control over the levels. To visually monitor the video levels, select Tools > Video Scopes, or press Option-9.

FIG-04-10 You can also display Final Cut Pro's built-in waveform monitor and vectorscope by clicking the Video Scopes button at the upper left of the Clip Settings tab.

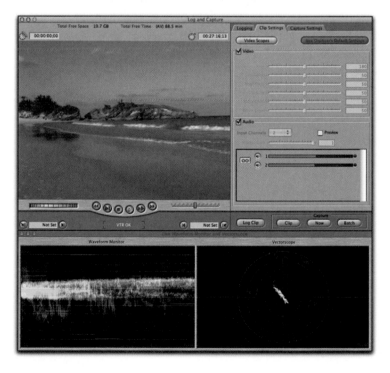

FIG-04-11 The Video Scopes provide a graphical view of the clip's video levels as the clip plays.

Capture Settings Tab

The Capture Settings tab allows you to confirm the settings for the method of device control, as well as the capture presets. You can also access the preferences for the scratch disks. Before you begin capturing video, you should get in the habit of verifying that your capture preset is correct and that there is adequate room on your scratch disk.

FIG-04-12 Use the Capture Settings tab as a quick way to modify your settings for device control, capture settings, and scratch disks.

The Video Capture Process

There are several different methods for capturing video. You can capture individual clips one at a time by setting in and out points. Final Cut Pro calls this method Capture Clip. You can also **batch capture** by logging all your footage first, setting all of your in and out points, and then telling the computer to automatically record each clip, one after another. This method is referred to as Batch Capture in Final Cut Pro. Finally, you can even capture a portion of a tape without using timecode, or even capture an entire tape at one time. Final Cut Pro calls this method Capture Now.

Capturing a Clip using Capture Clip

Before you begin capturing video, be sure to plug the four-pin end of the FireWire cable into your video camera. Then plug the six-pin end of your video cable into your computer.

Plug in your video source and power it on by putting it into VTR or VCR mode. Then load the tape with desired footage on it. After your video source is ready, select File > Log and Capture, or press Command-8, to activate the Log and Capture Window.

◆ *VTR stands for videotape recorder—a video camera or deck with timecode.*

TIP✪ *You can also hit the Space Bar on your keyboard to start or stop playing a clip.*

Once Final Cut Pro has established communication with your video device, it will say VTR OK at the bottom left of the Log and Capture window. Final Cut Pro will prompt you if it cannot communicate with your video source. To begin playing your videotape, click the Play button at the bottom of the Log and Capture window.

Use the Log and Capture window in Final Cut Pro to screen your video footage and determine which segments you wish to capture. To set the in point of a video clip while a tape is playing, click the Mark In button in the Log and Capture window, or press the "i" key on the keyboard when you see the frame where you would like the clip to begin. Alternatively, you can select Mark > Mark In. You can also set the out point while the video clip is playing by clicking the Mark Out button in the Log and Capture window, or by pressing the "o" key, when you see the frame where you would like the clip to end. You can also select Mark > Mark Out.

> *When setting in and out points, it is always a good idea to create some extra room by adding **handles**, or extra footage at the beginning and end of each clip. You may need to use these additional frames later in editing if you add transitions or effects. Editors typically add one- or two-second handles to the beginning or end of every clip.*

FIG-04-13 Click the Play button, or hit the Space Bar, to make Final Cut Pro play your video source.

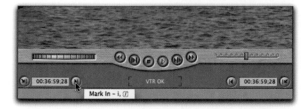

FIG-04-14 In this example, the in point was set at 36 minutes, 59 seconds, and 28 frames by clicking the Mark In button as the video clip was playing.

FIG-04-15 In this example, the out point was set at 37 minutes, 24 seconds, and 4 frames by clicking the Mark Out button as the video clip was playing.

TIP ✪ *To abort the video capture process once it has started, hit the ESC (escape) key.*

After you have set the in and out points of the video clip, you can capture that clip by clicking the Clip button in the Logging tab. But first check the Prompt box to the right of the Name field if you want to have Final Cut Pro automatically prompt you to name the clip.

Final Cut Pro will control your video source by automatically cueing the footage and capturing the clip. A window will appear, showing the progress of the capture. After the clip has been captured, it will be added to the project and will appear in the Project tab of the Browser window.

You can also capture a clip by manually entering its timecode. You may choose to do this if you want to add handles to the beginning and end of each clip. You would screen the footage, mark the in and out points, and then manually revise the timecode by adding a second or two to the in and out points of the clip. Manually entering the timecode is also useful when you are working from a camera log and the footage has already been screened and logged for you on paper.

FIG-04-16 If you would like to have Final Cut Pro prompt you each time to name the clip, check the Prompt box to the right of the Name field in the Logging tab.

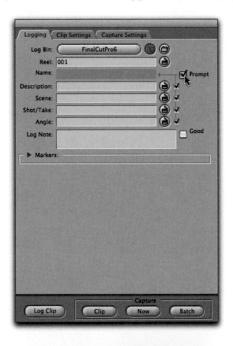

FIG-04-17 Once you have set the in and out points, you can capture the clip by clicking the Clip button in the Logging tab.

FIG-04-18 When the Log Clip dialog box opens, you can type a name for the clip in the Name field. You can also add notes about the clip in the Log Note field.

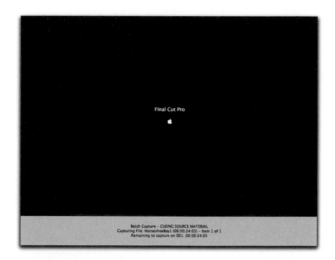

FIG-04-19 After clicking OK, Final Cut Pro will automatically control the video source and cue the clip by either fast-forwarding or rewinding as necessary.

FIG-04-20 You can then watch a preview of the clip as it captures. To abort the capture in progress, press the ESC key.

FIG-04-21 Final Cut Pro will automatically add the captured clip to the Project tab in the Browser window after it finishes capturing.

FIG-04-22 To manually enter the timecode numbers, first screen the footage and determine the in and out points. Then decide how big to make the handles. Click once to highlight the in point's timecode field.

FIG-04-23 Type over any existing timecode numbers with the new timecode. You do not have to enter the colons and semicolons. You also don't have to enter the leading zeros, but you do need to mark a place for the frames. In this example, the timecode is being changed to 39 minutes, 16 seconds, and zero frames, so the numbers 391600 are typed in.

FIG-04-24 After typing the numbers, hit the Return key and Final Cut Pro will automatically add the leading zeros, colons, and semicolon for you. Then click once to highlight the out point's timecode field.

FIG-04-25 Type in the new out point timecode. In this example, the out point's timecode is being changed to 39 minutes, 58 seconds, and zero frames, so the numbers 395800 are typed in.

FIG-04-26 After hitting Return, the leading zeros, colons, and semicolon will be entered automatically for you.

FIG-04-27 Once you have manually set the in and out points, you can capture the clip by clicking the Clip button in the Logging tab.

FIG-04-28 After the Log Clip dialog box opens, you can type a name for the clip in the Name field and add notes about the clip in the Log Note field.

FIG-04-29 After clicking OK, Final Cut Pro will automatically cue and capture the clip.

FIG-04-30 After it is finished capturing the clip, Final Cut Pro will add it to the Project tab in the Browser window.

FIG·04·31 By default, Final Cut Pro stores the captured clips in a series of Final Cut Pro folders inside the Capture Scratch folder inside the user's Final Cut Pro Documents folder.

TIP *To troubleshoot problems capturing video, visit Apple's Web site at www.apple.com/support/finalcutpro.*

Capturing Multiple Clips Using Batch Capture

In addition to capturing one clip at a time, you can also log all of your clips first and then have Final Cut Pro perform a batch capture. This is also the capture method you would use if you were working from a batch list. A **batch list** is a special text file that contains information about all the captured clips in a project. It is different from an **EDL,** or **Edit Decision List,** which is a special file that contains basic information about how the project has been edited, primarily so that it can be moved from one editing system to another. Final Cut Pro can import and export both batch lists and EDLs.

FIG·04·32 Click the Play button, or hit the Space Bar, to make Final Cut Pro play your video source.

To create a batch capture, first log your clips by setting each in and out point and clicking the Log Clip button at the bottom of the Logging tab, or press F2. After all of your clips have been logged, click the Batch button. Alternatively, you can select File > Batch Capture, or press Control-C.

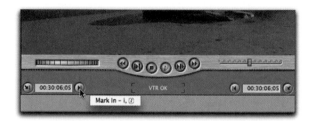

FIG-04-33 Click the Mark In button, or press the "i" key, to set the clip's in point.

FIG-04-34 Click the Mark Out button, or press the "o" key, to set the clip's out point.

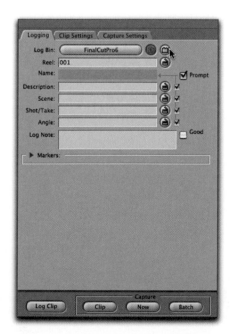

FIG-04-35 By default, the captured clips will be imported into the Project tab of the Browser window. To set a specific folder to store the clips in, click the New Bin icon to the far right of the Log Bin field in the Logging tab.

FIG-04-36 Bin 1 will automatically be generated and replace the project's name in the Log Bin field.

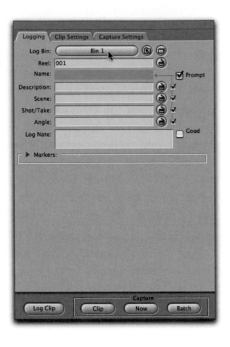

FIG-04-37 Bin 1 will be created in the Project tab of the Browser window and can be easily distinguished by the icon of a slate to the left of its name.

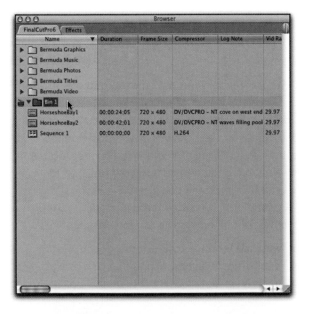

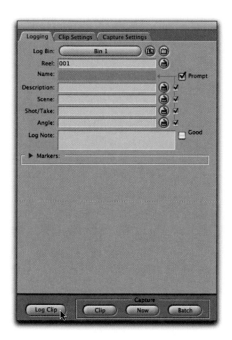

FIG-04-38 Then click the Log Clip button in the Logging tab, or press F2.

FIG-04-39 The Log Clip dialog box will open, where you can name the clip and add log notes.

FIG-04-40 Now the logged clip will appear in Bin 1 of the Project tab in the Browser window; the red line signifies it has not yet been captured.

FIG-04-41 Continue setting the in and out points for the next clip.

FIG-04-42 Click the Log Clip button again, or press F2.

FIG-04-43 Name the clip and add any log notes.

FIG-04-44 Continue this procedure until all of your clips have been logged and appear in the Project tab.

FIG-04-45 You can batch capture all of the clips at once or just some of them, like the three selected here.

FIG-04-46 When ready, click the Batch button, select File > Batch Capture, or press Control-C.

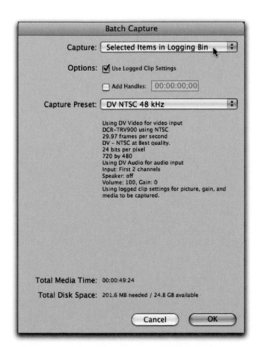

FIG-04-47 The Batch Capture window will open. In this example, Selected Items in Logging Bin should be chosen in the Capture pop-up menu.

FIG-04-48 Handles can be automatically added to the beginning and end of each clip by checking the Add Handles box under Options.

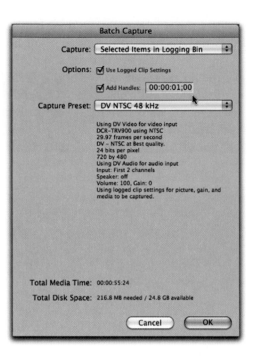

FIG-04-49 Once you have verified that your Capture Preset is correct, click OK.

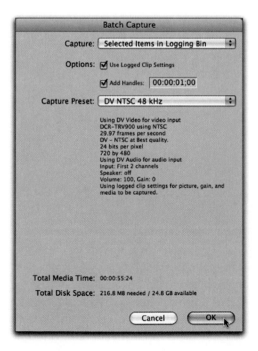

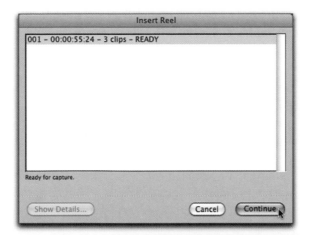

FIG-04-50 The Insert Reel dialog box will open, prompting you to load the tape if needed. Click Continue.

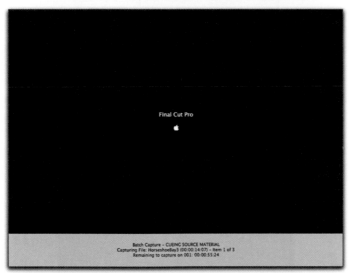

FIG-04-51 Final Cut Pro will automatically control the capture device and cue the footage.

FIG-04-52 A preview window will display the clips as they are captured.

FIG-04-53 If you want
to Batch Capture the
remaining clips, select
Offline Items in Logging
Bin from the Capture
pop-up menu.

FIG-04-54 After the
clips have been captured,
the Insert Reel dialog box
will open again. Click
Finished.

FIG-04-55 All of the
captured clips will appear
in the Project tab, with the
red line removed.

FIG-04-56 You can drag and drop additional clips into the bin like any other folder.

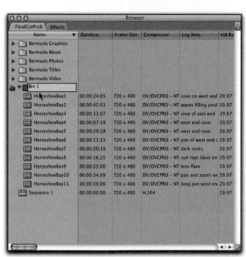

FIG-04-57 You can also rename the bin by clicking the name field once to select it and again to highlight the name.

FIG-04-58 Then type in the new folder name and press Return.

*Final Cut Pro has a sophisticated feature called **Media Manager,** which allows you to quickly do time-consuming tasks regarding your project and its media files. You can use Media Manager to copy entire projects or select items within projects, move all your media files into one folder on your scratch disk, and delete used portions of media files to save room on your hard drive. You can also use Media Manager to recompress media files with different settings. Finally, you can even create a copy of a sequence, so that lower-resolution clips can be recaptured later at full quality. However, because Media Manager is so advanced, be sure to practice with a sample project first to avoid costly mistakes. To activate Media Manager, select File > Media Manager.*

Capturing a Tape Using Capture Now

In addition to logging your clips and capturing them, you can also capture them on the fly using the Capture Now feature. This is especially useful if you are using a device that doesn't have timecode. It is also useful if you want to capture a large segment of a tape, or even an entire tape at one time.

Simply play your footage in the Log and Capture window and click the Now button to start the capture. Hit the ESC key when you want to end the capture. Final Cut Pro can even detect the places on the tape where the recording started and stopped. To use this feature to automatically divide a long video clip into segments, select Mark > DV Start/Stop Detect. Then highlight all of the marked segments in the Project tab and select Modify > Make Subclip, or press Command-U.

FIG-04-59 You can limit the duration of the Capture Now feature in the Scratch Disks tab of the System Settings. Select Final Cut Pro > System Settings, or press Shift-Q.

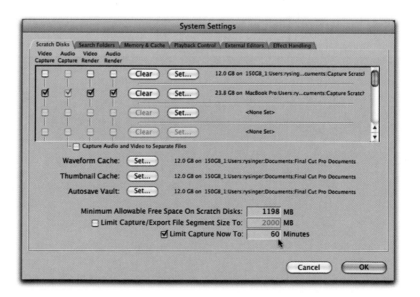

FIG-04-60 Name your clip in the Description field and press Return. It will automatically appear in the Name field, too.

FIG-04-61 Cue your capture device to the appropriate location, and click the Play button a few seconds before you would like the capture to begin.

FIG-04-62 Click the Now button in the Logging tab.

FIG-04-63 Your clip will automatically start capturing. Press the ESC key when you want to end the capture.

FIG·04·64 Your
clip will appear in the
Project tab of the Browser
window when it is finished
capturing. Click once to
select it.

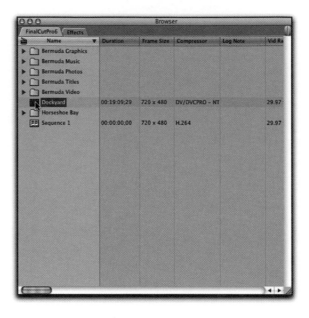

FIG·04·65 Then select
Mark > DV Start/Stop
Detect.

FIG·04·66 The
Scanning DV Movie(s)
dialog box will appear,
showing a progress bar.

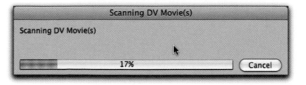

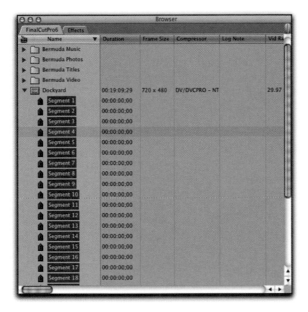

FIG-04-67 After it is finished, click the triangle to the left of the clip's icon to display the markers. Then select all of the clip's markers.

FIG-04-68 Select Modify > Make Subclip, or press Command-U.

FIG-04-69 All of
the segments will now
appear as subclips in the
Project tab of the Browser
window.

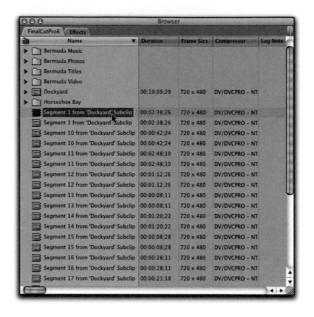

Summary

Whether your editing approach is to log your footage before you capture, or capture
the entire tape first and use subclips, the video capture phase is an important part of
video editing. Though logging and capturing can be tedious, Final Cut Pro gives you
the flexibility to choose whichever capture method you prefer, and makes the actual
task of capturing video straightforward and easy.

**KEYBOARD
SHORTCUTS**

Tools > Video Scopes	*Video Scopes (button)*	*Option-9*
File > Log and Capture		*Command-8*
Play (button)		*Space Bar*
Mark > Mark In	*Mark In (button)*	*i (key)*
Mark > Mark Out	*Mark Out (button)*	*o (key)*
Abort video capture		*ESC (key)*
Log Clip (button)		*F2*
File > Batch Capture	*Batch (button)*	*Control-C*
Modify > Make Subclip		*Command-U*

REWIND

1. What are scratch disks?
2. What does device control software do?
3. What are the steps for connecting capture devices using FireWire?
4. What are the advantages of logging your footage first?
5. What are in and out points?
6. What are the steps for capturing a single video clip in Final Cut Pro?
7. What is a batch capture?
8. What are the steps for batch capturing in Final Cut Pro?

9. Why would you use the Capture Now feature in Final Cut Pro?

10. What does Final Cut Pro's Media Manager do?

 **TAKE TWO**

1. Set your scratch disks and connect your FireWire video device.

2. Capture your video clips by setting in and out points. Also try batch capturing and capturing a large segment of a tape and making subclips.

3. Create a sample project and practice working with Media Manager.

CHAPTER 5

Basic Editing Techniques

Learn how to view and crop clips

Master drag-to-timeline editing

Comprehend three-point editing

Learn about Final Cut Pro's editing tools

Learn how to use the Trim Edit window

Understand how to link and unlink clips

Discover how to use markers

NOW THAT YOU know the parts of the editing interface and understand the functions of the different windows, editing in Final Cut Pro will seem less daunting. The program itself is quite powerful, offering many professional editing features and multiple ways of doing things. However, a simple approach is often the best way to begin.

Working with Clips and Sequences

The art of the edit is often determined by where to cut each shot. Very rarely is the entire clip that you capture used when you edit. Something as simple as trimming off a few frames can have a dramatic impact. First, decide approximately which portions of the clip you think you might use. Then, you further fine-tune your edit by trimming to the precise frame where you wish to make each cut.

Viewing and Cropping Clips

At any time you can use the Viewer window to **crop** a clip, or remove the unwanted portions, by changing the clip's original in and out points. The clip will have a new duration reflecting the changes you make; however, you can always revert to the captured clip's original duration later.

Click the Play button at the bottom of the Viewer window to play the clip. When you see where you would like the clip to begin, click the Mark In button at the lower left of the Viewer, press the "i" key, or select Mark > Mark In. Likewise, when you would like the clip to end, click the Mark Out button, press the "o" key, or select Mark > Mark Out. The clip will now have a new duration based on its new in and out points. To revert to the original duration of the clip, click on the Mark Clip button, press the "x" key, or select Mark > Mark Clip.

TIP *You can also manually enter the new in and out points by typing the timecode numbers in the Current Timecode field, and clicking the Mark In and Mark Out buttons.*

FIG-05-01 You can use the Viewer window to view and crop your clips. In the Video tab, you can view the current timecode of the clip as it plays and mark new in and out points.

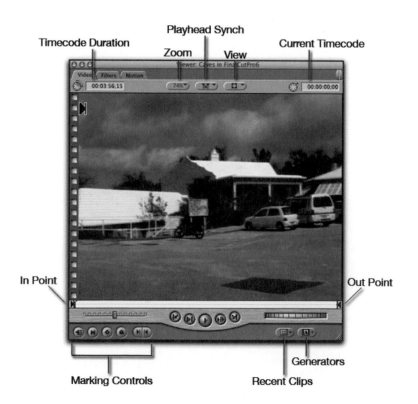

FIG-05-02 Click the Play button to find the portion of the clip you would like to use. Note the clip's original duration in the Timecode Duration field in the upper left corner.

FIG-05-03 When you see the frame where you would like the clip to start, click the Mark In button. The Current Timecode field in the upper right corner will change to reflect the new timecode of the in point.

FIG-05-04 When you see the frame where you would like the clip to finish, click the Mark Out button. After you have set new in and out points, note the new duration of the clip in the upper left corner.

FIG-05-05 To revert to the original in and out points of the clip, click on the Mark Clip button. Look in the upper left corner and notice that the clip has reverted to its original duration.

Editing Sequences

Different editors prefer different editing techniques; some rely on the mouse, others prefer keyboard shortcuts. When given multiple options, there is no right and wrong method, only the style that best suits you. However, those new to Final Cut Pro may find it helpful to start with the basics.

There are many different ways to manipulate clips in Final Cut Pro, but only two distinct approaches to editing. Editing performed in the Timeline window is called the drag-to-timeline method; editing performed in the Canvas window is called the three-point editing method. The **drag-to-timeline** approach is the fastest and easiest. You simply drag a clip from the Browser window to where you want it in the Timeline window.

Drag-to-Timeline Editing

To perform drag-to-timeline editing, select the clip in the Browser window by clicking once and holding down the mouse; drag it to the Timeline window, using the highlight as a visual guide to help you position the clip on the appropriate track. Do not let go of the mouse until you are certain that the clip is in the correct position! Once you position the clip over a track, an arrow will appear facing either down or to the right, depending on where you are on the track. Each track is subdivided into upper and lower portions; however, the dividing line is only visible when that part of the track is empty. If you position the clip over the upper portion of the track, with the arrow facing to the right, Final Cut Pro will perform an overwrite edit. If you position the clip over the lower portion of the track, with the arrow facing down, Final Cut Pro will perform an insert edit.

An **overwrite edit** places a clip at a specified point in the timeline, overwriting or replacing any media that is in the way on the track. As you position the clip over the track, the two-up display will appear in the Canvas window, showing you the two adjacent frames where the new clip will be placed. The frame on the right is where the overwrite will begin.

An **insert edit** also places a clip at a specified point in the timeline; however, it will not replace any existing media, but rather move that media to the right, further down the timeline and out of the way. In an insert edit, the two adjacent frames in the two-up display show exactly where the media on the track will be divided, so the new clip can be inserted, or placed, between them.

TIP ✪ *You can also drag clips directly from the Viewer window to the Timeline window.*

TIP ✪ *Do not let go of the mouse until you are certain that the correct edit will be performed at the right frame. Be careful not to accidentally perform an overwrite edit, or it will replace your existing media on the timeline!*

TIP ✪ *Make the Timeline window active, then select View > Level > 100% to view the timeline in one-second increments.*

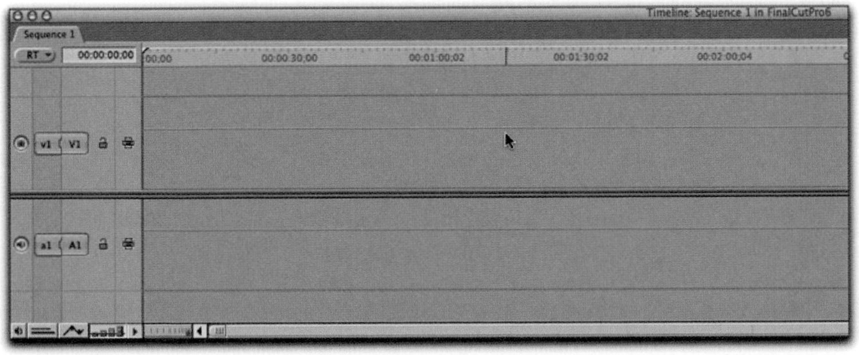

FIG-05-06 Note how the video track is subdivided in the Timeline window.

FIG-05-07 Select
a clip in the Browser
window and drag it to the
beginning of the timeline.
The arrow can face either
down or to the right, since
this is the first clip in the
sequence.

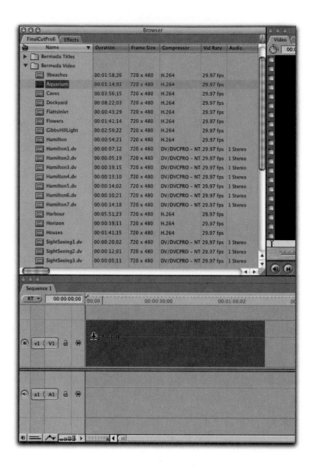

FIG-05-08 Drag a
second clip from the
Browser window and
position it so that it
overlaps with the previous
clip, with the arrow facing
down for an overwrite
edit.

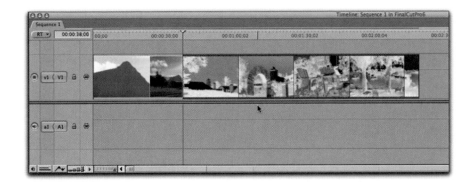

FIG-05-09 Notice how the new clip replaced part of the existing clip. Select Edit > Undo, or Command-Z, to undo the overwrite edit.

FIG-05-10 This time drag the second clip again so that it overlaps, but this time with the arrow facing to the right for an insert edit.

FIG-05-11 Observe how the two adjacent frames in the Two Up display change as you position the clip.

FIG-05-12 Notice how the existing clip was split and the new clip was inserted in the middle.

> ## Three-Point Editing
>
> *Drag-to-timeline editing requires four edit points, the in and out points of the two clips that are edited together. **Three-point editing,** on the other hand, only requires three edit points; the software automatically calculates the fourth edit point. The two primary edit types are insert and overwrite. Additional edit types are variations thereof. A **replace edit** is a type of overwrite edit that replaces the content of the sequence clip by aligning the frame at the playhead of the Viewer clip with the frame of the playhead of the sequence clip, even if no in and out points are set. A **fit to fill edit** is an edit where the speed of the clip is altered so that the clip fills, or takes up, a specified duration. Finally, a **superimpose edit** is an edit where a clip is placed on the track above a clip that is already on the timeline, at the frame where the playhead is positioned.*

Aligning Clips

If you position a new clip at the out point of an existing clip on the timeline, two small arrows will appear at the top and bottom of the track, signifying that the clips are placed directly next to one another, without any black frames left in between, and without the clips overlapping.

FIG-05-13 Notice how two arrows appear at the top and bottom of the track when two clips are placed directly next to each other.

Another way to avoid accidental black frames is to enable Final Cut Pro's snapping feature. **Snapping** allows the playhead to snap, or move directly, to edit points when it gets close to them. It also allows clips to snap together when they get close to each other on the timeline. You can enable the snapping feature by clicking on the Snapping button in the upper right corner of the Timeline window, pressing the "n" key, or selecting View > Snapping.

TIP ✪ *Disable the Snapping feature if you need to move a clip just a few frames at a time.*

FIG-05-14 To control Final Cut Pro's snapping feature, click on the Snapping button in the upper right corner of the Timeline window, press the "n" key, or select View > Snapping.

Adjusting a Clip's Duration

You can adjust a clip's duration directly on the timeline; however, you cannot extend the duration of a clip beyond its original captured length. Using the Selection tool, position the cursor over either the in or the out point of the clip; the cursor will change into two outward facing arrows. Then click, hold, and drag the clip to either the left or right to extend or shorten its duration. The new duration will be displayed as you drag. Release the mouse when you reach the desired duration.

TIP ✪ ***Clip duration*** *refers to the amount of time between a clip's in and out points.* ***Clip length*** *refers to the total time of the captured clip (from the Media Start to the Media End points).*

FIG-05-15 To extend the duration of a clip, position the cursor over the clip's out point, click and hold, then drag the cursor to the right.

FIG-05-16 This clip was extended 1 second and 25 frames, for a total duration of 1 minute, 28 seconds, and 16 frames.

Dividing a Clip

With the ability to undo any unwanted changes, you should feel free to experiment in Final Cut Pro. One commonly used technique in digital video editing is splitting a clip into two or more segments. This can be useful if you want to apply a filter to only part of a clip, or if you want to intersperse other media between segments of the clip. It can also be used to delete a portion of a clip or to move part of a clip to a different track.

To divide a clip into multiple sections, select the **Razor Blade tool** from the Tool palette, position it over the desired frame of the clip in the timeline, and click once to make a cut. A line with two facing red arrows will show that the clip has been divided. Any linked audio will automatically be cut along with the video portion. Repeat the process to make additional cuts. Keep in mind you can always undo any unwanted changes by selecting Edit > Undo, or pressing Command-Z. The **Razor Blade All tool** will cut all the media in each track along a specified point in the timeline.

TIP⚙ *After you are finished using the Razor Blade tool, be sure to exchange it in the Tool palette for the Selection tool. This will prevent you from accidentally dividing any clips the next time you click on a clip in the timeline. Just as you would with any sharp object, exercise caution!*

FIG-05-17 Use the Razor Blade tool in the Tool palette to divide a clip into two or more segments.

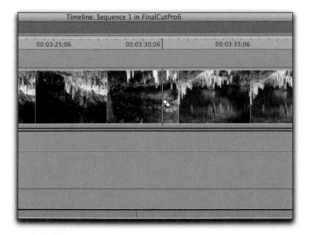

FIG-05-18 Position the Razor Blade tool over the appropriate frame in the timeline and click once to make the cut.

FIG-05-19 A line will appear with two facing red arrows, signifying that the clip has been divided.

Selecting and Moving Clips

After you divide a clip, you may want to create space between the sections. To move an individual clip (and any linked material) to anywhere on the track, use the Selection tool to click and hold the clip in the middle. If you grab the clip on either end, you may accidentally change its in or out point. Then drag the clip to the desired location. Any eligible track will highlight as you position the clip over it.

TIP ❂ *To choose the Selection tool, press the "a" key. To choose a special type of selection tool, press and repeat the "g" key until you get to the appropriate tool.*

Selection Tools

Selection tool—the default pointer that allows you to select, or choose, an item.

Range Selection tool—a type of Selection tool that lets you select multiple contiguous items, or parts thereof.

Group Selection tool—a type of Selection tool that lets you select entire multiple contiguous items.

Edit Selection tool—a type of Selection tool that lets you select an edit point between clips.

TIP ❂ *To select multiple contiguous clips with the Selection tool, hold down the Shift key. To select multiple noncontiguous clips with the Selection tool, hold down the Command key.*

FIG-05-20 Using the Selection tool, click the clip in the middle and hold down the mouse.

FIG-05-21 Drag the clip to the desired position on the track, using the highlight as a guide.

FIG-05-22 Release the mouse to drop the clip into place. Any linked material will move with it.

TIP ✪ *Press and repeat the "t" key until you select the appropriate Track Selection tool.*

TIP ✪ *When you are finished using any Track Selection tool, exchange it with the Selection tool so you don't inadvertently move anything.*

To slide all the clips from a chosen point along the same track, or all the clips from a chosen point on all the tracks, use the Track Selection tools. To move all the clips on all the tracks simultaneously forward down the timeline from a chosen point, select the All Tracks Forward tool from the Tool palette. Then position the All Tracks Forward tool where you would like to begin moving the clips. Click and hold as you drag forward down the timeline to your right. Let go of the mouse when you reach the location where you would like to reposition the clips. All clips to the right of the selection point on all the tracks will move in tandem with one another. Use the Select Track Forward tool if you would like to move clips forward along a single track from a chosen point.

Track Selection Tools

Select Track tool—*selects all the media on a single track.*

Select Track Forward tool—*selects all the media on a track from a chosen point forward.*

Select Track Backward tool—*selects all the media on a track from a chosen point backward.*

Select All Tracks Forward tool—*selects all the media on all the tracks from a chosen point forward.*

Select All Tracks Backward tool—*selects all the media on all the tracks from a chosen point backward.*

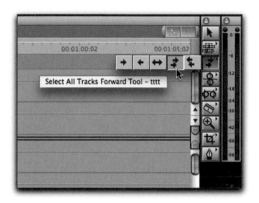

FIG-05-23 Select the All Tracks Forward tool to simultaneously move the clips from all tracks forward down the timeline from a chosen point.

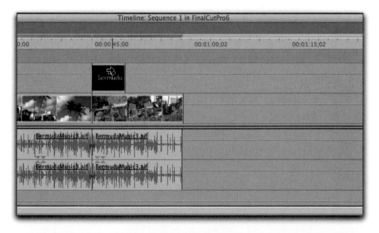

FIG-05-24 Position the All Tracks Forward tool where you would like to begin moving the clips.

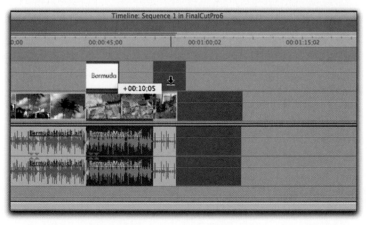

FIG-05-25 Then click, hold, and drag the clips forward down the timeline to the desired location.

FIG-05-26 The clips to the right of the chosen point on all the tracks will move forward in tandem with one another.

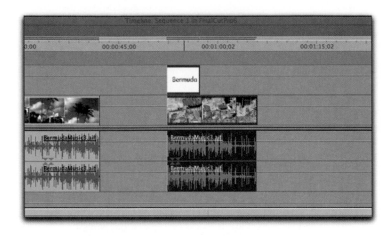

TIP ✪ *Another way to close a gap on a track is to Control-click within the gap, and select Close Gap from the shortcut menu.*

TIP ✪ *If you wish to have Final Cut Pro automatically close the gap when you delete a clip, select Sequence > Ripple Delete, or press Shift-Delete. Final Cut Pro will delete the clip and slide over all of the remaining clips so that no empty space is left.*

Deleting a Clip from the Timeline

In order to delete a clip from the timeline, use the Selection tool and click once on the clip to select it. The selected clip will be highlighted. Then select Sequence > Lift, or press the Delete key. You can also delete the clip by selecting Edit > Cut, or pressing Command-X.

After deleting the clip using one of these methods, a blank space, or **gap,** will be left on the timeline. You can remove the gap by clicking on it once with the Selection tool and pressing the Delete key. Alternatively, you can close the gap by positioning the playhead anywhere within the gap and selecting Sequence > Close Gap, or pressing Control-G.

FIG-05-27 Using the Selection tool, click once to select a clip to delete.

FIG-05-28 Press the Delete key, or select Sequence > Lift. A gap will be left on the timeline.

FIG-05-29 To delete the gap, click on it once with the Selection tool to highlight it.

FIG-05-30 Then press the Delete key to close the gap.

FIG-05-31 You can also remove a gap by positioning the playhead within the gap.

FIG-05-32 Then select Sequence > Close Gap, or press Control-G to close the gap.

TIP ✪ *Clips are automatically pasted into tracks that have Auto Select enabled. If Auto Select has not been set, the clips will be pasted into the tracks where they originated. Auto Select is the toggle to the far right of the track controls at the beginning of each track.*

Copying and Pasting a Clip

You can also copy and paste clips on the timeline. To copy a clip, select it and choose Edit > Copy, or press Command-C. You can also copy it by holding down the Option key *after* selecting the clip and then dragging the clip to a new location. To paste a clip, position the playhead where you want to paste it and choose Edit > Paste, or press Command-V. Keep in mind you can also cut (Command-X) and paste clips, instead of copying and pasting them.

FIG-05-33 To copy a clip, select it and choose Edit > Copy, or press Command-C.

FIG-05-34 Position the playhead on the track where you want to paste the clip.

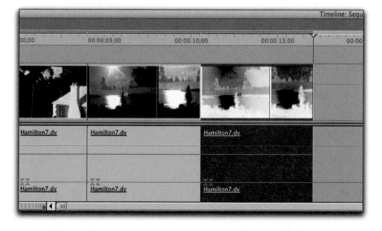

FIG-05-35 Then select Edit > Paste, or press Command-V.

Trimming Clips

After you have finished a rough edit by quickly positioning your clips on the timeline, you will want to fine-tune your edit by **trimming,** or adjusting the frames, at your edit points. There are several methods for trimming clips in Final Cut Pro. You can set new in and out points in the Viewer window. You can also use the Roll tool to adjust the edit point between two clips at the same time on the timeline; this is known as a **two-sided edit.** However, one of the preferred ways to perform a two-sided edit is to use the **Trim Edit** window.

First you'll need to learn how to quickly navigate between edit points on the timeline. Position the playhead on the timeline, and click the Go to Next Edit button in the Canvas window, or press Shift-E or the down arrow key. Alternatively, you can select Mark > Next > Edit. You can also click the Go to Previous Edit button in the Canvas window, or press Option-E or the up arrow key. You can also select Mark > Previous > Edit.

Once you are at the edit point, double-click between the two clips to launch the Trim Edit window. You can play the clip on either side and select a new in or out point. To select a new in point on the clip to the right, play the clip and click the Mark In button, or press the "i" key when you reach the frame.

 Keep in mind that in order to trim a clip, the captured clip must have sufficient frames to work from. That's why you should always add handles at the capture stage. If there aren't enough frames available, you will get a Media Limit error.

Trimming Tools

In addition to the Trim Edit window, Final Cut Pro has sophisticated Trimming tools. A **slip edit** *is a type of edit where the duration of the clip and its location stay the same, but both in and out points are changed at the same time. A* **slide edit** *is a type of edit in which the duration of the selected clip stays the same, and the clips to either side of it adjust their durations to make room. A* **ripple edit** *is a type of edit in which the duration of a clip is altered, and the start and end times of the other clips on the track change respectively to move with it. A* **roll edit** *is a type of edit in which the duration of the sequence stays the same, but the edit point between two clips shifts equally by subtracting frames from one clip and adding them to the other.*

FIG-05-36 To quickly navigate through the sequence to the next edit point, first position the playhead on the timeline.

FIG-05-37 Then, in the Canvas window, click the Go to Next Edit button, or press Shift-E or the down arrow key.

FIG-05-38 Then double-click on the edit point between two clips on the timeline.

FIG-05-39 The Trim Edit window will open. To change the in point of the clip on the right, first click the play button.

FIG-05-40 Click the Mark In button, or press the "i" key, when you reach the desired frame.

FIG-05-41 You can then view the new in point of the clip in the sequence.

Special Techniques

In addition to drag-to-timeline editing, cutting, copying, pasting, and trimming clips, there are some other common techniques you will want to master for basic editing. These include linking and unlinking clips, working with markers, creating a freeze frame, altering a clip's speed, and exporting a still frame.

Linking and Unlinking Clips

When you capture a video clip with audio, the video and audio portions are automatically linked. There may come a time when you wish to unlink the clip. Perhaps you only want to use the audio portion of a file, or perhaps you might wish to display a graphic over a portion of the video clip while the audio plays continually underneath it.

When you unlink a video clip and move either its video or audio portion, Final Cut Pro displays an **out-of-synch indicator,** which lets you know how many frames the audio and video portions are offset by. Because Final Cut Pro keeps track of the out-of-synch data after the audio and video clips are separated, you can synchronize them again at any time. To unlink a clip, select the clip and choose Modify > Link, or press Command-L. To turn a linked selection on or off, click the Linked Selection button or press Shift-L.

➡ *You can link up to 24 audio files with a single video file in Final Cut Pro. When you link multiple items together in the timeline, you can create a **merged clip.***

Getting Clips Back in Synch

There are three ways to get a clip back in synch. You can Control-click on the out-of-synch indicator in the shortcut menu. Then select Move into Synch and the tracks will line back up again. Alternatively, you can select the clip that is out-of-synch and type in the opposite timecode offset value. (You do not have to type the numbers into any special place. Just select the clip and begin typing. The Move field will automatically appear in the Timeline window once you start typing the numbers.) When you press Return, the clip will synchronize itself again. Finally, if you no longer wish to view the out-of-synch indicator, you can tell Final Cut Pro to think the clip synchronized by selecting the tracks of the clip and choosing Modify > Mark in Synch.

TIP ✪ *Hold down the Option key while making a selection to temporarily enable or disable linking. If you hold down the Option key after making the selection, you can duplicate the clip by dragging it to another location.*

FIG-05-42 Select the clip and choose Modify > Link, or press Command-L, to unlink a clip.

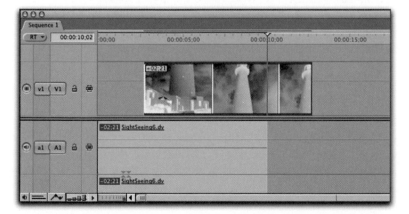

FIG-05-43 Deselect the clip and drag the video clip down the timeline to view the out-of synch indicator.

FIG-05-44 Click the Linked Selection button, or press Shift-L, to turn on or off a linked selection.

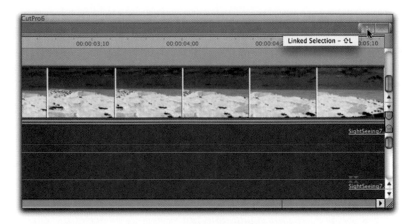

FIG-05-45 When the link has been turned off, you can offset the video and audio.

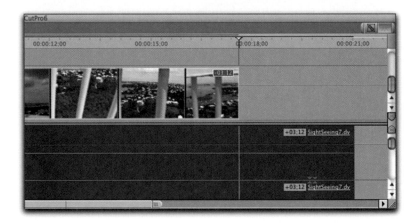

*A **split edit** is a technique that makes one of the linked audio or video portions longer than the other by setting different in or out points. This is often done for effect to soften edits; for example, you may want to hear the audio before you see the video image to soften the cut and make it less noticeable. To create a split edit, play the clip in the Viewer window and set your in point by pressing "i". (Use "o" for the out point.) Then press Control-i to split a video in point later than an audio in point. Or, to do the reverse, press Option-Command-i. Then drag the clip from the Viewer window to the timeline.*

Working with Markers

Markers are visual points of reference on clips or sequences. They can be used for synchronization, editing, or creating DVD chapter markers or compression markers. Clip markers are pink and can be added in either the Viewer or Timeline windows. Sequence markers are green and can be added in either the Canvas or Timeline windows.

To add a clip marker, open the clip in the Viewer window. Play the clip and position the playhead over the frame you wish to mark. Select Mark > Markers > Add, or press either the "m" key or the "`" (accent) key. You can also click the Add Marker button in the Viewer window. To add a sequence marker in the timeline, position the playhead over the frame you wish to mark in the timeline. Make certain the clip is not selected, or you will place a clip marker by mistake! Then select Mark > Markers > Add, or press either the "m" key or the "`" (accent) key. Or you can click the Add Marker button in the Canvas window.

Types of Markers

Note marker—*the default marker that is added to a clip or sequence.*

Chapter marker—*a marker that can be exported as a DVD chapter marker to DVD Studio Pro.*

Compression marker—*a marker that tells either Compressor or DVD Studio Pro where to create an MPEG I-frame during compression.*

Scoring marker—*a marker that provides Soundtrack Pro a visual cue for scoring.*

Audio peak marker—*a marker showing where audio is digitally clipping and the level should be reduced.*

Long-frame marker—*a marker showing an abnormally long frame created during capture that can cause potential playback and output problems.*

FIG-05-46 To place a clip marker, first position the playhead in the Viewer window over the frame you wish to mark in the clip.

FIG-05-47 Then click the Add Marker button in the Viewer window, press either the "m" or "`" (accent) key, or select Mark > Markers > Add.

FIG-05-48 The marker in the clip will appear pink.

FIG-05-49 To set a sequence marker, first position the playhead over the frame you wish to mark in the timeline.

FIG-05-50 In the Canvas window, click the Add Marker button, press either the "m" or "`" (accent) key, or select Mark > Markers > Add.

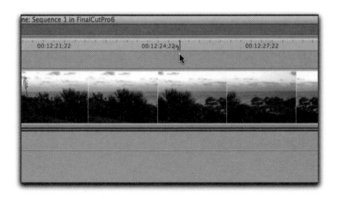

FIG-05-51 The marker will appear green in the timeline.

You can also enter details about markers, specify the marker type, or edit the marker. To make changes to the marker, first position the playhead over the marker and select Mark > Markers > Edit, or press either the "m" or "`" (accent) key. You can also Control-click the marker and choose Edit Marker from the shortcut menu. The Edit Marker dialog box will then open, and you can add any details or make changes to the marker.

TIP ✪ *To remove the marker type, delete the appropriate annotation text (i.e., <CHAPTER>) in the Comment field in the Edit Marker dialog box.*

FIG-05-52 Position the playhead over the marker and select Mark > Markers > Edit to open the Edit Marker dialog box.

You can also delete clip markers in the Viewer window. First, move the playhead to the marker. Then in the Viewer window, Option-click the Add Marker button, or select Mark > Markers > Delete (or Delete All). You can also press Command-` (accent) key, or press either the "m" or the "`" (accent) key to open the Edit Marker dialog box. Then click Delete.

To delete a sequence marker in the timeline, first make sure that no clips are selected. Then position the playhead over the marker. In the Canvas window, Option-click the Add Marker button, or select Mark > Markers > Delete (or Delete All). Alternatively, you can also press Command-` (accent) key, or press either the "m" or the "`" (accent) key to open the Edit Marker dialog box. Then click Delete.

You can also navigate using markers. To move a marker, first make sure snapping is turned on. Then position the playhead near the marker, and it will snap to it. The marker turns yellow when the playhead is directly over it. You can also Control-click in the Current Timecode field in the Canvas window. Then select the then marker from the shortcut menu. To move to the next marker, select Mark > Next > Marker, or press Shift-M or Shift-down arrow key. To move to the previous marker, select Mark > Previous Marker, or press Option-M or Shift-up arrow key.

Creating a Freeze Frame

Another editing technique is to create a **freeze frame,** which is a video clip that freezes, or holds, a particular frame for a specified duration. Use the Editing tab of the User Preferences window to set the default duration for freeze frames. You can adjust the duration of the freeze frame after it has been created at any time by typing in the Timecode Duration field in the Viewer window. To create a freeze frame, position the playhead over the frame you want to freeze in the Canvas window. Then select Modify > Make Freeze Frame, or press Shift-N. The freeze frame will be created and appear in the Viewer window. You can adjust its duration there, if need be; then drag it to the timeline.

FIG-05-53 In the Canvas window, position the playhead over the frame you wish to freeze.

FIG-05-54 Select Modify > Make Freeze Frame, or press Shift-N. To adjust the duration of the freeze frame, enter a new length in the Timecode Duration field in the Viewer window.

FIG·05·55 Drag the freeze frame to the desired location on the timeline.

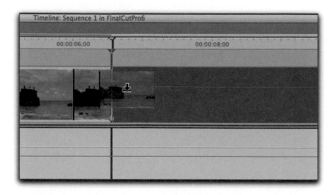

FIG·05·56 The finished freeze frame will assign a numerical timecode address to its name.

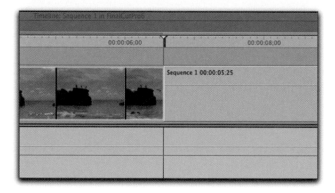

Altering a Clip's Speed

Another popular technique is to change the speed of a clip. If the speed is less than 100%, the clip will play slower than its original speed; if the speed is greater than 100%, the clip will play faster than its original speed. You have the option of making the clip's speed either constant or variable. **Constant speed** means the duration of the actual clip changes. A slow-motion clip will have a longer duration than the original clip, whereas a sped-up clip will have a shorter duration than the original clip. **Variable speed** means the actual clip duration doesn't change; instead, the clip's speed varies over time. Variable speed is not applied to the audio portion of a clip. You can still extend or shorten a clip by trimming, even with variable speed applied.

You also have several options when altering a clip's speed. You can play a clip backwards, by selecting the **Reverse speed** option. You can also enable **frame blending,** which reduces **strobing,** or the stuttering playback of slow motion clips. Frame blending works by using two frames on either side of duplicate frames and creates new frames that are a blending, or a composite, of both. Another way to combat strobing, which is particularly effective on clips at less than 20% speed, is to apply motion blur in the Motion tab of the Viewer window. **Motion blur** is an effect that blurs a clip with motion that has been keyframed. To alter a clip's speed, select the clip and choose Modify > Speed or press Command-J. You can also Control-click the clip and select Speed from the shortcut menu.

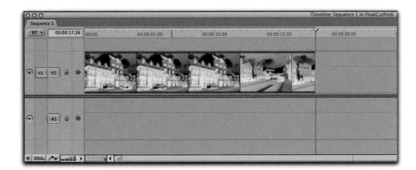

FIG-05-57 To alter a clip's constant speed, first select it. Take note of its original duration.

FIG-05-58 Select Modify > Speed, or press Command-J, to open the Speed dialog box. Choose Constant Speed from the pop-up menu. To make a clip play faster, enter a percentage greater than 100 in the Speed field.

FIG-05-59 The clip's new duration will be shorter because the modified clip is now playing faster than the original clip.

Exporting a Still Frame

Finally, you may on occasion wish to export a **still frame** of video, or a single frame, to be used as a still image with other applications. In order to export a still frame, position the playhead over the frame you wish to export in either the Viewer or the Canvas window. Then select File > Export > Using QuickTime Conversion. The Save dialog box will open. Select Still Image from the Format pop-up menu. Click on Options to choose a file format, such as JPEG, and to adjust the compression options if need be.

FIG-05-60 First position the playhead over the frame you wish to export in the Viewer window.

FIG-05-61 Then select File > Export > Using QuickTime Conversion. The Save dialog box will open. Select Still Image from the Format pop-up menu. Click the Options button to select the file format and settings.

FIG-05-62 The Export Image Sequence Settings dialog box will open. Choose the JPEG file format from the Format pop-up menu and click the Options button. You can ignore the frames per second field.

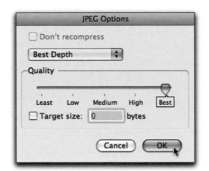

FIG-05-63 The JPEG Options dialog box will open. Adjust the Quality slider to Best and click OK.

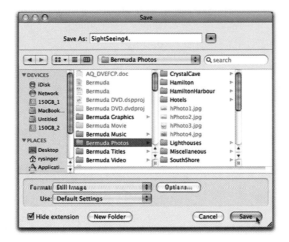

FIG-05-64 The Save dialog box will now open, where you can designate a name and place to save the still image; click Save.

Summary

There are many different ways to edit in Final Cut Pro. One method is not necessarily better than another, but it may better suit you. You may prefer drag-to-timeline editing instead of three-point editing. You may prefer to use the menus and buttons, as opposed to the keyboard shortcuts. However, regardless of which particular editing style you adopt, you need to make sure that you master the basic editing skills and techniques that are essential to every digital video editor.

Mark > Mark Clip	*Mark Clip (button)*	*x (key)*	**KEYBOARD SHORTCUTS**
Edit > Undo		*Command-Z*	
View > Snapping	*Snapping (button)*	*n (key)*	
Selection tool		*a (key)*	
Other Selection tools		*g (key repeated)*	
Select multiple contiguous clips		*Shift-Selection tool*	
Select multiple noncontiguous clips		*Command-Selection tool*	
Track Selection tools		*t (key repeated)*	
Sequence > Lift		*Delete (key)*	

Edit > Cut		*Command-X*
Sequence > Close Gap		*Control-G*
Sequence > Ripple Delete		*Shift-Delete*
Sequence > Lift		*Delete*
Edit > Copy		*Command-C*
Edit > Paste		*Command-V*
Mark > Next > Edit	*Go to Next Edit (button)*	*Shift-E or down arrow (key)*
Mark > Previous > Edit	*Go to Previous Edit (button)*	*Option-E or up arrow (key)*
Temporary unlink clip		*Selection tool + Option*
Modify > Link		*Command-L*
Selection on/off	*Linked Selection (button)*	*Shift-L*
Split edit; video in point later than audio in point		*Control-i*
Split edit; audio in point later than video in point		*Option-Command-i*
Split edit, video out point later than audio out point		*Control-o*
Split edit, audio out point later than video out point		*Option-Command-o*
Mark > Markers > Add	*Add Marker (button)*	*"m" (key), or "`" (accent key)*
Mark > Markers > Edit		*"m" (key), or "`" (accent key)*
Mark > Markers > Delete (or Delete All)		*Command-` (accent key)*
Mark > Previous > Marker		*Option-M or Shift-up arrow (key)*
Mark > Next > Marker		*Shift-M or Shift-down arrow (key)*
Delete marker		*Option-click the Add Marker (button)*
Modify > Make Freeze Frame		*Shift-N*
Modify > Speed		*Command-J*

REWIND

1. What is the drag-to-timeline method of editing?
2. What is the difference between an insert edit and an overwrite edit?
3. What is three-point editing?
4. What is a replace edit? What is a fit to fill edit? What is a superimpose edit?
5. What are the methods for trimming clips in Final Cut Pro?
6. What is a slip edit? What is a slide edit?
7. What is a ripple edit? What is a roll edit?
8. What is the purpose of linking and unlinking clips?

9. What is a split edit?
10. What is the purpose of using markers?

TAKE TWO

1. Practice drag-to-timeline editing and three-point editing.
2. Try editing using only the menus and buttons. Then try it again, using only the keyboard shortcuts.
3. Try each of these special techniques: linking and unlinking clips, working with markers, creating a freeze frame, altering a clip's speed, and exporting a still frame.

CHAPTER 6

Creating Video Transitions

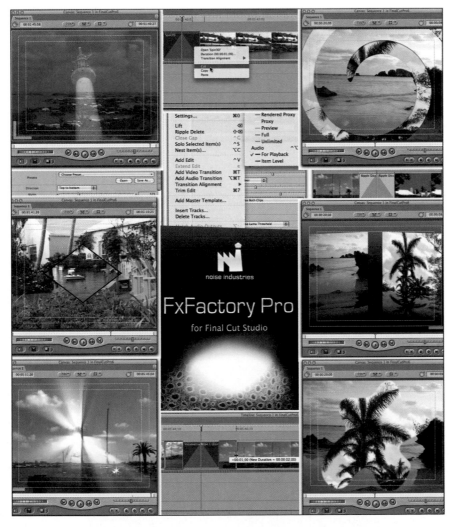

OBJECTIVES

Learn how to create video transitions

Understand how transitions are categorized

Understand third-party transitions

Examine how to customize transitions

Learn how to render transitions

ONCE YOU HAVE mastered the basics of arranging clips on the timeline, you can begin to add transitions. Editors have certain unspoken rules regarding transitions. For instance, you never want to place a transition between every clip. How often and where to add transitions is an artistic choice. Transitions should add to the overall effect of the edit, rather than becoming a nuisance or a distraction.

Understanding Transitions

A transition is a visual effect that acts as a bridge connecting one video layer to another. The simplest transition is a **cut,** where one video clip ends and another begins. You do not have to add a transition to the sequence in Final Cut Pro to view a cut; it is created automatically when two clips are placed next to each other on the timeline. Another common transition is a **cross dissolve,** where one clip is superimposed over another, with the first clip fading out as the second clip fades in.

FIG·06·01 This is the first video clip, before the transition starts.

FIG·06·02 The cross dissolve transition superimposes the two clips.

FIG-06-03 This is the second video clip, after the transition finishes.

The cut and the cross dissolve are subtle transitions and are used frequently when editing. Other, more noticeable transitions are used specifically for effect. There is no hard and fast rule as to how many transitions to place in an edit; it is dictated by the overall style of the piece and the feel the editor wishes to create.

In addition to choosing how many transitions to add, the duration of the transition is also another stylistic choice. Transitions typically last anywhere from 10 frames to 2 seconds, with the most common duration being between 15 frames and 1 second. Longer transitions can also be used sparingly for effect.

Types of Transitions

Transitions are usually grouped and categorized by style. Common types of transitions are dissolves, irises, and wipes. Final Cut Pro has an array of transitions to choose from, and most can be customized. In addition, you can purchase and use third-party transitions with Final Cut Pro.

Transition Categories

- *3D Simulation*
- *Dissolve*
- *Iris*
- *Map*
- *Page Peel*
- *QuickTime*
- *Slide*
- *Stretch*
- *Wipe*

FIG-06-04 Transitions are organized by category in the Effects tab of the Browser window.

FIG-06-05 The Diamond Iris transition is one style in the Iris category.

FIG-06-06 The Clock Wipe transition is a common style in the Wipe category.

 **SPOTLIGHT**

Gabriele de Simone, Founder, Noise Industries, LLC

FIG-06-07 Gabriele de Simone is the founder and lead software engineer of Noise Industries.

Gabriele de Simone is founder and lead software engineer of Noise Industries. Since the company's inception in 2004, Gabriele has brought innovative visual effects software to Apple Final Cut Studio, Final Cut Express, Avid Xpress Pro, and Media Composer editing products. By leveraging the modern graphics technologies in Mac OS X, Noise Industries ships the only software of its kind that allows end-users to customize and create visual effects plug-ins without writing a single line of code.

Before joining the video industry, Gabriele had most recently worked on metadata management software with Bruce Horn, creator of the original Finder and Mac desktop experience.

Born in the Gulf of Naples, Italy, Gabriele earned both an M.A. and a B.A. in computer science from Boston University.

FIG-06-08 Noise Industries makes FxFactory for Apple's Final Cut Studio and Final Cut Express, and Factory Tools for Avid Express Pro and Media Composer.

noise industries

1. Tell us about the products that are made by Noise Industries.

Our commercial products are FxFactory for Final Cut Studio and Final Cut Express, and Factory Tools for Avid Xpress Pro and Media Composer. Both are visual effects packages that build on modern graphics technology to deliver unprecedented speed and, increasingly, film-quality image processing. Both plug-in packages have features that are specific to their audience. Final Cut Studio users will find that superb host integration is very important to us: all plug-ins work just the same, whether they are applied inside Final Cut Pro or Motion. We also support high-precision rendering to work on media with 10-bits (or higher) of information for each color channel. Avid users will recognize that our AVX plug-ins provide many compositing features that cover important gaps in the Avid editing interface, such as real-time compositing modes and geometry adjustments.

2. What inspired you to create FxFactory?

The inspiration to write FxFactory came from some great graphics technologies delivered by Apple in recent times. A new trend in our industry has been to utilize graphics cards (GPUs) to perform tasks that were previously carried by the computer's processor (the CPU). Apple has done a great job of making this technology available for things that matter to us: high-quality effects for digital video applications. Motion embodies this trend more than any other application, and we decided to create the first major plug-in package designed on this foundation.

3. How is FxFactory different from other plug-in packages?

The first striking difference between FxFactory and other plug-in packages is that our visual effects tend to render very quickly. This is a side effect of a modern rendering architecture built from the ground up to use graphics cards for acceleration. However, our biggest innovation is to give customers the ability to create their own effects. All other plug-in packages offer a fixed set of plug-ins and functionality; FxFactory lets you modify and create plug-ins without writing a single line of code. Our customers take advantage of this feature by building plug-ins specific to their workflow. In some cases, they decide to distribute their creations, thus becoming plug-in vendors themselves. This is a revolutionary step for our industry: our customers end up becoming partners, and the entire editing community reaps the benefits. It's an ever-growing collection of visual effect plug-ins offered at a very low cost.

4. How has FxFactory been received in the industry?

FxFactory has been a stunning success with Final Cut Studio users. Perhaps you can't go wrong by providing hundreds of visual effects at an affordable price, superior host integration, and fast rendering times. More importantly, FxFactory is available as a free download: users have a chance to try every commercial plug-in and purchase only the effects they are interested in. We also offer some excellent free plug-ins, which give potential customers a big incentive for trying our product.

5. Tell us about some of the other developers who are making plug-ins for FxFactory.

Peter Wiggins, author of the Volumetrix plug-ins for Final Cut Studio, was an early Motion adopter as well as an experienced Shake and Final Cut Pro user. Long frustrated by what he saw as glaring omissions in other plug-in packages, he was able to use FxFactory to build the plug-ins he really wanted. When he released his Volumetric Light Spill plug-ins to the public, they became an instant success. Because FxFactory made it possible to build his plug-ins in weeks, rather than months, they are offered at a very low cost and are able to reach the widest of audiences.

The number of customers who become plug-in developers is growing rapidly, and with it the variety of visual effects that are available: Roger Bolton, who is behind the CoreMelt plug-ins, has dedicated an entire plug-in package to creating stunning slideshows; SUGARfx, a company founded by motion graphics artist Ricardo Silva, is specializing in "canned" motion graphics themes; the Japanese artist and animator Mamoru Kano is behind the eclectic collection of Futurismo plug-ins. Many other companies are working on FxFactory plug-ins, and a few of the high-end postproduction houses are taking advantage of our product to develop plug-ins for specific projects.

FIG-06-09 FxFactory won a *Videography* Vidy Award at the National Association of Broadcasters (NAB) show in 2007, demonstrating technology innovation and engineering excellence.

TIP✪ *You can try out FxFactory yourself! It's included in the back-of-the-book DVD. You are also eligible for a special discount on FxFactory Pro! See the DVD for details.*

There are now more than three hundred plug-ins currently available in FxFactory. Some are free and others are available for purchase. FxFactory Pro, which retails for $399, is unique because its plug-ins can be modified by end users. This professional package provides a large number of ready-to-be-used effects for Motion and Final Cut Pro and the ability for users to create their own effects. The open-ended architecture makes FxFactory versatile—fulfilling the needs for individual editors, who want a large selection of plug-ins for their projects, and postproduction houses, who want to improve their workflow with customizable effects.

Here are some of the transitions available in FxFactory.

FIG-06-10 First video clip.

FIG-06-11 Second video clip.

FIG-06-12 CoreMelt Editing Pack: Barcode Wipe.

FIG·06·13 CoreMelt
Editing Pack: Bubbles
Dissolve.

FIG·06·14 CoreMelt
Editing Pack: Clouds
Dissolve.

FIG-06-15 Noise Industries: Copy Machine.

FIG-06-16 Noise Industries: Disintegrate with Tiles.

FIG-06-17 CoreMelt
Editing Pack: Film
Dissolve.

FIG-06-18 CoreMelt
Editing Pack: Liquid
Dissolve.

FIG-06-19 Noise Industries: Paint Wipe.

FIG-06-20 CoreMelt Editing Pack: Panels Mix Off.

FIG-06-21 CoreMelt
Editing Pack: Radial Mask
Wipe.

FIG-06-22 Noise
Industries: Twirl Wipe.

FIG-06-23 CoreMelt
Editing Pack: Twisted
Dissolve.

FIG-06-24 Noise
Industries:
Videoconference.

FIG-06-25 CoreMelt
Editing Pack: Waterdrop
Distort Wipe.

FIG-06-26 Noise
Industries: Waves Wipe.

FIG-06-27 CoreMelt
Editing Pack: Zipper.

Working with Transitions

Transitions can be aligned on the timeline in several ways. You can choose to place the transition at the edit point between two clips, centering the transition on the cut. You can also add the transition to the out point of a clip, ending on the cut. Finally, you can place the transition on the in point of a clip, starting on the cut.

When attempting to place a transition at the edit point between two clips, you may, on occasion, receive the warning "Insufficient content for edit." This means that there are not enough overlapping frames at the edit point of the two clips to cover the duration of the transition. In this case, you can choose to shorten the duration of your clips to make room for the transition.

However, if you can't shorten your clips and you don't have enough extra frames to create the transition, you can apply the transition before and/or after the edit point, instead of at the edit point. Final Cut Pro will use frames of black instead of the second clip to create the transition. To make it easy to select the in point or out point of a clip, temporarily move the adjacent clip out of the way. To make the transition appear more seamless, apply the same transition to both the out point of the first clip and the in point of the second clip. You may need to reverse the transition's direction on the second clip by clicking on the directional arrow in the Transitions Editor.

 Digital video editors will often capture a little extra video at the beginning and end of a video clip (called handles) to create breathing room in case they should need the extra frames later in the editing process.

FIG-06-28 A dialog box will warn you if there are not enough frames available to create the transition.

FIG-06-29 If you don't have enough frames, you can shorten your clips to supply what's needed for the transition.

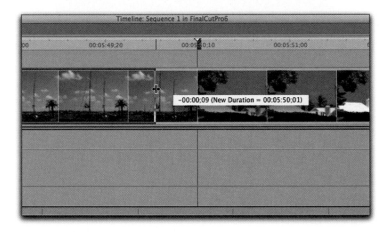

FIG-06-30 This Ripple Dissolve transition can now be applied at the edit point between clips, centered on the cut, because there are now sufficient frames for the transition.

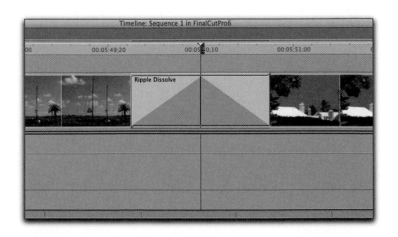

FIG-06-31 The alternative would be to add the transition to the out point of the first clip, so that it is ending on the cut. It's easier to select the in/out point if you temporarily move the adjacent clip.

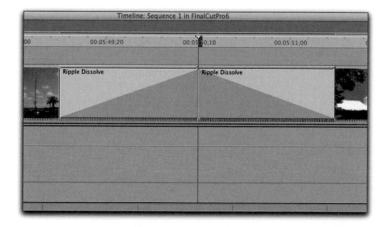

FIG-06-32 The same transition is then applied to the in point of the second clip. The direction of the Ripple Dissolve needed to be reversed on the second transition to make it appear seamless.

Adding Transitions to the Sequence

There are several ways to add transitions to your sequence. You can add them as you edit by selecting the "Insert with Transition" or "Overwrite with Transition" options in the Canvas window. Or you can add transitions to clips that are already in the Timeline window.

To add a transition to video clips that are already in your sequence, position your cursor over the edit point on the timeline and click once. The edit point will become highlighted. You can also position the playhead at the edit point in either the Timeline or Canvas windows. Then select Effects > Video Transitions and choose the type of transition you wish to apply. Alternatively, you can also drag the desired transition from the Effects tab of the Browser window directly to the edit point in the Timeline window. Transitions applied directly from the Effects tab of the Browser window will automatically be centered on the edit point. You can also Control-click the edit point in the Timeline window and Add Transition from the shortcut menu to apply a transition.

TIP✪ *In order to replace an existing transition with a new one, position the playhead over the transition in either the Timeline or Canvas windows, and apply the new transition.*

TIP✪ *To quickly navigate between edit points, use the Previous Edit and Next Edit buttons in the Canvas window.*

FIG-06-33 Position the cursor over the edit point in the Timeline window where you wish to place the transition and click once to highlight it.

FIG-06-34 Then select Effects > Video Transitions > Dissolve > Cross Dissolve to create a fade from black.

FIG-06-35 You can also drag transitions directly from the Effects tab to the edit point in the Timeline window.

FIG·06·36 Or you can Control-click the edit point in the sequence and choose Add Transition Cross Dissolve from the shortcut menu.

Using the Default Transition

The fastest way to place a transition in Final Cut Pro is by using the **default transition**—a predetermined transition of a specified length. The default video transition is a 1 second Cross Dissolve. To apply the default transition, press Command-T or select Effects > Default – Cross Dissolve. You can change the default transition type by selecting the desired transition in the Effects tab of the Browser window and selecting Effects > Set Default under Video Transitions. You can also Control-click the transition's icon and choose Set Default Transition from the shortcut menu.

TIP ✪ *The current default transition is underlined in the Effects tab of the Browser window.*

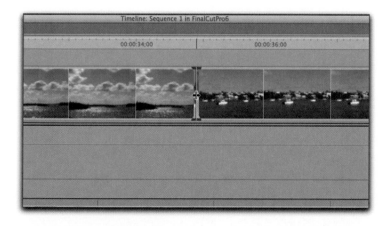

FIG·06·37 To apply the default video transition, first select an edit point by clicking on it.

FIG-06-38 Then
select Effects >
Default – Cross Dissolve,
or press Command-T.

FIG-06-39 The
1-second Cross Dissolve
is applied as the default
transition.

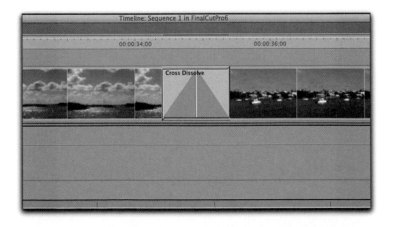

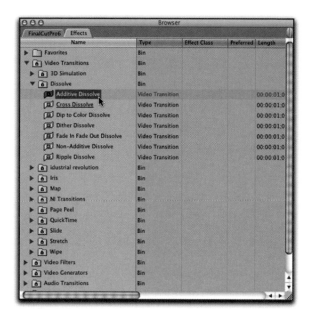

FIG-06-40 To change
the default transition,
select the desired
transition in the Effects
tab of the Browser
window.

FIG-06-41 Then
select Effects > Set
Default under the Video
Transitions portion of the
menu.

FIG-06-42
Alternatively, you can Control-click the desired transition's icon and choose Set Default Transition from the shortcut menu.

FIG-06-43 The new default transition, the Additive Dissolve, is now underlined in the Effects tab of the Browser window.

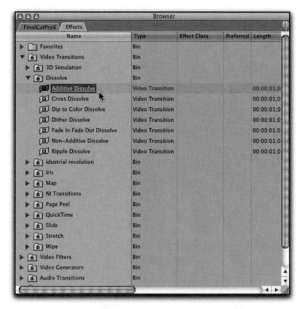

Moving, Copying, and Deleting Transitions

You can move, copy, and delete transitions in Final Cut Pro. Moving a transition is easy. Simply select it and drag it from its current location to the new edit point in the Timeline window. Remember, you will need enough extra frames to center the transition over the edit point. You can also move the transition to before or after the edit point.

To copy a transition, select the transition in the Timeline window by clicking it once to highlight it, then select Edit > Copy, or press Command-C. You can also Control-click the transition and choose Copy from the shortcut menu. To paste the transition to a new location, select the edit point where you would like to paste the transition by clicking on it once, then select Edit > Paste, or press Command-V. You can also Control-click the transition or edit point and choose Paste from the shortcut menu. Alternatively, you can also copy a transition from one edit point to another, by holding down the Option key and dragging the transition to the desired edit point on the timeline.

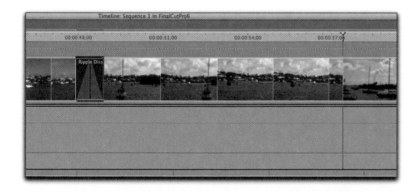

FIG-06-44 To move a transition, select it and drag it from its current location to a new edit point on the timeline.

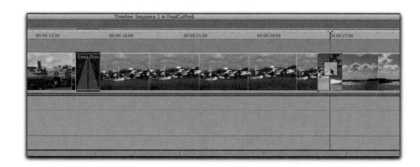

FIG-06-45 To copy a transition, select it, and select Edit > Copy, or press Command-C.

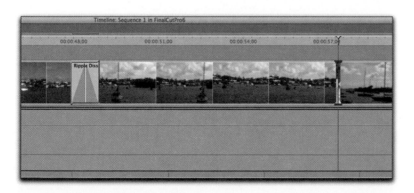

FIG-06-46 Then select the edit point on the timeline where you would like to paste the transition.

FIG-06-47 To paste the transition, select Edit > Paste, or press Command-V.

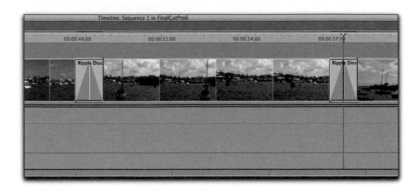

FIG-06-48 Alternatively, to copy the transition, Control-click the transition and choose Copy from the shortcut menu.

FIG-06-49 Alternatively, to paste the transition, Control-click the transition or edit point and choose Paste from the shortcut menu.

FIG-06-50 To delete a transition, first select it by clicking on it once in the timeline.

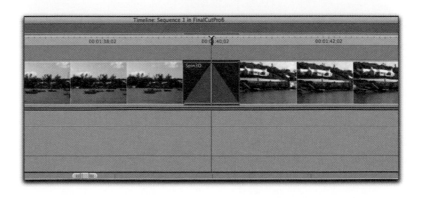

FIG-06-51 Then select Edit > Clear, or press the Delete key.

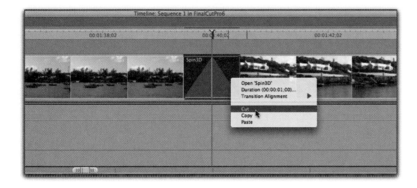

FIG-06-52
Alternatively, you can Control-click the transition and choose Cut from the shortcut menu.

To delete a transition from a sequence, select the transition you want to remove in the Timeline window and click once to highlight it. Then select Edit > Clear, or press the Delete key. You can also Control-click the transition and choose Cut from the shortcut menu.

Changing a Transition's Duration

Typically transitions last anywhere from 10 or 15 frames to 1 or 2 seconds. The default duration of a transition is 1 second. Often, you will want to change a transition's duration. You can quickly shorten or lengthen a transition by clicking on either edge and dragging it inward or outward. Dragging it outward lengthens it, while dragging it inward shortens it.

TIP ✪ *When applying transitions to still images and titles, keep in mind that the duration of the transition shortens the amount of time the image or title is visible on the screen. Be sure to take this into consideration so that there is sufficient time to view the image or title before it disappears.*

FIG-06-53 You can adjust the duration of a transition by clicking on either edge and dragging it inward or outward. As you drag the edge of the transition, the new duration will temporarily appear as a guide.

Using the Transition Editor

Once a transition has been added to the timeline, you can customize it by double-clicking on the transition to activate the Transition Editor. You can also click once to select the transition, and select View > Transition Editor. Alternatively, you can Control-click the transition and choose Open from the shortcut menu. The transition's settings will appear in the Viewer window, where you can select different options.

In addition to changing the duration of a transition, you can also select the percentage values for the start and end of the transition. A complete transition from one video clip to another starts at 0 and ends at 100 percent. You can also adjust the alignment of a transition, or trim frames around the edit point. As you adjust a transition's duration or edit point in the Transition Editor, the Two-Up display will appear in the Canvas window. Many transitions will also have additional options that you can customize, such as direction and color.

You can zoom in on the Transition Editor by selecting View > Zoom In, using the Zoom In tool, or pressing Command-+(plus). You can zoom out by selecting View > Zoom Out, using the Zoom Out tool, or pressing Command-−(minus). To zoom to fit the ruler in the Transition Editor, press Shift-Z.

FIG-06-54 Position your cursor over the transition and double-click to open the Transition Editor, or select the transition by clicking once and select View > Transition Editor.

FIG-06-55 Alternatively, you can Control-click the transition and choose Open from the shortcut menu.

FIG-06-56 The options for the transition will display in the Viewer window.

FIG-06-57 As you adjust the transition's duration or edit point, you can use the Two-Up display in the Canvas window as a guide.

Previewing and Rendering Transitions

Depending on what type of transition you select, you may want to preview it or render it to see what it will actually look like. Many transitions can be viewed in real-time, but some more complex transitions may not. To save time, you can still preview those frames of the transition, although not in real-time. You can preview individual frames of a transition by dragging the playhead across the transition in the timeline. As you do so, you can view those frames in the Canvas window. Alternatively, you can also position the playhead and select Mark > Play > Every Frame, or press Option-P or Option-\, to play back every frame of the transition; however, it will not play back in real-time. Press the space bar to stop the playback at anytime.

FIG-06-58 Certain transitions will have additional properties that you can customize. This third-party transition, Volumetrix Wipe 1 (Zoom), is made by idustrial revolution and has many properties you can modify.

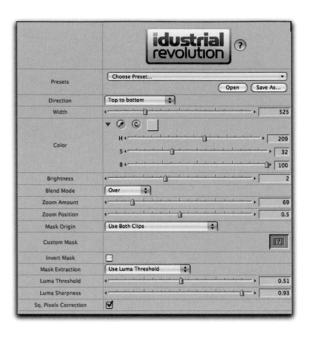

TIP ✪ *To cancel a render in progress, press the Escape (Esc) key.*

In order to play back the transition in real-time, you may need to render it. A transition that requires rendering will have a red line in the render bar at the top of the Timeline window. In digital video, a render means to process effects like filters and transitions so that they can be played back in real-time. To render the transition, select it in the Timeline window and select Sequence > Render Selection > Both (selecting Both means that both the video and the audio will be rendered). Or you can press Command-R to render the selection. A dialog box will open to show the progress of the render. After a transition has been rendered, you can play it back from the Timeline window and watch it in real-time in the Canvas window. A blue line in the render bar signifies that the transition has been rendered.

➔ *If the Caps Lock key is engaged, rendering is automatically disabled.*

FIG-06-59 To preview individual frames of a transition, drag the playhead across the transition in the timeline.

FIG-06-60 You can view the previewed frames in the Canvas window.

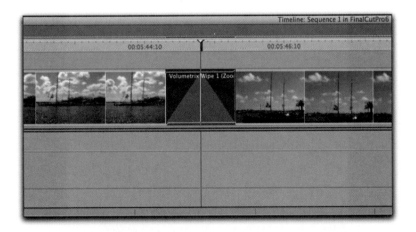

FIG-06-61 A red line in the render bar signifies a transition that requires rendering. To render the transition, first select it, then select Sequence > Render Selection > Both, or press Command-R.

FIG-06-62 A dialog box will show the progress of the render.

FIG-06-63 After the render has finished, a blue bar will appear in the render bar over the transition.

FIG-06-64 Before the Volumetrix transition starts.

FIG-06-65 Several frames into the transition.

FIG-06-66 Nearly halfway into the transition.

FIG-06-67 More
than halfway into the
transition.

FIG-06-68 Near the
end of the transition.

FIG-06-69 After the Volumetrix transition ends.

Summary

Whether you use built-in transitions or purchase third-party plug-in packages like Noise Industries FxFactory, there are endless options for customizing your edit in Final Cut Pro. Understanding the way transitions work, and how and when to use them, will help you to better develop your own unique editing style.

Effects > Default – Cross Dissolve		*Command-T*	**KEYBOARD SHORTCUTS**
Edit > Clear		*Delete key*	
View > Zoom in	*Zoom In tool*	*Command-+(plus)*	
View > Zoom out	*Zoom Out tool*	*Command-–(minus)*	
Zoom to fit		*Shift-Z*	
Mark > Play > Every Frame		*Option-P or Option-*	
Sequence > Render Selection > Both		*Command-R*	
Cancel render		*Esc key*	

1. What is a transition?

2. What are some common types of transitions?

3. What are third-party transitions?

4. Why are handles important when you are using transitions?

5. What is a default transition?

6. What is a fade to/from black?

7. What ways can you customize transitions?

8. What does the Transitions Editor allow you to do?

REWIND

9. How do you preview a transition?

10. How do you render a transition?

TAKE TWO

1. Practice adding different types of transitions to your sequence.

2. Try moving, copying, pasting, and deleting transitions.

3. Use the Transition Editor to customize your transitions.

CHAPTER 7

Using Layers and Transparency

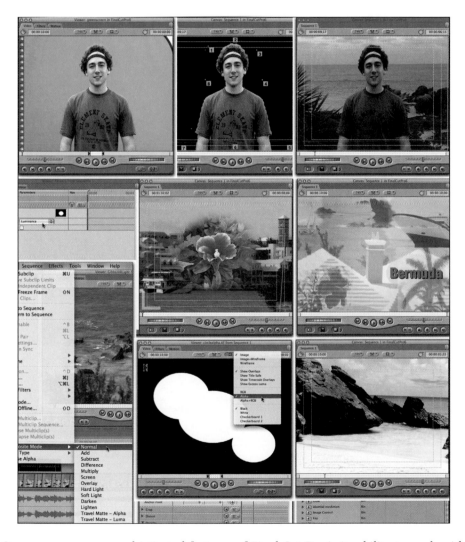

OBJECTIVES

Learn how to work with
tracks and layers

Examine transparency
and composite modes

Learn how to create and
use alpha channels

Learn how to work with
layered Photoshop files

Understand keying,
mattes, and masks

ONE OF THE more sophisticated features of Final Cut Pro is its ability to work with multiple video or graphic clips to create special effects. You can easily composite and layer clips in Final Cut Pro, as well as utilize alpha channels, mattes, and masks. You can even work with layered Adobe Photoshop files.

Compositing

Compositing, or **layering,** is the technique of combining multiple video layers into a single layer to achieve a special effect. The layers can be still titles, graphics, and/or video. Final Cut Pro allows you to work with up to 99 layers, or tracks, at one time.

Working with Tracks

Because each sequence can have up to 99 video tracks and 99 audio tracks, it is important to understand how to work with tracks in Final Cut Pro. You can add and delete tracks, lock tracks to prevent unwanted changes, temporarily disable tracks, and resize tracks in the Timeline window.

FIG-07-01 You can add a single track at a time by dragging a clip to the unused area above the current video track. Drag a clip to the unused area below the current audio track to add an additional audio track.

FIG-07-02 Final Cut Pro will automatically add a track to accommodate the media.

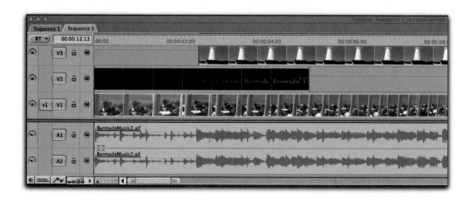

TIP✪ *Hold down the Option key when you click the Lock Track control to lock all the video and audio tracks except that track.*

TIP✪ *To lock a video track, press F4 and the number of the track you want to lock (1-9). To lock all the video tracks in the sequence, press Shift-F4. To lock an audio track, press F5 and the number of the track you want to lock (1-9). To lock all the audio tracks in the sequence, press Shift-F5.*

FIG-07-03 Or, Control-click above the current video track and choose Add Track from the shortcut menu. Control-click below the current audio track to do the same.

FIG-07-04 Select Sequence > Insert Tracks to add multiple tracks to a sequence. The Insert Tracks dialog box will open, allowing you to specify the track type, location, and number of tracks.

FIG-07-05 To delete a single track, Control-click in the area to the left of the track and choose Delete Track from the shortcut menu. After the track is deleted, the remaining tracks will automatically be renumbered.

FIG-07-06 To delete multiple tracks, select Sequence > Delete Tracks and choose from the options in the Delete Tracks dialog box.

FIG-07-07 When you click on the Lock Track control to the left of the track, a crosshatch pattern appears over the locked track, and any accidental changes are prevented. No edits can be made until you click again on the Lock Track control to unlock it.

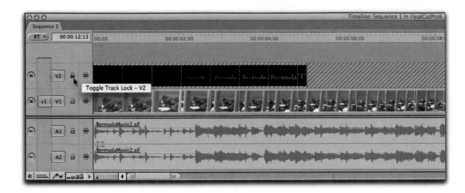

FIG-07-08 You can disable a track or tracks to hide the content during playback and output at any time. You can still see and edit the items on the track, but you won't see or hear them playback in the Canvas window. To disable a track, click on the Track Visibility control to the left of the track.

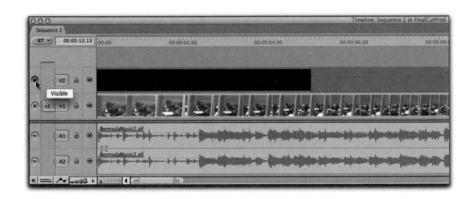

FIG-07-09 In order to see more or fewer tracks at one time, you can resize a video track by dragging the upper boundary near the track controls. To resize an individual audio track, drag the lower boundary of the track near the track controls.

TIP ✪ *Disabling a track is useful when you want to isolate a track or view an alternate edit. It is also useful if you don't want to wait for clips to render before playing back your sequence.*

FIG-07-10 Only the chosen video track has been resized.

FIG-07-11 You can also click on the Track Height control to resize all the tracks by clicking on the appropriate size icon at the bottom left of the Timeline window.

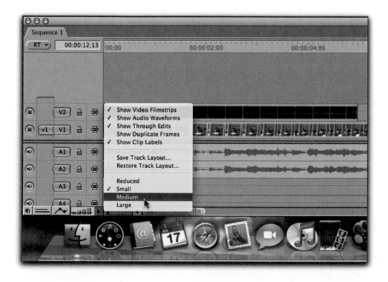

FIG-07-12 Alternatively, you can Control-click the Track Height control to choose from the Track Height shortcut menu.

TIP ✪ *To enable one track while disabling all the others, hold down the Option key while clicking the Track Visibility control.*

FIG-07-13 Another method is to click and hold the triangle to activate the Track Layout pop-up menu, and choose the appropriate track height.

TIP ✪ *Hold down the Option key to resize all the video tracks or all the audio tracks at once. Hold down the Shift key to resize all the video and all the audio tracks at the same time.*

TIP ✪ *When layering video clips, the clip with the highest track number is at the front of the video frame.*

TIP ✪ *Hold down the Shift key as you drag a clip up or down a track to maintain its timing in the sequence.*

TIP ✪ *Hold down the Command key while adjusting the Opacity Overlay to have more precise control of its numerical value.*

Layering Clips

When you layer clips in Final Cut Pro, there are three methods for combining, or compositing, those layers—opacity, composite modes, and alpha channels. **Opacity** determines how transparent a clip is. A **composite mode** is a feature that uses the chrominance and luminance values of two clips to determine how those clips are blended together. An **alpha channel** contains extra information that is saved with the file, designating a part of the image to have the option of becoming transparent.

Opacity

You can adjust the opacity of every clip on a video track in Final Cut Pro. Adjusting the opacity allows you to blend one or more layers into a single image. There are two methods to adjust the opacity in a clip: either drag the Opacity Overlay in the Timeline window or adjust the Opacity setting in the Motion tab of the Viewer.

FIG-07-14 Click the Clip Overlays control in the Timeline window to make the opacity controls active.

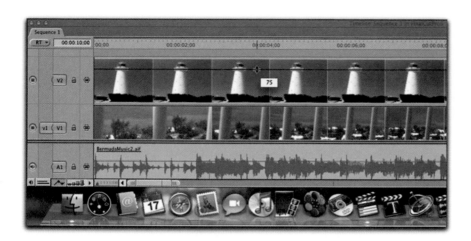

FIG-07-15 Then drag the opacity level at the top of the clip up or down to the desired value. Hold down the Command key while dragging to be more precise.

FIG-07-16 Alternatively, you can double-click the clip to activate its controls, and click on the Motion tab in the Viewer window. Then adjust the Opacity slider or enter a numerical value.

FIG-07-17 Whether you control the opacity directly on the timeline or in the Viewer window, you can view the results of the composited clips in the Canvas window.

Composite Modes

The second method for compositing layers is to use the composite mode feature in Final Cut Pro. The default composite mode is Normal, meaning the clip is completely opaque and does not blend with the clip beneath it. The other available composite modes are Add, Subtract, Difference, Multiply, Screen, Overlay, Hard Light, Soft Light, Darken, Lighten, Travel Matte – Alpha, and Travel Matte – Luma.

FIG-07-18 First, place your layers on the timeline, with the layer you wish to blend on top.

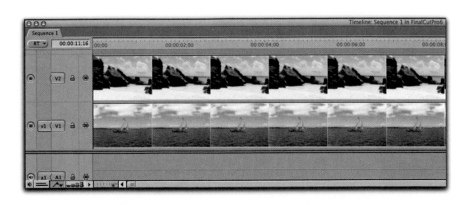

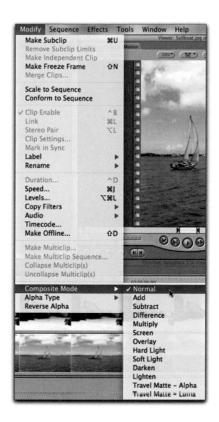

FIG-07-19 Select the clip on V2 to make it active, then select Modify > Composite Mode and choose the type you wish to try.

FIG-07-20 This clip is on track V1, the background layer.

FIG-07-21 This clip is on track V2, the foreground layer—the layer to which the composite mode will be applied.

FIG-07-22 In Add mode, the whites, or light values, are emphasized from both images, and the blacks, or dark values, are made transparent. Midrange color values that overlap are lightened.

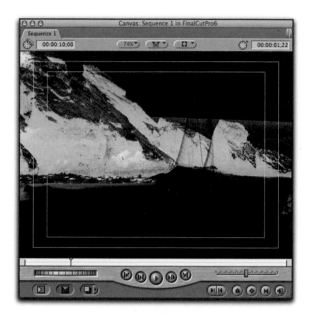

FIG-07-23 In **Subtract mode,** all the overlapped colors are darkened. The whites in the foreground image turn black, and the blacks in the foreground image become transparent. The blacks in the background image are preserved, while the whites in the background image invert the color values in the foreground image, like a film negative.

FIG-07-24 In **Difference mode,** the order of the clips is irrelevant. It is similar to Subtract mode; however, the darkened areas are less so.

FIG-07-25 In **Multiply mode,** the darkest parts of each overlapping image are emphasized. Lighter areas in both images become more transparent, with white showing through completely, while the blacks from both images are preserved. As in Difference mode, clip order has no effect.

FIG-07-26 In **Screen mode,** the lightest parts of each overlapping image are emphasized. Darker areas in both images become more transparent, with black showing through completely, while the whites from both images are preserved. Clip order is irrelevant in Screen mode.

FIG-07-27 In **Overlay mode,** whites and blacks in the foreground image become translucent, while whites and blacks in the background image replace the overlapping areas in the foreground image. Overlapping lighter midrange values are screened, while overlapping darker midrange values are multiplied.

FIG-07-28 In **Hard Light mode,** the whites and blacks in the background image interact with the overlapping midrange values, while the whites and blacks in the foreground image do not interact with the overlapping midrange values. The lighter midrange values of the background clip are screened, and the darker midrange values are multiplied.

FIG-07-29 In **Soft Light mode,** the whites and blacks in the foreground image become translucent, while lights and blacks in the background image replace the overlapping areas in the foreground image. Overlapping midrange color values are mixed together, differentiating Soft Light mode from Overlay mode.

FIG-07-30 In **Darken mode,** the darkest parts of each overlapping image are emphasized, and the whites in both images allow the overlapping areas to become transparent. Lighter midrange values are more translucent, while darker midrange values are less so. The order of the clips has no effect in Darken mode.

FIG-07-31 In **Lighten mode,** the lightest parts of each overlapping image are emphasized. The lightest pixels from each clip are preserved in the composited image. Clip order is irrelevant in Lighten mode.

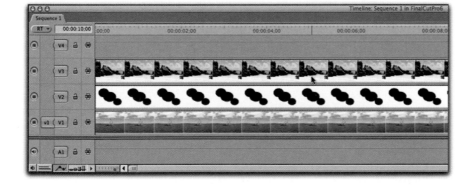

FIG-07-32 In Travel Matte – Alpha mode, at least two layers are needed to make the final image, but three or more layers are typically used. The optional background layer can be a single layer or multiple composited layers, and only a portion of it will be visible, if it is used. The middle layer requires an alpha channel, which provides the transparency. The foreground layer is on top of the background layer and is the clip to which the composite mode is actually applied.

FIG-07-33 The alpha channel from the track below the clip to which the Travel Matte – Alpha mode is applied will be used to create the transparency. The black portion of the alpha channel becomes transparent, revealing the foreground image, while the white portion of the alpha channel retains the background image. If a background image is not used, the default background color will be displayed in its place.

FIG-07-34 In Travel Matte – **Luma mode,** the luminance information from the clip below is used to create the transparency.

Alpha Channels

When you import files into Final Cut Pro, the software will automatically detect if a clip has an alpha channel. Programs like Adobe Photoshop and Adobe Illustrator allow you to create alpha channels in still images. Most 3D animation and motion graphics programs will also allow you to create alpha channels. However, there are different types of alpha channels, and which program you use will determine which type is created.

SPOTLIGHT

Creating Alpha Channels in Photoshop

You can easily create alpha channels in Adobe Photoshop, and video editors frequently work with the program. Photoshop even has custom video options for creating new files, such as NTSC DV 720 × 480 (with guides), which allow you to see the action and title safe areas of the image to be displayed on video. The following steps illustrate how to create an alpha channel in Adobe Photoshop.

FIG-07-35 Start with an existing image or create a new image to apply an alpha channel to.

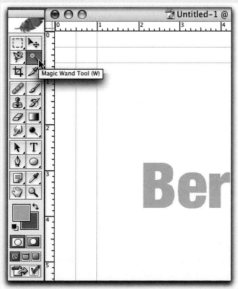

FIG-07-36 You can use the Magic Wand tool or other Selection tools like the Magnetic Lasso tool to assist you in creating the alpha channel.

FIG-07-37 Select all the areas in the image that you wish to become transparent. If you are using the Magic Wand tool, hold down the Shift key to make multiple selections.

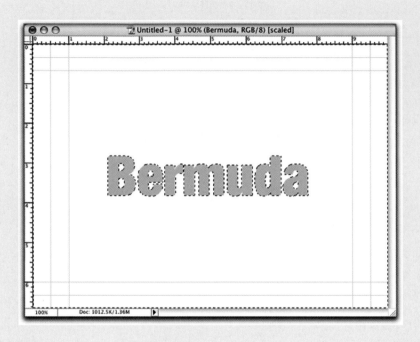

FIG-07-38 Choose Select > Save Selection.

FIG-07-39 The Save Selection dialog box will open. Name your selection "alpha".

FIG-07-40 You can view your selection in the Channels palette by selecting "alpha". The black part of the alpha channel becomes transparent, while the white part retains the image.

FIG-07-41 If you should need to reverse your original selection, click the triangle to activate the Channels pop-up menu and select Channel Options.

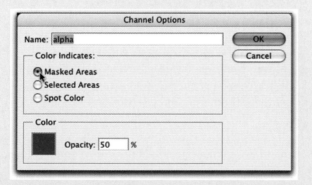

FIG-07-42 The Channel Options dialog box will open. Toggle between Masked Areas and Selected Areas to reverse the black and white portions of the alpha channel, if need be.

FIG-07-43 Once you are satisfied with your alpha channel, select File > Save As. The Save As dialog box will open. Name your file and save it in Photoshop format. Be sure the Alpha Channels box is checked before clicking Save.

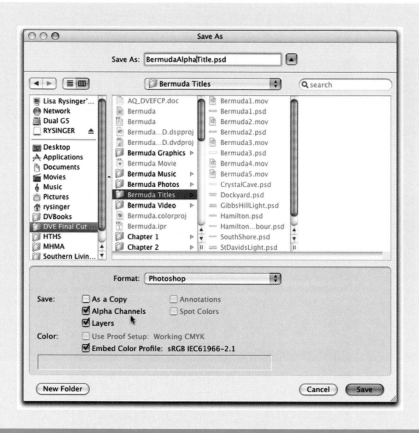

Final Cut Pro automatically determines the alpha channel type as it imports the file, so it is not vital that you know what type of alpha channel was created. However, it is important to understand the alpha channel types, just in case the wrong type is selected and you need to correctly identify and change it later.

In a **straight alpha channel,** or unmatted alpha channel, the transparency information is kept in a separate channel, not with the color information in the red, green, and blue channels. This is the preferred type of alpha channel, because the edges are the cleanest.

In a **premultiplied alpha channel,** or matted alpha channel, the transparency information is kept in a separate channel but is also premultiplied with a color, typically white or black.

 *If the wrong type of alpha channel is selected, it may show artifacts, especially around the edges. An **artifact** is a compression anomaly that creates distortion in an area of an image.*

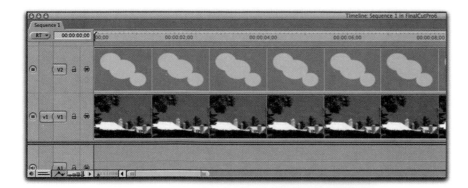

FIG-07-44 In the Timeline window, place the background clip on track V1 and the alpha channel clip on track V2.

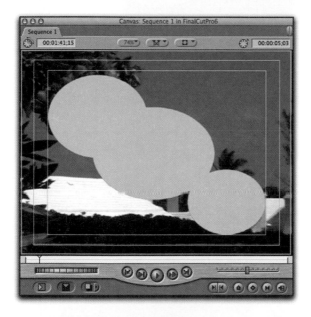

FIG-07-45 By default, Final Cut Pro will automatically enable the alpha channel, and you can view the composited footage in the Canvas window.

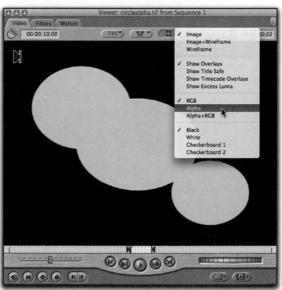

FIG-07-46 Double-click on the alpha channel in the sequence to activate it in the Viewer window. Select Alpha from the View pop-up menu.

FIG-07-47 The black part of the alpha channel becomes transparent. The white part of the alpha channel retains the image.

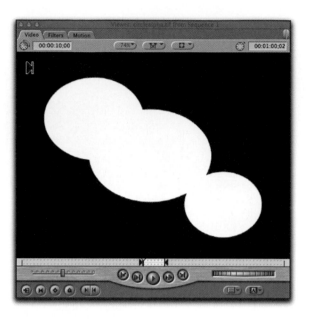

FIG-07-48 In order to view the alpha channel's properties, select it in the Browser window and select Edit > Item Properties > Format, or Control-click it and choose Item Properties > Format from the shortcut menu. You can also press Command-9.

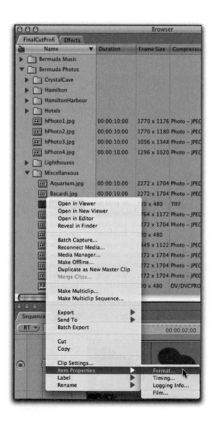

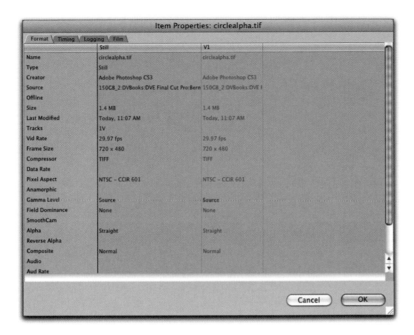

FIG-07-49 The Item Properties dialog box will open, allowing you to view the details of the clip.

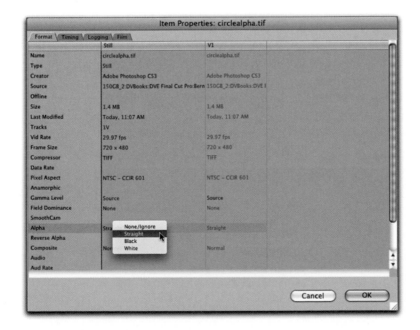

FIG-07-50 If you should ever need to change the designated alpha channel type, Control-click the Alpha row in the second column. However, it is recommended you use the alpha channel type that Final Cut Pro has predetermined.

FIG-07-51 You can also reverse the alpha channel by Control-clicking the Reverse Alpha row in the second column and choosing Yes from the shortcut menu.

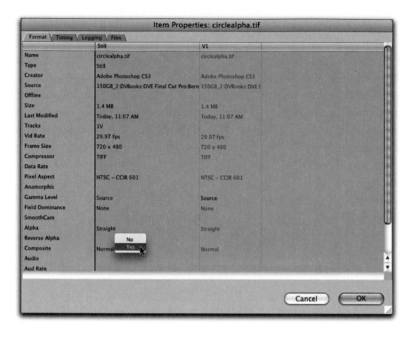

FIG-07-52 Or you can select the clip in the sequence and select Modify > Reverse Alpha.

FIG-07-53 The alpha channel will reverse itself, and you can view the change in the Canvas window.

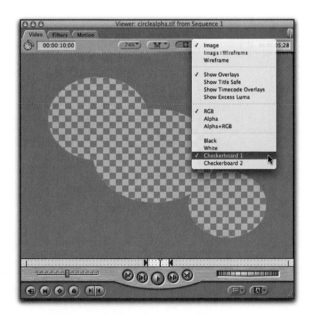

FIG-07-54 Also, you may find it useful to enable the Checkerboard pattern in the Viewer to view which part of the alpha channel is transparent, as opposed to the default Black background.

Layered Photoshop Files

In addition to creating alpha channels in Adobe Photoshop, video editors will often work with layered Photoshop files. Having the ability to work with the individual layers of the Photoshop file allows you to apply effects to each layer in Final Cut Pro. You can take a layered still file and apply motion, as well as filters and other effects, to one or more of its layers.

TIP ✪ *If you wish to work with a layered Photoshop file as a single layer, you must first flatten it in Adobe Photoshop before importing it into Final Cut Pro.*

FIG-07-55 When a
layered Photoshop file
is imported into Final
Cut Pro, its layers are
composited together and it
becomes a sequence in the
Browser window.

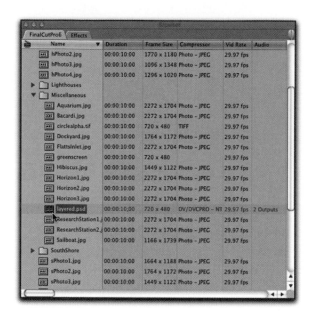

TIP ✪ *Once you have
imported a layered
Photoshop file into Final
Cut Pro, do not attempt to
add or delete layers—you
may get unexpected
results. Instead, return
to Photoshop to add or
delete the layers.*

FIG-07-56 Drag the
layered Photoshop file to
the Timeline window to
add it to the sequence.

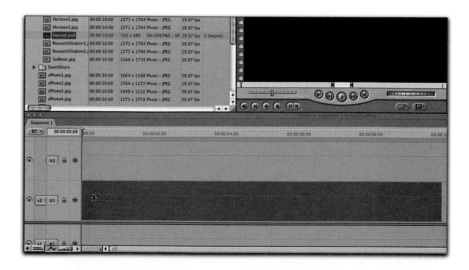

FIG-07-57 You can view the composited layers in the Canvas window.

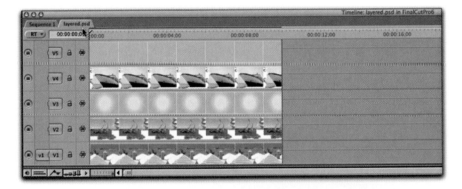

FIG-07-58 In order to view and manipulate the individual layers in the Photoshop sequence, double-click on the file and a new sequence window will open.

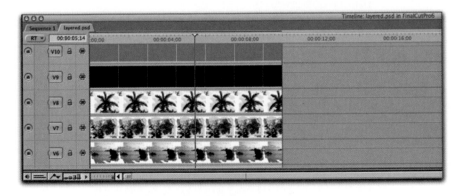

FIG-07-59 You can scroll through the layers in the sequence. Photoshop's background layer will appear on V1. The layers will retain their original hierarchy from Photoshop, with the top layer having the highest track number.

Keying, Mattes, and Masks

In addition to working with composite modes and alpha channels, Final Cut Pro also allows you to use keys, mattes, and masks to work with layers. **Keying** is a technique in which chrominance or luminance is used to make part of a video clip transparent.

A **matte,** also called a **holdout matte,** is a created effect that uses information in one layer of video to reveal part of another layer of video. A **mask** is a clip created specifically to define transparent areas in another clip. Think of a mask as being just the black and white portion of the alpha channel, while an alpha channel is both a standalone image and a defined area of transparency. The terms matte and mask are often used interchangeably.

 *A color matte is different from a holdout matte, which is used for keying. A **color matte** is any single color, such as black, that fills a video frame.*

Chroma and Luma Keying

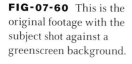 **TIP** ✪ *The Matte Choker filter and Spill Suppressor filter can be helpful when working with footage that is difficult to key.*

TIP ✪ *Select a video format that is either uncompressed or minimally compressed to get a high-quality key.*

Chroma keying is a postproduction technique in which any specified color is keyed out, or made transparent. **Luma keying** uses the luminance, or brightness and darkness values, to create the transparency. Bluescreen and greenscreen are commonly used chroma keys. **Bluescreen** is a keying technique used to isolate a subject that was filmed against a blue background, which will later be replaced with other footage. Likewise, **greenscreen** is a keying technique used to isolate a subject that was filmed against a green background.

> *When shooting footage that will later be keyed, it is extremely important to have even and adequate lighting. Both the subject and the bluescreen or greenscreen background should be separately lit. It is recommended to have at least five to ten feet between the subject and the background to reduce the amount of colored light spilling onto the subject. A straw-colored filter is often applied to the backlight of the subject to counteract any spill from the bluescreen, whereas a magenta-colored filter is likewise used for greenscreen.*

FIG-07-60 This is the original footage with the subject shot against a greenscreen background.

FIG-07-61 The greenscreen clip is placed on track V2 and the background video is on track V1.

FIG-07-62 Select Color Smoothing from the Key folder under Video Filters in the Effects tab of the Browser window. Use 4:1:1 or 4:2:2 for your respective footage. It will improve the overall quality of the key.

FIG-07-63 Drag the filter from the Browser to the greenscreen clip in the sequence to apply it.

FIG-07-64 Double-click the greenscreen clip on the timeline to activate its setting in the Viewer window. Then select the Filters tab to view the Color Smoothing filter.

FIG-07-65 Now follow the same steps to apply the Chroma Keyer filter. Click on the Visual button to access the visual controls.

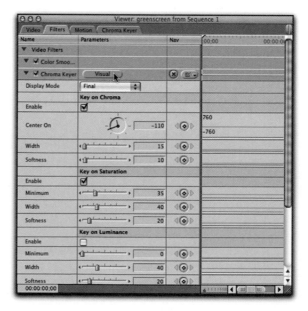

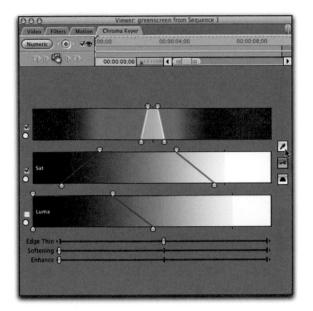

FIG-07-66 You can revert to the numeric controls by clicking on the Numeric button, if desired. Now click on the Eye Dropper tool on the right.

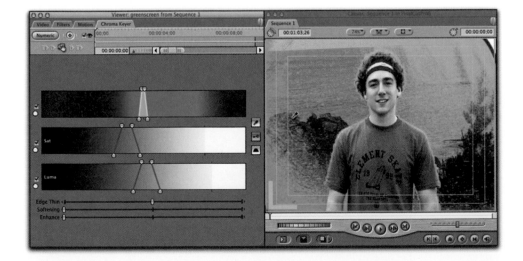

FIG-07-67 Click on the greenscreen to key it, and the visual controls on the right will change accordingly.

FIG-07-68 Hold down the Shift key to make multiple selections with the Eye Dropper tool. Continue until most of the green is removed, but do not get too close to the edges of the subject in the foreground.

FIG-07-69 Now adjust the top handles of the Color Range, Saturation, and Luma controls to continue removing the overall range of green and the edge fringing. Be careful not to encroach too much on the edges of the foreground image.

FIG-07-70 Now adjust the bottom handles of the Color Range, Saturation, and Luma controls to further enhance the key by blurring the range of difference between the keyed-out colors.

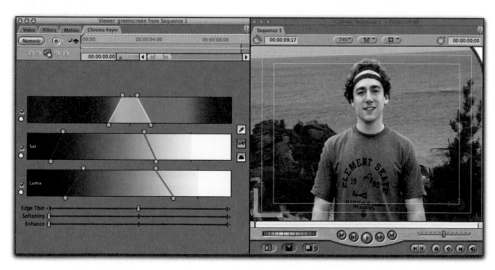

FIG-07-71 In order to see the edges of the foreground image better, Zoom in on the Canvas.

FIG-07-72 Now adjust the Edge Thin slider to decrease the color fringing around the edges and the Softening slider to blur the edges. If you overdo these adjustments you will lose detail in your image. If you are not satisfied with the progress, you may need to also apply the Matte Choker filter at this point.

FIG-07-73 Once you are satisfied, use the Enhance slider to desaturate the spill that remains around the edges. If you are not satisfied with the progress, you may need to apply the Spill Suppressor filter at this point.

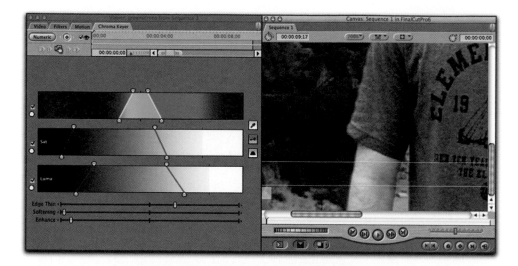

FIG-07-74 Now apply the Four-Point Garbage Matte filter to eliminate any unwanted areas in the background; use the Eight-Point Garbage Matte if more precise control is needed. Select point 2 in the controls on the left to address the problem in the upper right corner of the frame.

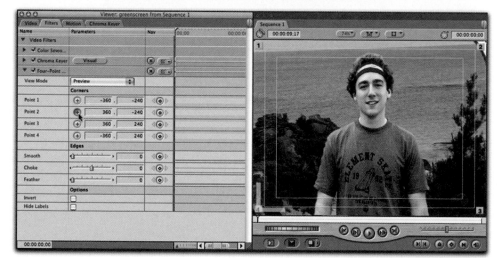

FIG-07-75 Now click on point 2 in the Canvas window and drag it inward until the object in the background is keyed out.

FIG-07-76 To make the keyed footage look more realistic, filters may need to be applied to the foreground and background images. For example, a Blur filter may need to be applied to the background clip to simulate the focus of the composited image. Now apply the Color Corrector filter to the greenscreen clip.

FIG-07-77 Adjust the Level Controls to more closely match the lighting of the background image. The foreground image was shot in full sun at midday; the background image was shot at twilight on a partly cloudy day.

FIG-07-78 Now apply the Color Corrector filter to the background layer. A Blur filter is not needed in this instance, since the plant to the left of the background frame is in focus in the foreground.

FIG-07-79 Increase the saturation of the background image to more closely match the saturation in the foreground image.

FIG-07-80 This is the result of the final composite with all the filters applied.

Matte Filters

Matte filters are frequently used with the Chroma Keyer filter in Final Cut Pro. The three most common are the Four-Point Garbage Matte, the Eight-Point Garbage Matte, and the Matte Choker. A **garbage matte filter** is used to help crop out the foreground subject by manipulating defined points, typically four or eight. A **choker filter** is used to eliminate the colored fringing that occurs around the edges of the foreground subject.

FIG-07-81 The Four-Point Garbage Matte should be used when only the edges of the frame need to be cropped out.

FIG-07-82 The Eight-Point Garbage Matte should be used when you need to come in closer to the subject in the foreground.

FIG-07-83 The Matte Choker filter can also be used to help alleviate the color fringing around the edges of the subject. A black background has been temporarily selected, in lieu of the background clip, to assist in viewing the progress of the key.

FIG-07-84 Adjust the Edge Thin and Edge Feather sliders to improve the key.

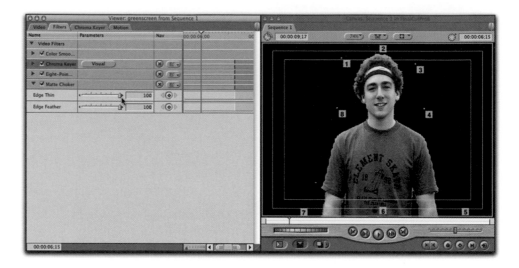

Mask Filters

Final Cut Pro also has filters to help you work with masks and alpha channels. **Image Mask** uses either the luma or alpha channel in one clip to create an alpha channel in another. **Mask Feather** allows you to feather, or soften, the edges of the clip's alpha channel by blurring them. **Mask Shape** allows you to use a simple shape, such as a circle or square, as an alpha channel. **Soft Edges,** on the other hand, feathers only the edges of the video clip, ignoring any alpha channel information.

FIG-07-85 Place the background clip on track V1 and the clip you wish to mask on V2.

FIG-07-86 To apply Image Mask, drag it from the Matte folder under Video Filters in the Effects tab of the Browser window to the clip on V2.

FIG-07-87 Double-click on the flowers clip and select the Filters tab in the Viewer window to access the controls of the Image Mask filter.

FIG-07-88 Now drag Circle in the Shapes folder under Video Generators in the Effects tab to the Mask icon in the Image Mask controls in the Viewer.

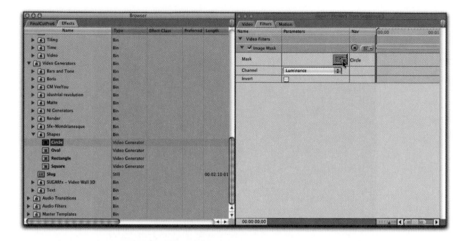

FIG-07-89 Make sure Luminance is selected from the Channel pop-up menu to view the shape.

FIG-07-90
Alternatively, you can drag an image with an alpha channel to the Mask icon.

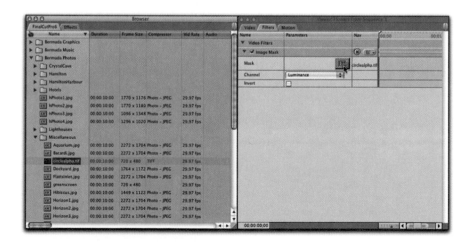

FIG-07-91 Now select Alpha from the Channel pop-up menu to view this image.

FIG-07-92 You can also apply the Mask Feather filter to blur and soften the edges of the alpha channel.

FIG-07-93 Or instead, you can use the Mask Shape filter to apply simple shapes, like Oval.

Summary

Final Cut Pro features an arsenal of effects to help you composite multiple layers of video. The ability to work with alpha channels and layered Photoshop files, coupled with Final Cut Pro's sophisticated tools for transparency, keying, matting, and masking, provides limitless editing options.

KEYBOARD SHORTCUTS

Lock all video tracks	*Shift+F4*
Lock all audio tracks	*Shift+F5*
Edit > Item Properties > Format	*Command-9*

REWIND

1. What is compositing, or layering?
2. What is opacity, or transparency?
3. Name and define three composite modes.
4. What is an alpha channel?
5. What are the different types of alpha channels?
6. Why use a layered Photoshop file?
7. What are chroma keying and luma keying?
8. Discuss the lighting tips for bluescreen and greenscreen.
9. What is a matte?
10. What are the mask filters?

TAKE TWO

1. Practice working with layers and using tracks. Be sure to try different composite modes.
2. Practice creating and using alpha channels. Also try using an alpha channel as an image mask.
3. Practice chroma keying. Be sure to use filters on the foreground and background images.

CHAPTER 8
Adding Motion

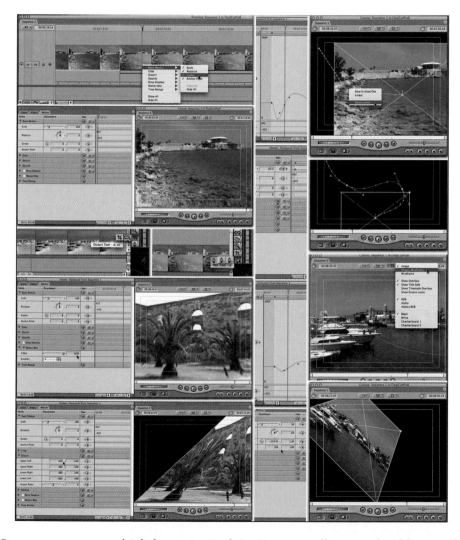

OBJECTIVES

Learn how to apply motion using the Viewer

Discover how to adjust motion parameters

Learn how to apply motion using the Canvas

Understand how to use keyframes

ONCE YOU HAVE multiple layers in Final Cut Pro, you will want to be able to apply motion to them. Motion can be applied to any video track. It can be used on video, photographs, still images, titles, and animation. You can adjust the scale of a clip, as well as its position on the horizontal and vertical axes. You can also control the

211

rotation of a clip and even its opacity, or how transparent it appears. Motion effects add another dimension to an editing project and offer limitless creative possibilities.

Creating Motion Using the Viewer

TIP ✪ *To reset any of the motion attributes to their default parameters, click the red X in the Navigation column.*

One of the ways to apply motion in Final Cut Pro is to use the Motion tab in the Viewer window. Every clip has different attributes, like scale and rotation, and each of these attributes has parameters that can be adjusted. The default settings for the clip are 100 for both the Scale and Opacity, and 0 for the Rotation, Crop, Aspect Ratio, Drop Shadow, and Motion Blur. Both the Center and Anchor Point is 0,0.

FIG-08-01 Double-click on a clip in the Timeline window to activate its settings in the Viewer window. Then click the Motion tab to view the default parameter settings.

Creating Basic Motion

Under the Basic Motion attribute, there are four parameters you can manipulate: Scale, Rotation, Center, and Anchor Point. **Scale** changes the overall size of a clip. It has a range from 0 to 1000. **Rotation** revolves a clip around its center. You can rotate up to 24 full revolutions in either direction (positive or negative). Each full revolution is 360 degrees. **Center** marks the clip's position in the frame, using the x,y coordinate system. Finally, **Anchor Point** is used to mark the point around which the clip will move or rotate. Its default is the center of the clip, but that can be changed to any other x,y coordinate.

Cartesian Geometry

*Final Cut Pro allows you to use the **Cartesian coordinate system**, or analytical geometry, to position clips within the video frame. This system uses an x,y coordinate-based system, where x is the horizontal axis and y is the vertical axis. The center of the frame is always 0,0. To move a clip down in Final Cut Pro, enter a positive number for the y-coordinate; to move a clip up, enter a negative number for the y-coordinate. To move a clip to the right in Final Cut Pro, enter a positive number for the x-coordinate; to move a clip to the left, enter a negative number for the x-coordinate.*

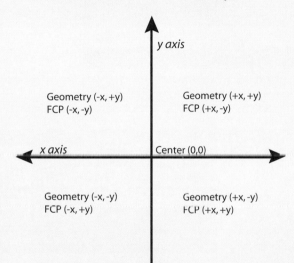

Cartesian Coordinates
Final Cut Pro vs. Geometry

y axis

Geometry (-x, +y)
FCP (-x, -y)

Geometry (+x, +y)
FCP (+x, -y)

x axis   Center (0,0)

Geometry (-x, -y)
FCP (-x, +y)

Geometry (+x, -y)
FCP (+x, +y)

FIG-08-02 Please note: the y-axis values are reversed in Final Cut Pro when compared to traditional geometry. The lower quadrants in Final Cut Pro have positive values, whereas the lower quadrants in geometry have negative values.

FIG-08-03 This is the original clip without any motion settings applied.

FIG-08-04 A Scale setting of 50 has been applied to the clip.

FIG-08-05 The clip has been rotated 55 degrees.

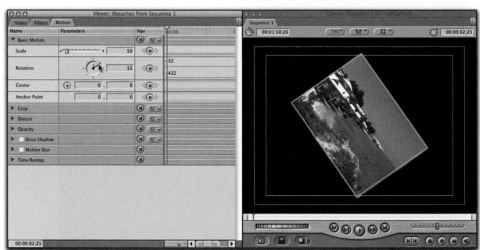

FIG-08-06 The Center setting has been changed to −152.45,1.34.

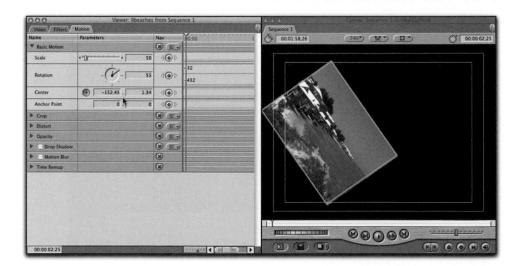

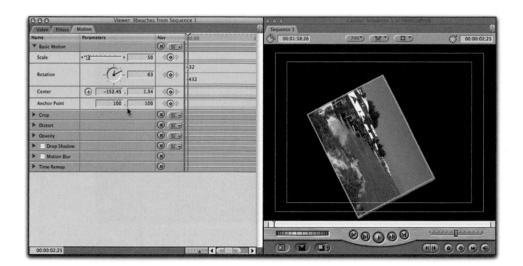

FIG-08-07 The Anchor Point setting has been changed to 100,100, and the clip has been rotated 63 degrees.

Additional Motion Attributes

In addition to Basic Motion, other attributes include Crop, Distort, Opacity, Drop Shadow, Motion Blur, and Time Remap. The **Crop attribute** allows you to crop or remove the outside portion of a clip and soften the edges by feathering. Its parameters are Left, Right, Top, Bottom, and Edge Feather and each range from 0 to 100.

The **Distort attribute** can change the shape and/or proportions of the clip. Its parameters are Upper Left, Upper Right, Lower Right, Lower Left, and Aspect Ratio. The Aspect Ratio can range from −10,000 to 10,000. The other parameters depend on the pixel dimensions of the video frame. In a standard DV frame of 720 x 480, the x-value can range from −360 to 360, while the y-value can range from −240 to 240.

The **Opacity attribute** adjusts the degree of transparency of the clip. A solid, or opaque, clip is the default. It can range from 0 to 100, with 0 being completely transparent and 100 being completely opaque.

The **Drop Shadow attribute** creates a drop shadow behind the clip. Its parameters are Offset, Angle, Color, Softness, and Opacity. The Offset can range from −100 to 100. The Angle can range from −720 to 720. The Color can be chosen with the Eyedropper tool or the Color Picker, and the Hue, Saturation, and Brightness can also be adjusted. Both the Softness and the Opacity can range from 0 to 100.

The **Motion Blur attribute** can apply blurring to motion in any clip, regardless of whether the motion is part of the original clip or an effect you created. The parameters are % Blur, ranging from 0 to 1000, and Samples in increments from 1 to 32.

The **Time Remap attribute** allows you to change the speed of a clip. You can create either constant speed changes, or variable speed changes. The Time Remap parameters are Setting, Duration, Speed %, Source Duration, Reverse, and Frame Blending. The Time Graph Output parameters are Time, Source Frame, and Velocity %.

FIG-08-08 This is the original clip without any motion settings applied.

FIG-08-09 This clip has been cropped to Right 35 and Top 17.

FIG-08-10 This clip has been distorted to Upper Left 200, −240.

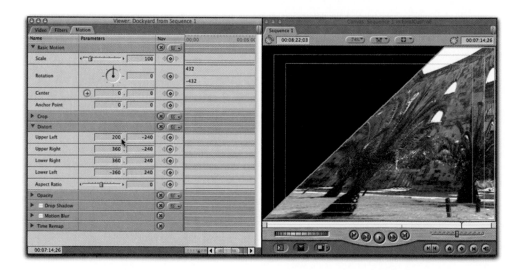

FIG-08-11 The Opacity setting has been changed to 40.

FIG-08-12 An aqua drop shadow has been applied to the clip.

FIG-08-13 The Motion Blur setting has been changed to 1000.

FIG-08-14 In the
Time Remap setting, the
Speed % has been changed
to 50.00.

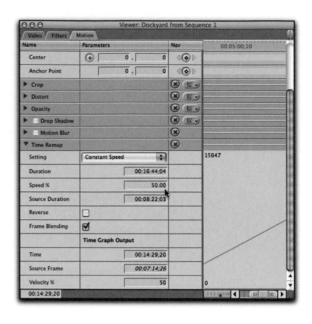

Creating Motion Using the Canvas

TIP *You can also press Shift-Z, with either the Canvas or Viewer window active, to reset the zoom level to Fit to Window.*

In addition to using the Motion tab of the Viewer to apply motion to a clip, you can also create motion directly in the Canvas window. You can zoom into the Canvas window to help you better view and position your clips. Select View > Level and choose a percentage from the submenu to zoom in or out on the Canvas. You can also use the View pop-up menu to zoom in or out. Or, with the Canvas window active, press Command-+ (plus sign) to zoom in or Command-− (minus sign) to zoom out.

Wireframe Modes

In order to apply motion in the Canvas window, you must select one of the wireframe modes. An aqua border will appear around your clip showing any motion parameters that have been applied. Select Image+Wireframe mode for general use. However, if you have high-resolution clips and you don't want to wait for your image to update, choose Wireframe mode.

> *While using one of the wireframe modes, the number in the center of the clip indicates which video track it is on.*

FIG-08-15 Select either View > Image+Wireframe or View > Wireframe, or you can make your selection from the View pop-up menu. You can also press W to toggle between Image, Image+Wireframe, and Wireframe modes.

Selection, Crop, and Distort Tools

Once you are in one of the two wireframe modes and the aqua border has appeared around your clip, you can use tools to manipulate the clip's handles. The Scale/Distort handles are one of the four corner points of the clip that allow you to scale or distort the clip, using the Selection or Distort tools respectively. The Center handle is a point in the middle of the clip that allows you to reposition the clip in the Canvas, using the Selection tool. The Rotation handles are one of four handles around the edges of the clip that allow you to rotate the clip around its center point, using the Selection tool. You can also drag one of the clip's four sides with the Crop tool to crop the clip.

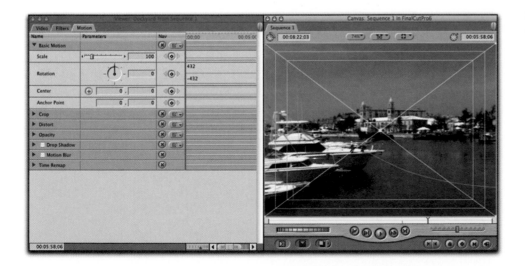

FIG-08-16 This is the original clip without any motion settings applied.

FIG-08-17 Use the
Selection tool in the Tool
palette to select one of the
Scale/Distort handles.

FIG-08-18 Position
your cursor over one of the
four corner points until a
cross hair appears.

FIG-08-19 Then click and drag to scale the clip proportionally. If you do not want to constrain the clip's proportions, hold down the Shift key while you drag the clip.

FIG-08-20 Use the Selection tool to select the clip. Position your cursor near the middle of the clip until the move symbol appears.

FIG-08-21 Then click and drag to move the clip into a new position.

FIG-08-22 Use the Selection tool to select one of the Rotational handles of the clip. As you position your cursor, it will change to a rotational arrow.

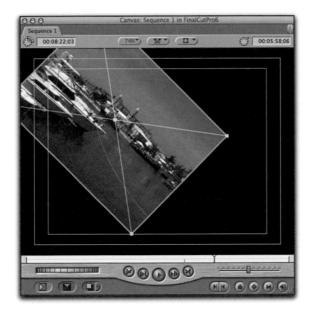

FIG-08-23 Then click and drag the edge of the clip to rotate it. Hold down the Shift key while you click and drag to rotate in 45-degree increments. Be sure to release the mouse before the Shift key.

FIG-08-24 Select the Distort tool in the Tool palette.

FIG-08-25 Then select one of the Scale/Distort handles. Your cursor will change to the distort symbol as you hover over one of the four corner points.

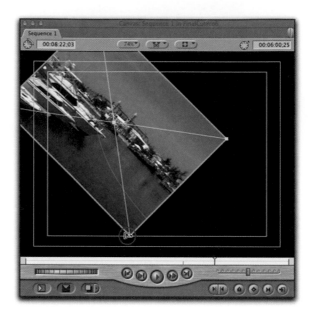

FIG-08-26 Simply click and drag any point to distort the clip.

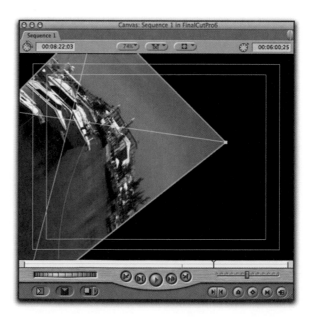

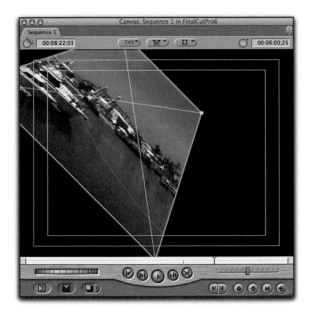

FIG-08-27 Or, to change the perspective of the clip, hold down the Shift key as you click and drag to change all four points simultaneously.

FIG-08-28 Select the Crop tool in the Tool palette.

FIG-08-29 To crop the side of the clip, position the cursor over one of the edges until the crop symbol appears.

FIG-08-30 Then click and drag one of the edges.

FIG-08-31 To crop two sides at a time, click and drag one of the corners of the clip instead. Hold down the Shift key while dragging a corner to maintain the clip's aspect ratio.

Creating Motion Using Keyframes

Used in both digital video and 3D animation, a **keyframe** is a video frame that marks a place in time where a particular change, such as size or shape, occurs. You can use keyframes to create animated motion effects in Final Cut Pro. The scale, position, and other motion settings, like opacity and distortion, can all be keyframed or changed over time. In addition to using keyframes to animate motion effects, you can also use these same keyframe techniques to animate filters over time.

Setting Keyframes

Keyframing requires at least two or more points where some parameter has been changed. In its simplest form, you would create a start and end point and change one parameter, such as scale. The start point may be 100 and the end point 50. The clip is four seconds long. Final Cut Pro will automatically interpolate all the frames in between the two keyframes you set. Therefore, halfway into the clip, at 2 seconds, Final Cut Pro will have determined that the scale at that frame should be 75. However, say you wanted the scale to shrink more quickly at first, and then slow down. You could then add an additional keyframe at 1 second and set it to 75. You could continue adding keyframes allowing you easy, precise control over any parameter you wish to animate over time—Final Cut Pro will do the hard work for you.

FIG-08-32 To keyframe motion effects in a clip, first double-click the clip to activate it in the Viewer. Then click on the Motion tab. This is the original clip without any motion settings applied.

FIG-08-33 The first keyframe will be placed at the beginning of the clip. Advance the playhead to the beginning of the clip in the Timeline window. Then click the Keyframe button for the Scale parameter in the Motion tab of the Viewer window. It will turn green.

FIG-08-34 Advance the playhead in the Timeline to the end of the clip. Change the Scale parameter to 50. Final Cut Pro will automatically add the second keyframe for you and interpret all the frames in between. The keyframe will appear as a green diamond in the keyframe graph area to the right.

FIG-08-35 You can view the animated motion effect in the Canvas window.

FIG-08-36 You can navigate back and forth between keyframes by clicking the arrows on either side of the Keyframe button. To move to the keyframe on the left, click the Previous Keyframe button, or press Option-K. To move to the keyframe on the right, click the Next Keyframe button, or press Shift-K.

FIG-08-37 To add another keyframe to the 1-second mark, first advance the playhead in the Timeline window.

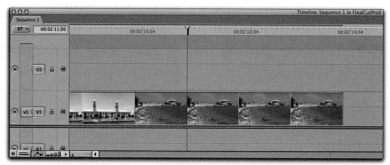

FIG-08-38 Resize the Viewer window so that the keyframe graph area is easier to see by clicking and dragging the right side of the Viewer toward the Canvas window. Then change the Scale parameter in the Motion tab of the Viewer window to 75. Final Cut Pro will automatically add the keyframe for you and reinterpret all the other frames in the animated effect.

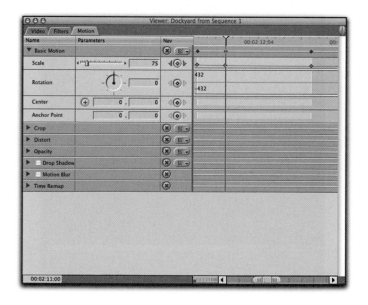

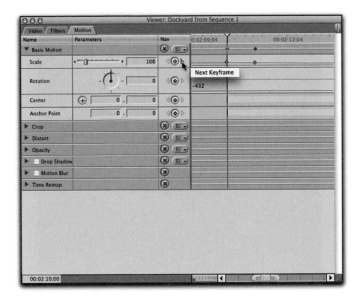

FIG-08-39 You can delete a keyframe at any time by navigating to it with the Previous Keyframe or Next Keyframe buttons.

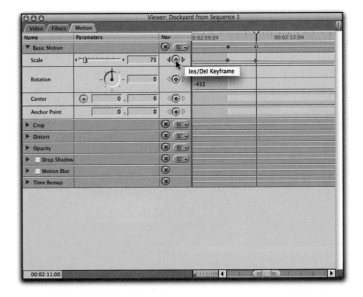

FIG-08-40 Then click the Keyframe button to delete the keyframe.

FIG-08-41 The keyframe will be deleted from the keyframe graph area, and the motion settings will automatically be updated to reflect the previous state before the keyframe was applied.

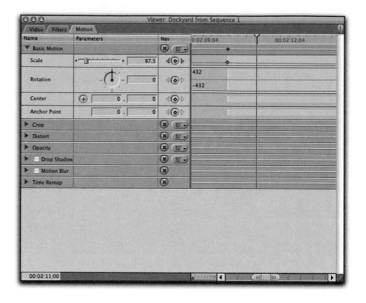

FIG-08-42 You can also delete a keyframe by positioning the cursor over it until the cross hair appears.

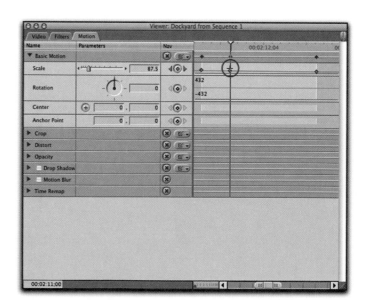

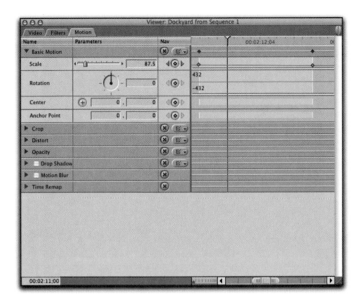

FIG-08-43 Then click and drag the keyframe out of the keyframe graph area and release the mouse. The keyframe will disappear.

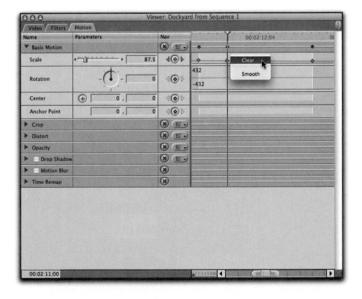

FIG-08-44 Another way to delete a keyframe is to Control-click it and choose Clear from the shortcut menu.

FIG-08-45 You can also reposition a keyframe. First, position the cursor near the keyframe until a cross hair appears.

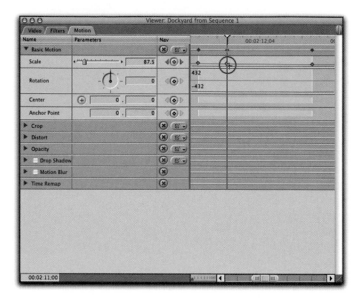

FIG-08-46 Then click and drag the keyframe into its new position. A box will appear as you drag, showing the timecode duration of the change you are making.

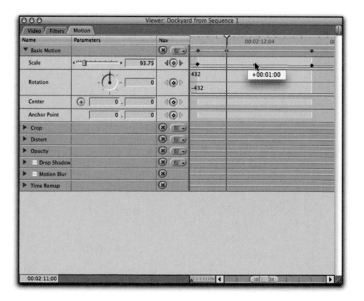

FIG-08-47 You can also add motion keyframes directly in the Canvas window by clicking on the Add Motion Keyframe button. It will keyframe all the motion parameters by default.

FIG-08-48
Alternatively, you can also choose a specific motion parameter by Control-clicking the Add Motion Keyframe button and making a selection from the shortcut menu.

FIG-08-49 It is often easier to create a motion path directly in the Canvas window. A **motion path** is a line defined by two or more points, which illustrates movement. First, select one of the wireframe modes from the View pop-up menu.

FIG-08-50 With the Selection tool, click and drag the clip into the position where you would like the motion to start. Then click the Add Motion Keyframe button.

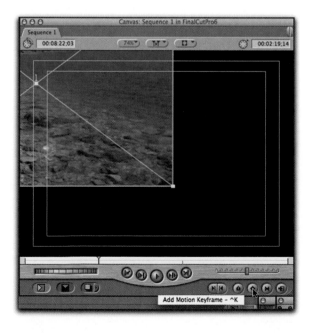

FIG-08-51 Move the playhead in either the Timeline window or Canvas window to the next position where you would like to add a keyframe. Then reposition your clip in the Canvas. Final Cut Pro will automatically add the next keyframe and create the motion path.

FIG-08-52 You can continue adding keyframes to your motion path.

FIG-08-53 To move
a keyframe in a motion
path, use the Selection tool
to drag it anywhere in the
Canvas.

FIG-08-54 You can
delete a keyframe directly
in the Canvas window
by Control-clicking the
keyframe and choosing
Delete point from the
shortcut menu.

Keyframe Tools

You can use the Pen tools in the Tool palette to add, delete, and modify keyframes.
The **Pen tool** allows you to add keyframes by simply clicking in the keyframe graph
area. The **Pen Delete tool,** or **Delete Point tool,** allows you to delete a keyframe by
clicking it. The **Smooth Point tool** allows you to smooth a keyframe. **Smoothing** is

the process of adding Bézier handles to specific keyframes; this allows the user to define the amount of Bézier curve applied between the keyframes of certain motion and filter effects, making the change appear more gradually. In order for an effect to be smoothed, it must have a single value, such as Scale or Opacity. An effect with multiple values, such as Anchor Point, which has both an x and y value, cannot be smoothed.

FIG-08-55 Press the P key to select the Pen tool.

FIG-08-56 Press the P key twice to select the Pen Delete tool, which is also known as the Delete Point tool.

FIG-08-57 Press the P key three times to select the Smooth Point tool.

Bézier Handles and Curves

Named after Pierre Bézier, who conceived the mathematical formula, a **Bézier curve** is a line with handles used to create a curve between two points. A **Bézier handle** is the control that is used to modify the curve of a line, which increases the bend of the line as the handle is dragged farther away from its vertex point. Keyframes at the start and end of an effect have one-sided Bézier handles. Keyframes in the middle of an effect have two-sided Bézier handles.

FIG-08-58 Resize the Scale parameter area by dragging down the lower dividing line in the keyframe graph area.

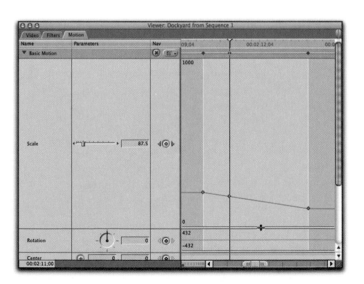

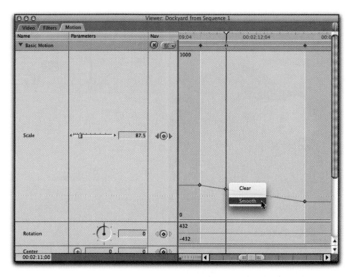

FIG-08-59 To smooth a keyframe, Control-click the keyframe, and choose Smooth from the shortcut menu.

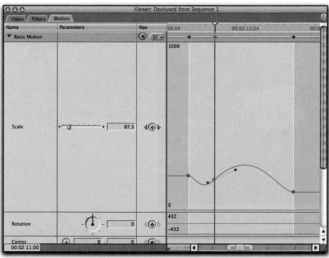

FIG-08-60 Then drag the Bézier handle to change the shape of the curve.

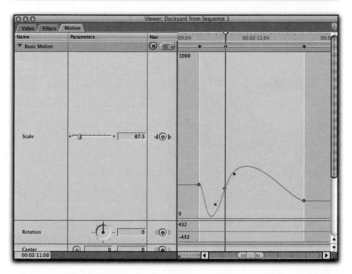

FIG-08-61 If you want to manipulate one side of a Bézier curve independently of the other, press and hold the Shift key as you drag.

FIG-08-62 If you want to change the angle between one side of a Bézier curve and the other, press and hold the Command key as you drag.

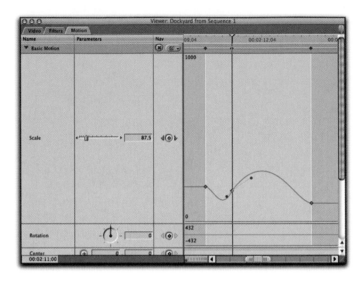

FIG-08-63 If you want to change the length and the angle of one Bézier handle independently of the other, press and hold Shift-Command as you drag.

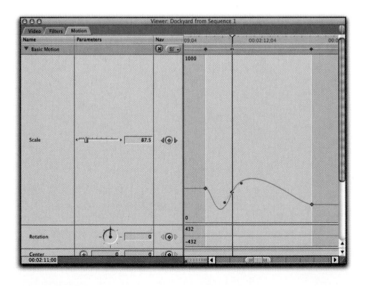

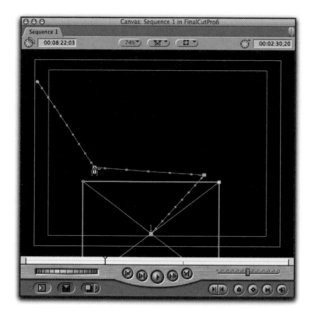

FIG-08-64 You can also smooth motion paths using Bézier handles in the Canvas window. Using the Smooth Point tool, select a point along the motion path.

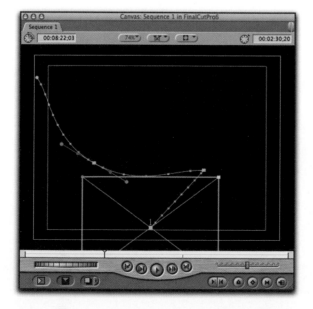

FIG-08-65 Then adjust the Bézier handles to smooth out the motion.

FIG-08-66 You can smooth the entire motion path, if desired.

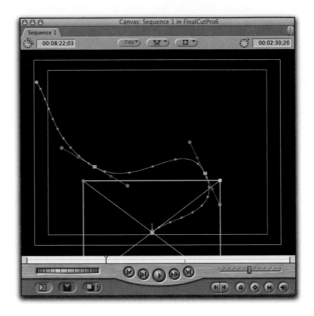

Timeline Keyframe Editor

You can also edit both motion keyframes and filter keyframes directly in the Timeline window. The keyframe graph area is divided into two sections: a blue line represents the motion bar and a green line represents the filters bar. Use the Selection tool to drag keyframes along the motion bar to move them. You can also double-click on the motion bar to open that clip's Motion tab in the Viewer. These techniques also apply to the filters bar.

FIG-08-67 Click the Clip Keyframes control to make the keyframe graph area visible in the Timeline. A blue line represents the motion bar.

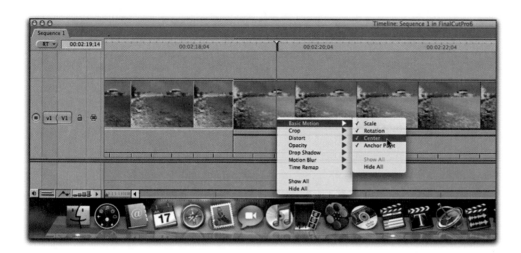

FIG-08-68 You can also isolate which keyframes are visible by Control-clicking on the motion bar and choosing from the shortcut menu.

Summary

The ability to create motion effects is another key feature of Final Cut Pro. Motion can be simple or sophisticated. It can involve one layer or multiple layers, providing the editor with many options. And those creative choices multiply exponentially when you add the powerful technique of using keyframes to your editing arsenal.

Toggle between wireframe modes	*W*	**KEYBOARD SHORTCUTS**
Scale clip, unconstrained proportions	*Shift-drag*	
Rotate clip, 45-degree increments	*Shift-drag*	
Distort clip, all points simultaneously	*Shift-drag*	
Crop clip, maintain aspect ratio	*Shift-drag*	
Previous Keyframe button	*Option-K*	
Next Keyframe button	*Shift-K*	
Toggle between Pen tool modes	*P*	
Change one side of Bézier curve independently	*Shift-drag*	
Change the angle of Bézier curve	*Command-drag*	
Change the length and angle of one Bézier handle	*Shift-Command-drag*	

1. What are the Basic Motion parameters?
2. Describe the Crop parameter.
3. Describe the Distort parameter.
4. Describe the Opacity parameter.
5. Describe the Drop Shadow parameter.
6. Describe the Motion Blur parameter.
7. What is Time Remapping?
8. What are x,y coordinates?

 REWIND

9. What is a keyframe?

10. What is a motion path?

TAKE TWO

1. Practice creating motion using the Viewer.
2. Practice creating motion using the Canvas.
3. Practice creating motion using keyframes.

CHAPTER 9

Creating Effects Using Video Filters

OBJECTIVES

Discover the different
types of video filters

Understand third-party
filters

Learn how to apply and
remove filters

Learn how to keyframe
filters

Discover Color

IN ADDITION TO motion effects, Final Cut Pro offers editors an arsenal of different
filter effects that can change the look of an image. Filter effects can be either artistic
or functional. You can color correct a clip, which the viewer may never notice, or you
can apply a Stylize filter to create a dramatic impact. Filter effects are one of Final
Cut Pro's most powerful features.

Types of Video Filters

A filter is an effect that makes changes to the individual pixels of a clip, altering its chrominance, luminance, or the very look of the image itself. You can change its color, create a blur, add a glow, or just about anything else you can imagine.

Final Cut Pro organizes its filters by type in the Video Filters folder in the Effects tab of the Browser window. Categories include Blur, Border, Channel, Color Correction, Distort, Glow, Image Control, Key, Matte, Perspective, QuickTime, Sharpen, Stylize, Tiling, Time, and Video.

➡️ *FxPlug filters are effects that are hardware-accelerated using Apple's OpenGL, CoreGraphics, and CoreImage technologies.*

➡️ *Video filters that appear in bold in the Effects tab of the Browser window can play back in real-time.*

➡️ *Third-Party filters are additional effects created by developers like CoreMelt and Noise Industries.*

FIG-09-01 Video filters are organized by type in the Video Filters folder in the Effects tab of the Browser window.

FIG-09-02 This is the original image without any filters applied.

Blur

Blur filters can add a blur to the entire clip or just a portion of it. They include Compound Blur, Defocus, Directional Blur, Gaussian Blur, Movement Blur, Prism, Radial Blur, Soft Focus, Wind Blur, and Zoom Blur.

FIG-09-03 The Gaussian Blur filter allows you to blur one or all of the channels of the clip, including the alpha channel.

FIG-09-04 The Zoom Blur filter makes it appear as if the image is moving toward you or away from you.

Border

Border filters add a border to the edges of your clips. They include Basic Border and Bevel.

FIG-09-05 The Basic Border filter draws a border around the edges of the clip. You can select both the thickness and color of the border.

Channel

Channel filters manipulate the individual red, green, blue, and alpha channels of your clips. They include Arithmetic, Channel Blur, Channel Mixer, Channel Offset, Channel Swap, Color Offset, Compound Arithmetic, and Invert.

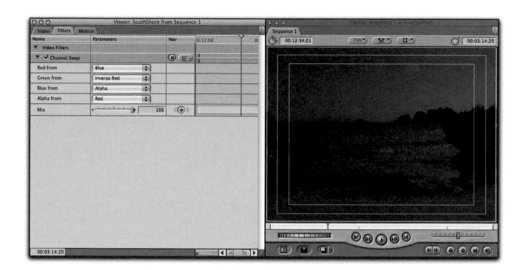

FIG-09-06 The Channel Swap filter allows you to exchange the red, green, blue, and alpha channels—and their inverses.

Color Correction

Color Correction filters allow you to control the color balance of your clips by manipulating the blacks, whites, and midtones. They include Broadcast Safe, Color Corrector, Color Corrector 3-way, Desaturate Highlights, Desaturate Lows, RGB Balance, and RGB Limit.

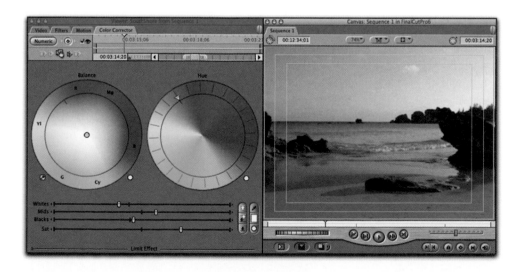

FIG-09-07 The Color Corrector filter offers basic color correction—balance, hue, whites, midtones, blacks, and saturation.

FIG-09-08 The RGB Balance filter lets you independently manipulate the highlights, midtones, and blacks of each color channel—red, green, and blue.

Distort

Distort filters are artistic in style and allow you to create the illusion of texture. They include Bumpmap, Cylinder, Displace, Earthquake, Fisheye, Insect Eye, Pond Ripple, Refraction, Ripple, Scrape, Stripes, Target, Twirl, Wave, and Whirlpool.

FIG-09-09 The Pond Ripple filter simulates ripples in water, allowing you to adjust both the number and size of the ripples.

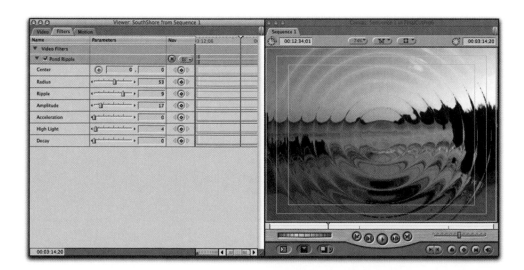

Glow

Glow filters are artistic in style and allow you to create glow effects. They include Bloom, Dazzle, Light Rays, Outer Glow, and Overdrive.

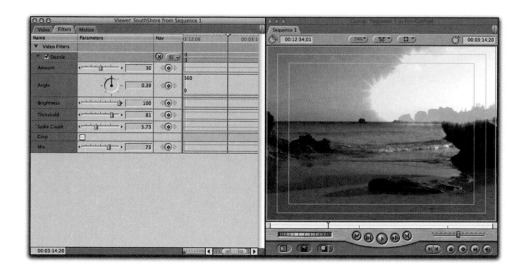

FIG-09-10 The Dazzle filter adds star-like accents in the highlights of an image, creating a surreal look.

Image Control

Image Control filters allow you to adjust the chrominance and luminance values of your clips. They include Brightness and Contrast, Color Balance, Color Reduce, Desaturate, Gamma, Gamma Correction, Gradient Colorize, HSV Adjust, Levels, Proc Amp, Reduce Banding, Sepia, Threshold, Tint, YIQ Adjust, and YUV Adjust.

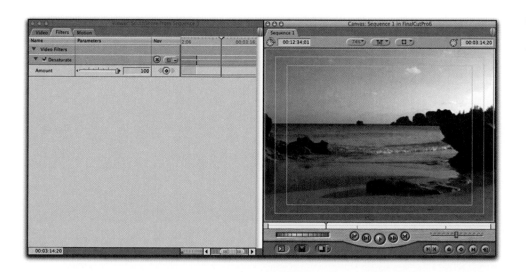

FIG-09-11 The Desaturate filter removes the color from a clip.

FIG-09-12 The Threshold filter reduces the colors in an image to any two colors, allowing you to control the degree of contrast and the midtones.

Key

Key filters allow you to isolate a subject and key out its background. They can be used in conjunction with Matte filters. Key filters include Blue and Green Screen, Chroma Keyer, Color Key, Color Smoothing – 4:1:1, Color Smoothing – 4:2:2, Difference Matte, Luma Key, Spill Suppressor – Blue, and Spill Suppressor – Green.

FIG-09-13 The Difference Matte filter keys out the similar areas between two images.

Matte

Matte filters allow you to mask out areas of a clip for compositing. They can be used in conjunction with Key filters. Matte filters include Eight-Point Garbage Matte, Extract, Four-Point Garbage Matte, Image Mask, Mask Feather, Mask Shape, Matte Choker, Matte Magic, Soft Edges, and Widescreen.

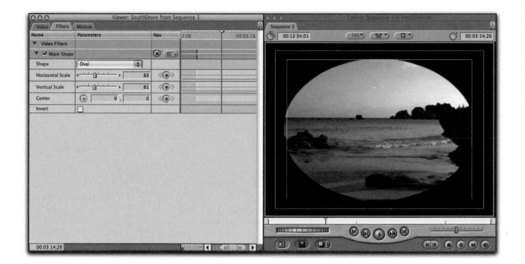

FIG-09-14 The Mask Shape filter allows you to choose a shape—such as a diamond, oval, or rectangle—to act as a mask, which becomes transparent.

FIG-09-15 The Widescreen filter allows you to letterbox an image, choosing from the standard academy ratios.

Perspective

Perspective filters allow you to move a clip in space within its frame. They include Basic 3D, Curl, Flop, Mirror, and Rotate.

FIG-09-16 The Basic 3D filter allows you to move the image along the x, y, and z–axes, making it appear three-dimensional.

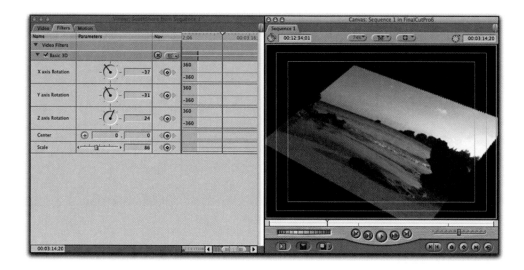

FIG-09-17 The Flop filter allows you to turn over an image horizontally or vertically. Note that any type within the images will be reversed.

QuickTime

QuickTime filters are additional effects included with QuickTime Pro. They include Blur, Brightness and Contrast, Color Style, Color Tint, ColorSync, Edge Detection, Emboss, General Convolution, HSL Balance, Lens Flare, RGB Balance, and Sharpen.

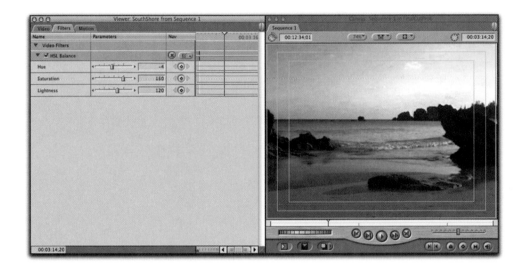

FIG-09-18 The HSL Balance filter allows you to control the hue, saturation, and lightness of an image.

Sharpen

Sharpen filters bring out detail in clips by manipulating the contrast. They include Sharpen and Unsharp Mask.

FIG-09-19 The Sharpen filter increases the contrast between adjacent pixels, making the image appear sharper.

Stylize

Stylize filters are artistic in style and allow you to create special effects. They include Add Noise, Anti-alias, Bad TV, Circles, Color Emboss, Crystallize, Emboss, Extrude, Find Edges, Indent, Line Art, MinMax, Noise Dissolve, Posterize, Relief, Replicate, Slit Scan, Slit Tunnel, Solarize, Vectorize Color, and Vignette.

FIG-09-20 The Posterize filter reduces the number of colors in a clip through a mapping process.

FIG-09-21 The Solarize filter increases the highlights and shadows and reduces the midtones of a clip.

Tiling

Tiling filters are artistic in style and allow you to create geometric effects. They include Kaleidoscope, Kaleidotile, Offset, and Random Tile.

FIG-09-22 The Offset filter divides the clip into tiles and changes their horizontal and vertical origins.

Time

Time filters are artistic in style and allow you to create effects that appear over time. They include Echo, Scrub, Strobe, Trails, and WideTime.

Video

Video filters can be either artistic in style or functional for solving video-related problems. They include Blink, De-interlace, Flicker Filter, Shift Fields, SmoothCam, Stop Motion Blur, Strobe, Timecode Generator, Timecode Reader, and Viewfinder.

FIG-09-23 The Viewfinder filter simulates the viewfinder of a camcorder.

 **SPOTLIGHT**

FxFactory

FxFactory is Noise Industries's visual effects software for Final Cut Express and Final Cut Studio. There are now more than three hundred plug-ins currently available in FxFactory. Some are free and others are available for purchase. FxFactory Pro, which retails for $399, is unique because its plug-ins can be created and modified by end users. This professional package provides a large number of ready-to-be-used effects for Final Cut Express, Final Cut Pro, and Motion.

 You can try out FxFactory yourself! It's included in the back-of-the-book DVD. You are also eligible for a special discount on FxFactory Pro! See the DVD for details.

FIG-09-24 Noise Industries makes FxFactory for Apple's Final Cut Studio and Final Cut Express, and Factory Tools for Avid Express Pro and Media Composer.

FIG-09-25 FxFactory won a *Videography* Vidy Award at the National Association of Broadcasters (NAB) show in 2007, demonstrating technology innovation and engineering excellence.

FIG-09-26 This is the original image without any filters applied.

FIG-09-27
CoreMelt Editing Pack: The CM Blur > Depthblur Gradient filter blurs the image through a gradient, specifying the blur amount at two points.

FIG-09-28
CoreMelt Editing Pack:
The CM Color
Correction >
Advanced Vignette
filter creates a vignette
effect with control
over its shape, color,
size, orientation, and
edges.

FIG-09-29
CoreMelt Editing
Pack: The CM Color
Correction > Bleach
Bypass filter increases
the contrast and
lowers the saturation
to simulate a lab's
bleach bypass process.

FIG-09-30 Noise
Industries: The NI
Color Correction >
Threshold with Colors
filter reduces your
image to two colors
and lets you control
the brightness, opacity,
and sharpness.

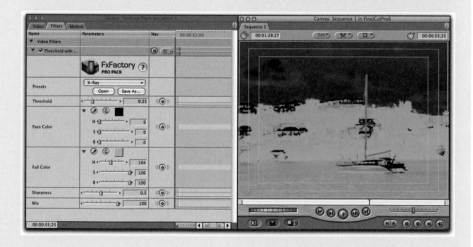

FIG-09-31 Noise Industries: The NI Distort > Chromatic Aberration filter selectively distorts, blurs, and blends channels around a mask. The Halo preset was chosen here.

FIG-09-32 Noise Industries: The NI Distort > Perspective Reflection filter repositions the image and simulates a reflection over a glass surface.

FIG-09-33 CoreMelt Motion Pack: The CM Glow > Core Glow filter allows you to choose separate colors for the inner glow and the outer glow.

FIG-09-34
CoreMelt Motion Pack: The CM Glow > Godrays filter is a more intense light rays filter, which allows you to control the length and emission point of the rays.

FIG-09-35
CoreMelt Motion Pack: The CM Glow > Optical Glow Edges filter creates a glow effect around the edges of images, allowing you to control the threshold and width.

FIG-09-36 Noise Industries: The NI Halftones > CMYK Halftone filter creates a color halftone of the image. This clip uses the Disco Lights preset.

FIG-09-37
CoreMelt Motion
Pack: The CM Image
Behaviors > Optical
Glow Across filter
creates an optical glow
across an image—
through a matte
shape—at a specified
speed.

FIG-09-38
CoreMelt Editing
Pack: The CM Image
Processing > Camera
Shake filter creates
animated motion,
simulating a camera
being shaken by
an explosion or an
earthquake.

FIG-09-39 Noise
Industries: The NI
Sharpen > Sharpen
Chroma filter sharpens
only the chrominance
values in the source
image and leaves the
luminance values
alone.

FIG-09-40
CoreMelt Motion Pack:
The CM Stylize > 3D
Lit Sphere filter wraps
the image around the
shape of a sphere and
allows you to
reposition the light
source.

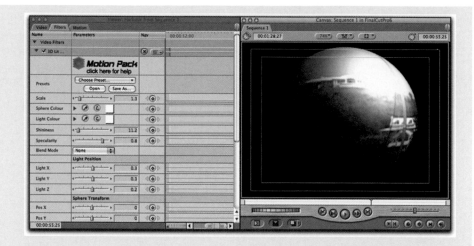

FIG-09-41
Noise Industries: The
NI Stylize > Night
Vision filter simulates
what the image would
look like if it were
viewed through
night-vision goggles.

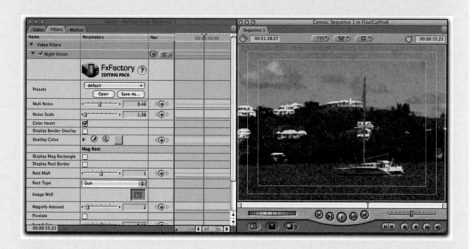

FIG-09-42 Noise
Industries: The NI
Stylize > Pencil Sketch
filter simulates what
the image would look
like if it were sketched
with colored pencils.

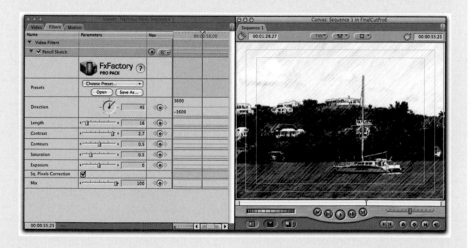

FIG-09-43 Noise Industries: The NI Stylize > Spot Light filter adds a directional spotlight to the image, allowing you to control its position, intensity, and color.

FIG-09-44 When you launch FxFactory Pro, all of your plug-ins will be categorized and listed by package. To open any package, select it from the column on the right and click the Open icon at the top of the window.

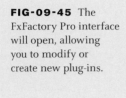

FIG-09-45 The FxFactory Pro interface will open, allowing you to modify or create new plug-ins.

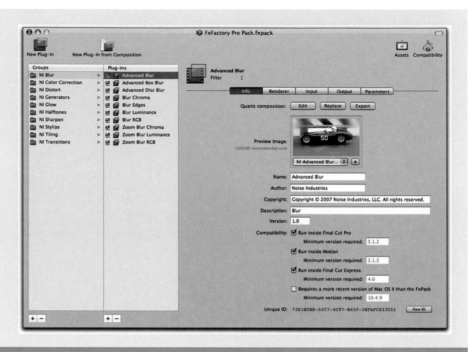

Applying Video Filters

TIP❖ *To render a video clip with a filter or filters applied, select the clip and select Sequence > Render Selection > Video, or press Command–R.*

Once you understand the different types of video filters, you will better understand how to apply them. You can apply a single filter to a clip, or you can apply multiple filters to the same clip to get different looks.

Adding Filters

To add a video filter to a clip, drag it from the Effects tab of the Browser window to the clip in the sequence. Alternatively, you can select the clip in the sequence and select Effects > Video Filters and choose the desired filter from the submenus.

FIG-09-46 Video filters are stored by type in the Video Filters folder in the Effects tab of the Browser window.

TIP ❂ *You can also apply filters directly to clips in the Browser window; however, understand that if the filter has been applied to the master clip, it will be applied every time that clip appears in the sequence.*

FIG-09-47 This is the original clip without any filters applied.

TIP ❂ *You can elect to display the filters bar by clicking the Toggle Clip Keyframes button at the lower left of the Timeline window. See the Timeline Keyframe Editor in Chapter 8 for more information.*

FIG-09-48 Select the desired filter in the Effects tab of the Browser window.

FIG-09-49 Then drag the filter to the clip in the sequence in the Timeline window.

FIG-09-50 To access the filter's parameters, double-click on the clip in the sequence and click the Filters tab in the Viewer.

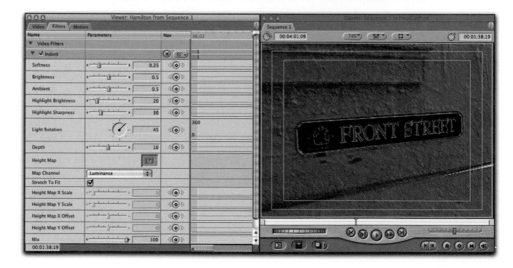

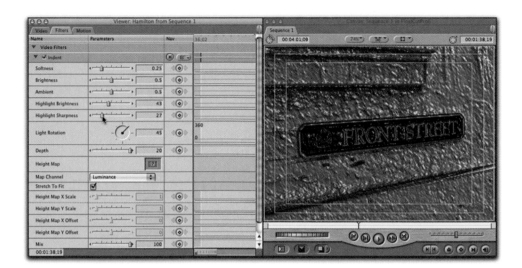

FIG-09-51 You can adjust a filter's parameters using the sliders and other controls.

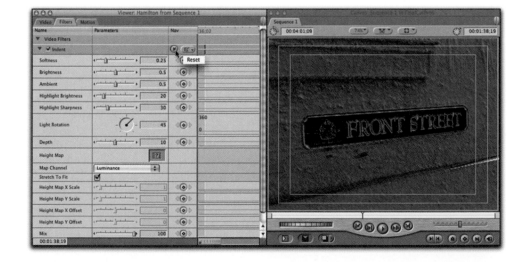

FIG-09-52 Click on the Reset button to return to the default settings for the filter.

Reordering Filters

When multiple filters are applied to the same clip, you can change their order. Depending on which filters have been applied, reordering filters can change the overall look of the image and produce different results.

FIG-09-53 The Desaturate filter was first applied to this clip, stripping it of all its color. Then the Color Balance filter was added and adjusted to increase the green midtones.

FIG-09-54 The Color Balance filter has been selected and is being placed before the Desaturate filter, indicated by the dark gray line.

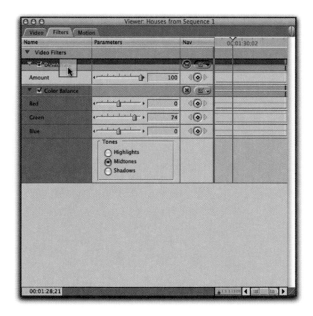

FIG-09-55 After the filter order has been changed, the image loses all of its color.

Disabling Filters

Final Cut Pro gives you the option of temporarily disabling filters to better ascertain their effect. This ability can be especially useful when experimenting with filters in combination. To disable a filter, deselect the check box to the left of the filter's name in the Filters tab of the Viewer.

FIG-09-56 This video clip has the Threshold filter applied. Note the check in the box to the left of the filter's name.

FIG-09-57 Click the box to the left of the filter's name to deselect it, and the filter will be temporarily disabled.

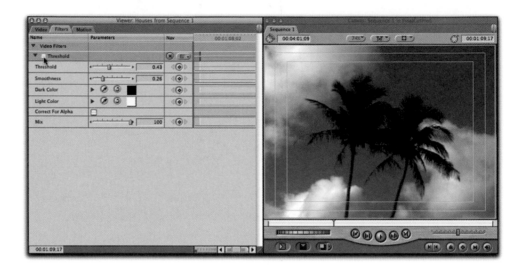

Removing Filters

TIP ✪ *Don't forget, you can always undo an action by selecting Edit > Undo, or by pressing Command–Z.*

If you are certain you no longer wish to use a filter, you can delete it by selecting the filter in the Filters tab and pressing the Delete key. You can also select the filter and choose either Edit > Cut or Edit > Clear. Alternatively, you can Control-click a filter and choose Cut from the shortcut menu.

FIG-09-58 This video clip has the Solarize filter applied.

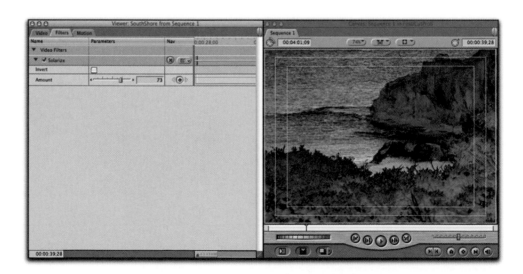

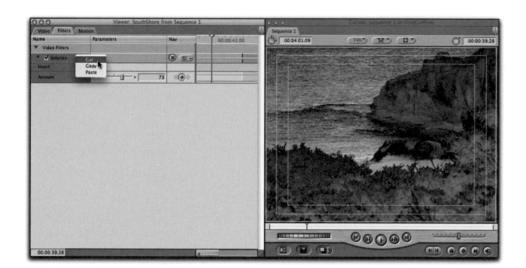

FIG·09·59 Control-click the filter and choose Cut from the shortcut menu to remove it.

FIG·09·60 The Solarize filter has been removed from the video clip.

Copying and Pasting Filters

You may also find it useful to copy and paste your filters from one clip to another. To copy and paste a filter, first Control-click the filter you wish to copy and choose Copy from the shortcut menu. Then select a clip in the sequence where you would like to paste the filter. Control-click the clip and choose Paste Attributes from the shortcut menu. Make sure the Video Attributes Filters box is checked in the Paste Attributes dialog box and click OK.

Alternatively, you can select the clip in the sequence whose filter or filters you wish to copy and select Edit > Copy, or press Command–C. Then select the clip in the sequence where you wish to paste the filter or filters and select Edit > Paste Attributes, or press Option–V. The Paste Attributes dialog box will open. Make sure the Video Attributes Filters box is checked and click OK.

FIG-09-61 This clip has the Posterize filter applied.

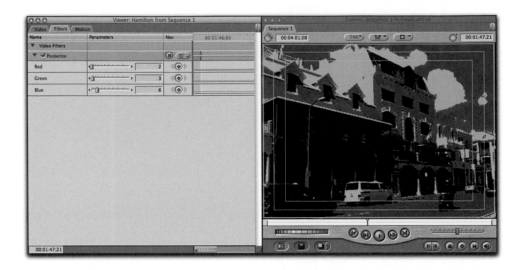

FIG-09-62 Control-click the filter and choose Copy from the shortcut menu.

FIG-09-63 Select a clip in the sequence where you would like to paste the filter.

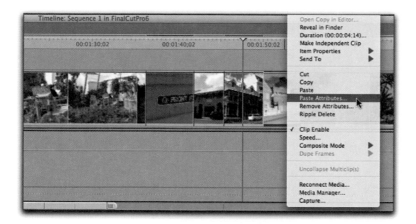

FIG-09-65 The Paste Attributes dialog box will open. Make sure the Video Attributes Filters box is checked and click OK.

FIG-09-66 The Posterize filter, with the same parameters, will be applied to the new clip.

TIP *Option-Control-3 copies all the filters from the previous clip and pastes them to the current clip. Option-Control-4 copies all the filters from the current clip and pastes them to the next clip.*

Keyframing Filters

Just as you keyframed motion effects, you can also keyframe filters in Final Cut Pro. This technique gives you many options as an editor. You can choose to gradually apply a filter, increasing its intensity over time. Or you can choose to vary a filter over time during the entire clip, or just a portion of it. Keyframing filters can even give still clips the illusion of motion.

FIG-09-67 To keyframe filter effects in a clip, first double-click the clip to activate it in the Viewer. Then click on the Filters tab. This is the original clip with the Compound Blur filter applied. The Amount parameter has been set to 0.

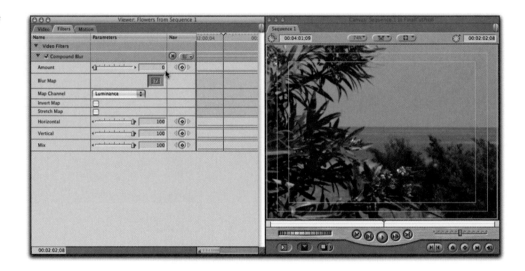

FIG-09-68 The first keyframe will be placed at the beginning of the clip. Advance the playhead to the beginning of the clip in the Timeline window. Then click the Keyframe button for the Amount parameter in the Filters tab of the Viewer window. It will turn green.

FIG-09-69 Advance the playhead in the Timeline to the end of the clip. Change the Amount parameter to 10. Final Cut Pro will automatically add the second keyframe for you and interpret all the frames in between. The keyframe will appear as a green diamond in the keyframe graph area to the right. Note that the Invert Map box has also been checked to create this effect.

FIG-09-70 You can view the keyframed Compound Blur effect in the Canvas window.

FIG-09-71 You can navigate back and forth between keyframes by clicking the arrows on either side of the Keyframe button. To move to the keyframe to the left, click the Previous Keyframe button, or press Option-K. To move to the keyframe to the right, click the Next Keyframe button, or press Shift-K.

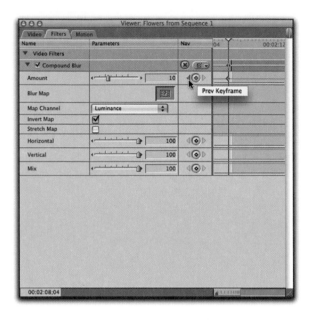

FIG-09-72 To add another keyframe in between, first advance the playhead in the Timeline window to the desired position.

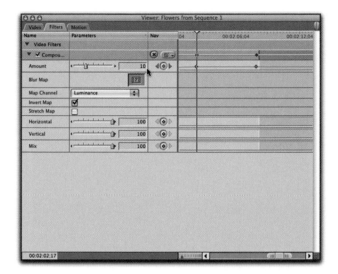

FIG-09-73 Resize the Viewer window so that the keyframe graph area is easier to see by clicking and dragging the right side of the Viewer toward the Canvas window. Then change the Amount parameter in the Filters tab of the Viewer window to 10. Final Cut Pro will automatically add the keyframe for you and reinterpret all the other frames in the keyframed effect. Now the Compound Blur filter will increase gradually during the first part of the clip and then maintain a setting of 10 for the remainder of the clip.

Please refer to Chapter 8 for additional information on keyframes, such as how to delete and reposition keyframes, using keyframe tools, manipulating Bézier handles and curves, and using the Timeline Keyframe Editor.

 **SPOTLIGHT**

Color

Color is Apple's professional color grading and finishing application. It is quite sophisticated and will allow you to create a signature look for a project. You can work in SD, HD, or 2K and preview the results in real time. With GPU-accelerated processing, high-quality rendering is fast. When your project requires more than Final Cut Pro's built-in Color Correction and Image Control effects offer, Color is the solution.

FIG-09-74 This is the window layout for a single monitor configuration in Color.

FIG-09-75 You can navigate through your files in the Setup tab by clicking the folder with the red arrow in the upper left corner. Click the Import button to add a media file to your project.

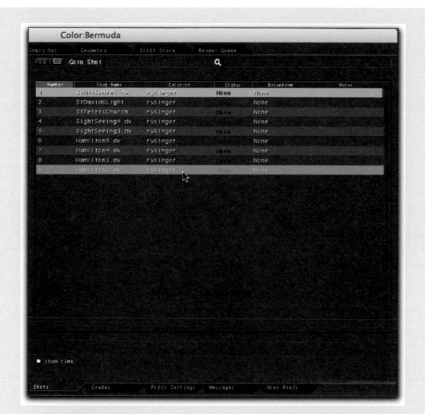

FIG-09-76 All the files that have been added are listed in the order they were imported.

FIG-09-77 The files are also automatically added to the timeline in the order in which they were imported.

FIG-09-78 In the Scopes window, the waveform monitor can be viewed in Overlay mode, which displays the red, green, and blue channels together. The video preview is above it, and the vectorscope is below it. Other scopes, such as 3D Color Space and Histogram, may be accessed at any time by Control-clicking either of the displayed scopes.

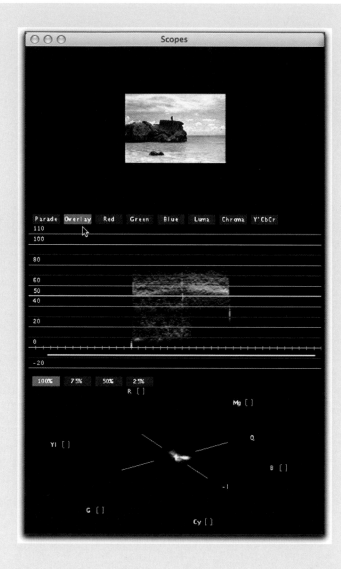

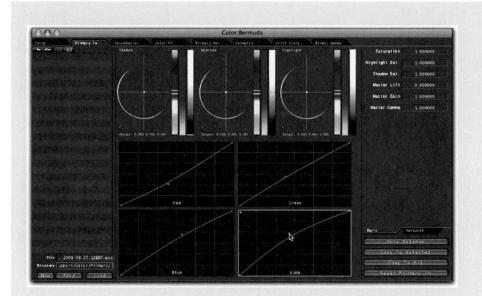

FIG-09-79
By clicking on the Primary In tab, you can make primary color grade adjustments.

FIG-09-80 If you click on the Color FX tab, you can choose from more than twenty custom-effect looks.

Summary

Effects are the most valued feature of any digital video program because they give unlimited creative power and freedom to the editor. Experimenting with Final Cut Pro's filter effects requires both time and patience. And there are many third-party plug-ins that can also be acquired and learned. However, mastering filter techniques is well worth the effort. You will refine your skills as an editor, and your projects will be all the better for it.

KEYBOARD SHORTCUTS	Edit > Paste Attributes	*Option–V*
	Copy all filters from previous clip and paste them to current clip	*Option-Control-3*
	Copy all filters from current clip and paste them to next clip	*Option-Control-4*

REWIND

1. What is a video filter?
2. List the different video filter categories in Final Cut Pro.
3. Describe three video filter categories.
4. What are FxPlug effects?
5. What are third-party filters?
6. What is FxFactory?
7. Why is filter order important?
8. What ways can you customize filters?
9. Why is keyframing filters useful?
10. Describe Color.

TAKE TWO

1. Experiment with Final Cut Pro's filters. Be sure to try varying the filter order and using keyframes.
2. Experiment with FxFactory's filters.
3. Practice using Color.

Creating Titles and Graphics

Learn techniques for creating titles and graphics for digital video

Learn about design conventions

Understand the function of Title Safe indicators

Learn how to use Final Cut Pro's text generators

Discover third-party text generators

Discover LiveType and Motion

CREATING TITLES AND graphics is an important part in the editing process, and with Final Cut Pro, you have many options. Final Cut Pro comes with built-in titling tools, called text generators. In addition, you can use third-party plug-ins, such as those by Boris, to create titles. Final Cut Pro also comes with the standalone titling program LiveType. And you can also create stunning motion graphics with Final Cut Studio's Motion.

Titles and Graphics

So, what exactly is a title, and how is it differentiated from credits or a graphic? A **title** is a text file, which can be a single word or multiple words or phrases, that provides additional information, such as names and dates, or clarifies important concepts or terms. **Credits** are a list of names of the people who worked on a video or film project and what their individual roles were.

Graphics, on the other hand, may include type, but can also be made up of computer-generated imagery. **Two-dimensional graphics** are computer-generated images that are created along the vertical Y-axis and the horizontal X-axis. **Three-dimensional graphics** and animation also include a third axis—the Z-axis—which represents depth.

Titles and graphics are commonly designed with alpha channels so that their backgrounds can be removed and replaced with other images. Popular two-dimensional graphic design programs include Adobe Photoshop and Adobe Illustrator. Three-dimensional animation programs include Autodesk's Maya and NewTek's LightWave.

Design Conventions

Regardless of which program you use, there are design conventions that apply to creating titles and graphics specifically for digital video. They must be followed to ensure that your titles won't be cut off or displayed poorly on the screen.

Title Safe Indicators

To ensure that your titles are displayed properly, keep in mind that televisions and video equipment were designed to overscan the video image so that any imperfections around the edges wouldn't be seen. Therefore, digital video programs like Final Cut Pro have the option of displaying a **Title Safe indicator** that is 20% smaller than the full frame, thus alerting you to the parts of the image that run the risk of being cut off.

The outermost boundary is called the **action safe area,** and any video image within the action safe area will be displayed in its entirety. The innermost boundary is the **title safe area.** This separate line was created specifically for titles because they run the risk of becoming distorted if they are too close to the edges of the frame.

 Your computer display(s) must be set to "millions" of colors to be able to see the Title Safe indicators. If you should need to change your display settings, select Apple Menu > System Preferences, click on Displays, and choose Millions from the Colors pop-up menu.

Broadcast Safe Colors

In addition to ensuring that your titles and graphics fit properly within the video frame, you also want to make sure that the colors you choose are safe to broadcast. Keep in mind that the computer monitor has a greater color depth, and that the colors you see on your display may not be the same as those the television set reproduces. Most digital video editing programs, and some graphic design programs like Adobe Photoshop, have a filter you can apply to ensure that the images use **broadcast safe colors.**

FIG-10-01 To enable the Title Safe indicators, select View > Show Title Safe or choose Show Title Safe from the View pop-up menu in the Viewer window.

FIG-10-02 Select Effects > Video Filters > Color Correction > Broadcast Safe to apply the Broadcast Safe filter to a clip.

Sans-Serif Fonts

Another factor to consider when designing titles and graphics for video is selecting the appropriate font. Thin lines do not reproduce well in video and tend to flicker on the screen. Thicker fonts are preferable, as is using the bold style. Likewise, serif fonts should not be used for video. A **serif font** has thin lines on the points of the letters. A **sans-serif font** does not have thin lines on its points (sans is Latin for without), and is therefore ideal for video.

⬦ *Final Cut Pro uses TrueType fonts, so be sure to install the TrueType versions as opposed to the PostScript versions when installing additional fonts.*

FIG-10-03 Arial and Helvetica are sans-serif fonts that are ideal for video.

Serif Fonts (Not Ideal for Video)	Sans-Serif Fonts (Ideal for Video)
Baskerville	Arial
Century	Futura
Garamond	Gills San
Goudy	Helvetica
Palatino	Myriad

TIP ✪ *Never use true white (Red-255, Green-255, Blue-255) for a text color because it tends to shimmer, especially over black. Instead, either reduce the opacity to 90% or lower the red, blue, and green values so that the white has a slight grayish tinge on your display. Because of the difference in color depth, it will appear white when reproduced on video.*

Design Techniques

In addition to selecting a bold, sans-serif font, there are other ways to ensure that the text can be easily read. Choosing the appropriate color is very important to help set off the text from its background. Drop shadows and/or outlines are also commonly added to the type to help the text stand out. Additionally, shapes and gradients are often applied behind the text to separate it from busy backgrounds and to give the illusion of depth.

FIG-10-04 In the original image, the text is the same color as the sand and difficult to read.

FIG-10-05 The aqua blue color of the ocean is a better choice to help the text stand out.

FIG-10-06 A black drop shadow and outline also help distinguish the text from the background.

FIG-10-07 Gradients and shapes are often placed behind the text to give the illusion of depth to the image and further accentuate the type.

TIP✪ *You can specify the default duration for the generated text in the Still/Freeze Duration field of the Editing tab in the User Preferences dialog box.*

Text Generators

A **text generator** is a feature in Final Cut Pro that creates a title clip on a video track, which can be manipulated like any ordinary video clip. Because the title clips are automatically composited with whatever video layers you place behind them, the text-generated clips will require rendering. Frame size does not have to be specified, because the text-generated clips will automatically adopt the frame size that has been chosen for the sequence.

FIG-10-08 Simply drag a text generator from the Effects tab of the Browser window to the desired track in the Timeline window to apply it.

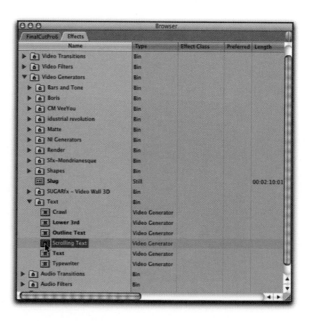

Final Cut Pro's Text Generators

The six text generators that are built into Final Cut Pro are Crawl, Lower 3rd, Outline Text, Scrolling Text, Text, and Typewriter. **Crawl** creates a single line of text that moves horizontally across the frame. **Lower 3rd,** commonly used to identify a person or place, automatically positions the text in the lower third of the frame. **Outline Text** creates an outline around text that does not move. **Scrolling Text** is used to create movie credits that roll vertically up or down the frame. **Text** creates text in a single position in the frame. Finally, **Typewriter** simulates the effect of typing directly on the screen by displaying one character at a time.

FIG-10-09 Crawl will display the desired text along a single moving line. You can specify the font, size, style, and color. You can also control the spacing, location, and direction of the text.

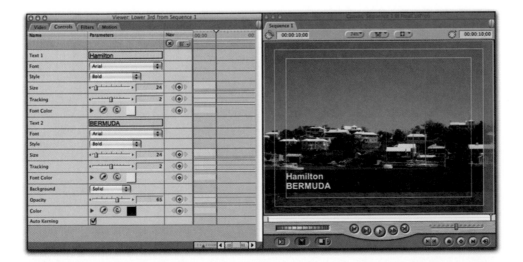

FIG-10-10 You can add two lines of text using Lower 3rd, specifying the font, style, size, tracking, and color. You can also choose the background and control its opacity and color.

FIG-10-11 You can create multiple lines of outlined text that does not move with Outline Text. You can specify the font, style, alignment, and size. You can also control the tracking, leading, aspect, line width and softness, and center. You can even change the text color and opacity, and add a background layer that can be manipulated.

FIG-10-12 Scrolling Text lets you create multiple lines of text that scroll up or down the screen. You can specify the font, size, style, alignment, and color. You can also control the spacing, leading, indent, gap width, fade size, and direction.

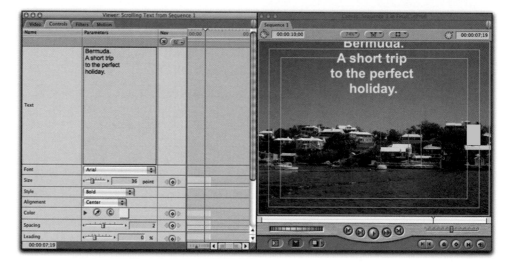

FIG-10-13 You can create multiple lines of text that do not move with Text. You can specify the font, size, style, alignment, and color. You can also control the origin, tracking, leading, and aspect.

FIG-10-14 Typewriter allows you to make text appear on the screen one letter at a time. You can specify the font, size, style, alignment, and color. You can also control the spacing, location, indent, and pause.

Third-Party Text Generators

In addition to using Final Cut Pro's built-in text generators, you can also use third-party text generators. Boris has four generators that ship free with Final Cut Pro: three text generators—Text Scrambler, Title 3D, and Title Crawl—and one shape generator, Vector Shape. You can also purchase additional plug-ins from developers like Noise Industries.

FIG-10-15 Boris Title 3D is one of the third-party generators that comes free with Final Cut Pro. You can manipulate individual characters of text on the X, Y, and Z-axes.

FIG-10-16 Noise Industries's Star Titler lets you easily simulate the scrolling text from the opening of the *Star Wars* movies.

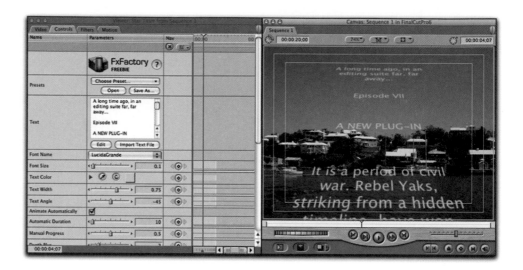

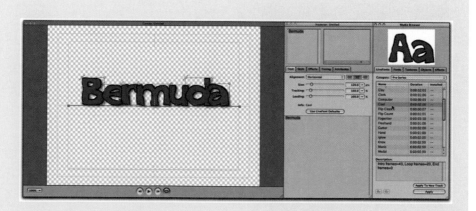

SPOTLIGHT

LiveType

LiveType is a standalone application that creates professional-quality titles and graphics. It features LiveFonts and FontMaker to create animated fonts that utilize color and motion. You can apply keyframed motion behaviors, such as fades and zooms, to regular fonts, and even manipulate individual characters. LiveType also includes hundreds of textures and graphics. After creating and rendering your titles and graphics in LiveType, you can export the movies for use in Final Cut Pro or another application.

FIG-10-17 You can choose from a selection of preanimated LiveFonts to apply to your text.

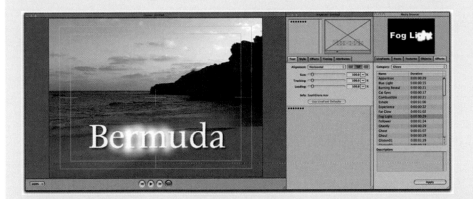

FIG-10-18 A glow motion behavior and a drop shadow have been applied to this text. A movie has also been temporarily placed in the background to act as a guide for framing.

FIG-10-19 A texture has been applied to the background, and a drop shadow has been applied to the text.

FIG-10-20 An animated object has been placed behind the text and in front of the background movie. An outline, a drop shadow, and a glow have also been applied to the text.

 **SPOTLIGHT**

Motion

Motion ships with Final Cut Studio and is Apple's real-time 3D motion graphics design program. It comes with more than 150 filters and effects.

FIG-10-21 You can elect to work from a customizable template instead of creating a new project from scratch.

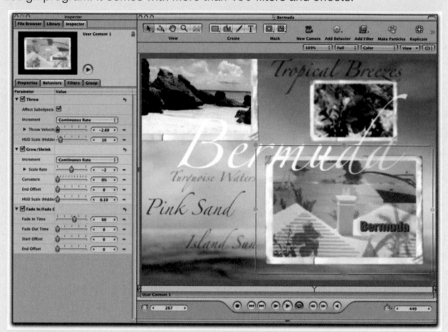

FIG-10-22 In this new project, a gradient, an outline, and a drop shadow have been applied to the text.

FIG-10-23 Noise Industries's Matte Shape Generator has been applied next and made partially transparent.

FIG-10-24 Noise Industries's Star Shine Generator has also been applied to further enhance the look of the matte.

FIG-10-25 Finally, the Aurora 2 particle emitter has been applied in front of the background layer, but behind the text and matte. The Color Range has been modified to reflect the colors in the image, and the opacity has been reduced.

You can also purchase additional effects from third-party developers. After creating your titles and graphics in Motion, you can export the movies for use in Final Cut Pro or another application.

Summary

You have many options for designing titles and graphics for digital video. You can create them in a graphic design or animation program, or you can choose to use one of Final Cut Pro's built-in generators, or a third-party plug-in package. Or you can choose to use a standalone program like LiveType or Motion. However, regardless of which program you choose, be sure to use the proper conventions for broadcast, and take special note of the Title Safe indicators.

 **REWIND**

1. What is the difference between titles and credits?
2. What are graphics?
3. What are the action safe and title safe areas?
4. Why is the Broadcast Safe filter important?
5. What are serif and sans-serif fonts?
6. What design techniques should you use to ensure that your text can be easily read?
7. What is a text generator?
8. List and describe Final Cut Pro's built-in text generators.

9. Describe LiveType.
10. Describe Motion.

---

1. Practice creating titles with Final Cut Pro's text generators.
2. Practice creating titles and graphics in LiveType.
3. Practice creating titles and graphics in Motion.

TAKE TWO

CHAPTER 11

Working with Audio and Music

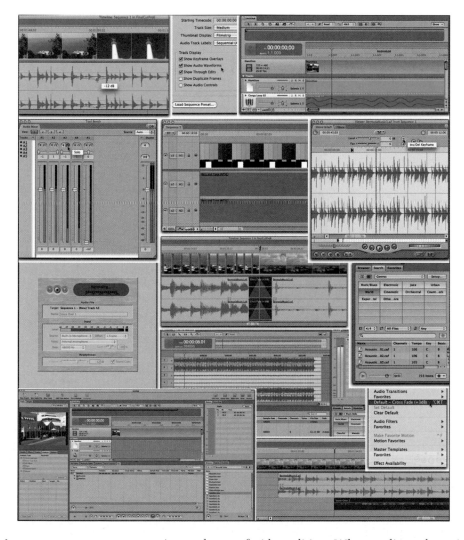

AUDIO AND MUSIC are an integral part of video editing. When audio and music
are done correctly, they enhance the project but often go unnoticed. When there is
a problem with distortion or the dialogue is too low to be heard over the music, bad
audio can ruin an entire video project. Therefore, it is important to spend the time to
understand audio and learn how to manipulate it in Final Cut Pro.

TIP An extensive discussion of audio mixing can be found in Final Cut Pro's User Manual, Volume III, Part I: "Audio Mixing."

Understanding Audio

Final Cut Studio includes Soundtrack Pro 2 for editing professional audio, music, and effects. For those who want additional audio capabilities, Apple also offers Logic Express and Logic Studio, which are geared toward musicians who write, record, and edit their own music.

Final Cut Pro also has built-in audio capabilities. You can create up to 99 audio tracks, add audio filters, and create cross fades.

 Logic Studio includes Logic Pro 8, Mainstage, Soundtrack Pro 2, Studio Instruments, Studio Effects, and Sound Studio Library.

Audio Terminology

Amplitude—how strong, or loud, the sound wave is.

Bit Depth—binary numbers, or bits, that represent the audio sample; the higher the bit depth, the better the representation.

Decibel—a numerical expression (dB), based on voltage or power, that represents how loud a sound is.

Frequency—the pitch of a sound wave, measured in hertz (Hz), or cycles per second.

Phase—the timing between two sound waves, measured in degrees.

Sample Rate—how often a signal is measured, or sampled, per second, measured in kHz; the higher the sample rate, the higher the quality.

Sound Wave—the vibration an object causes in the air, which is audible to the human ear, and includes amplitude, frequency, and phase.

Audio Meters

Maintaining proper audio levels is one of the most important aspects of editing audio. Audio levels refer to the volume of the audio. If the levels are too high, the audio can sound distorted; if the levels are too low, the audio can be difficult to hear. And when different audio tracks have a wide range of levels, the audio can sound disjointed.

Final Cut Pro features several types of **audio meters,** which monitor the audio's decibel level. The **input audio meters** allow you to monitor the audio levels in the Log and Capture window. In the Audio Mixer window, there are individual **track meters** for each track in the sequence and **Master audio meters** for each audio output channel in the sequence. And a **floating audio meter** shows the output levels of the Viewer or Canvas and Timeline windows.

Final Cut Pro uses **digital full scale audio meters** that measure the signal in dBFS (decibels full scale) and can range from −60 dBFS up to 0 dBFS, which is different from **analog audio meters,** which measure the signal in dB (decibels) and can range from −30 dB up to +7 dB. Any audio above 0 dBFS is **clipped audio,** and the original shape of the waveform cannot be recovered. On analog equipment, 0 dB is the optimal level of the device, whereas with digital meters, 0 dBFS is the maximum level before clipping occurs. In comparison, 16-bit audio, such as digital DV audio, often uses the −12 dBFS level, which would equate to a 0 dB analog level, whereas 20-bit or 24-bit audio would use a −18 or −20 dBFS level.

Final Cut Pro's floating audio meter and Master audio meter alert you to peaks above 0 dBFS with a **clipping indicator** that lights up during playback and will remain lit until you start playback again.

> *Final Cut Pro's track and Master audio meters will display levels above 0 dBFS, all the way up to 12 dBFS.*

FIG-11-01 The input audio meters can be viewed in the Clip Settings tab of the Log and Capture window.

FIG-11-02 The number of track meters corresponds with the number of audio tracks in the sequence. They can be viewed in the Audio Mixer tab of the Tool Bench window by selecting Tools > Audio Mixer, or by pressing Option-6.

FIG-11-03 The Master audio meter can also be viewed in the Audio Mixer tab of the Tool Bench window by selecting Tools > Audio Mixer, or by pressing Option-6.

FIG-11-04 The floating audio meters can be displayed or hidden at any time by selecting Window > Audio Meters, or by pressing Option-4.

FIG-11-05 The clipping indicator will light up red in the Master audio meter whenever the digital audio level exceeds 0 dBFS.

Audio Levels

It's important to maintain proper audio levels throughout the production and postproduction process: recording, capturing, editing, and outputting. If you begin by recording poor-quality audio, you will be hard-pressed to clean it up in the postproduction process.

 The amount of dynamic range of the audio mix depends on what type of sound system the audio will be played back through. Typically, the theatrical Dolby Digital dynamic range is 20 dB, average videotape is 12 dB, and television broadcast is 6 dB.

Audio Peaks

If you should need to check for audio levels above 0 dBFS, which could sound crackly due to clipping, Final Cut Pro can automatically analyze an audio clip and mark any high peaks. Simply select an audio clip in the Browser window, or double-click on an audio clip in the sequence to open it in the Viewer window, and select Mark > Audio Peaks > Mark. To remove the markers, select Mark > Audio Peaks > Clear.

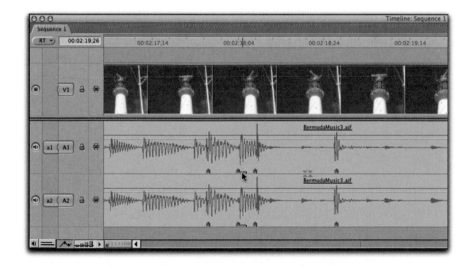

FIG-11-06 Final Cut Pro will mark with red the peaks in the audio file that are clipped.

Normalization Gain

Sometimes your audio may be too low. You have the option of manually amplifying the level using the Gain audio filter. Or, you may use Final Cut Pro's Normalization Gain command, which is a nondestructive way to apply a gain filter to a clip without modifying the original file. The Normalization Gain command ensures that the clip's levels are increased optimally, without running the risk of becoming distorted, which could happen if you adjust the Gain filter manually.

FIG-11-07 To use the Normalization Gain feature, first select the audio clip in the sequence and then select Modify > Audio > Apply Normalization Gain. A dialog box will open where you can enter a value in the Normalize field. The default is 0 dBFS. Then click OK.

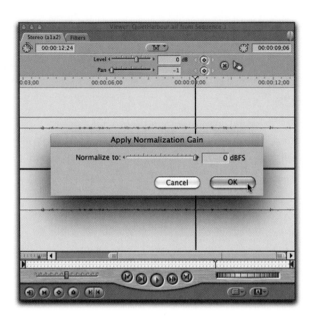

Color Bars and Tone

While it is important to manage the audio levels during the editing process, it is also important to ensure that the levels are correct when preparing a project for broadcast or duplication. Therefore, you have the option of adding **color bars** and **tone** at the beginning of the sequence, which serve as a reference for calibrating color and audio levels at another facility.

FIG-11-08 To add color bars and tone to the beginning of the sequence, go to the Effects tab of the Browser window, open the Video Generators folder, then open the Bars and Tone folder and select the proper format, such as NTSC, for your project. Then drag the generator to the beginning of the sequence in the Timeline window.

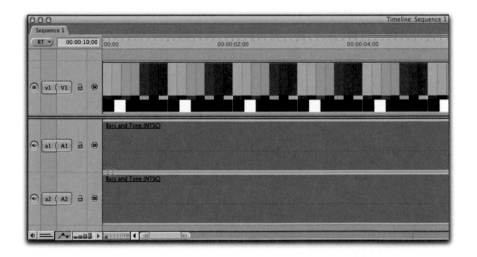

Audio Mixer

Once you understand audio levels, you can use the Audio Mixer to adjust the levels of each audio track and mix the audio tracks down by combining them into the desired number of audio output channels. To open the Audio Mixer, select Tools > Audio Mixer, or press Option-6.

The audio output channels are designated in the audio output preset of the sequence. To modify the sequence settings, first select the sequence in the Timeline window, then select Sequence > Settings, or press Command-0. Then select the Audio Outputs tab and choose the desired audio output channels.

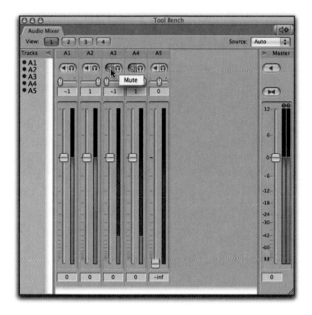

FIG-11-09 You can mute the audio for a particular track by clicking the Mute button, and that track will be silent while the rest of the audio tracks in your sequence play.

FIG-11-10 To isolate one audio track to play and mute all the others, click the Solo button for the track you wish to hear.

FIG-11-11 You can also adjust the audio levels for a track using the faders. Alternatively, you can enter a numerical value in the field below each fader.

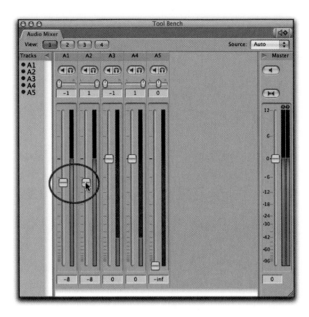

FIG-11-12 You can adjust the levels for each audio output channel using the Master fader.

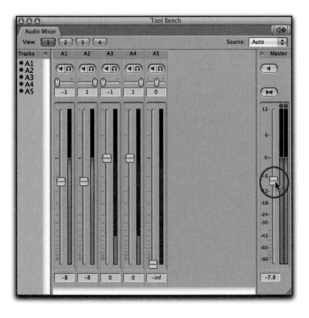

FIG-11-13 You can change an audio clip's stereo pan using the panning slider, which adjusts both tracks simultaneously. Or you can enter a numerical value in the field below the panning slider.

Working with Audio in the Timeline and Viewer

In addition to using the Audio Mixer, you can also work with audio directly in the Timeline and Viewer windows. You may wish to adjust the display options in the Timeline window to make it easier to edit the audio. If you choose to display clip overlays, you can manipulate the audio level overlays directly in the Timeline window. Likewise, if you choose to display audio waveforms, you can have a visual cue to line up an edit.

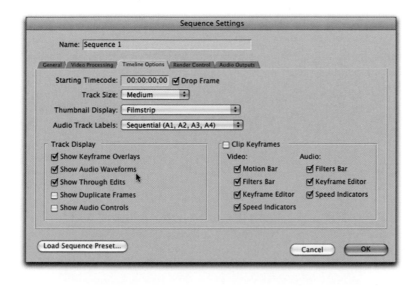

FIG-11-14 First select the sequence and then select Sequence > Settings, or press Command-0. The Sequence Settings dialog box will open. Then select the Timeline Options tab and make sure Show Keyframe Overlays and Show Audio Waveforms options are checked.

FIG·11·15 You can also click the Clip Overlays button to display the audio level overlay, which appears as a pink line. Or with the Timeline window active, press Option-W.

FIG·11·16 To adjust the overall audio level, select the pink line and drag it up or down until you reach the desired decibel level.

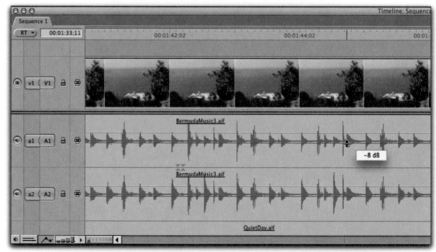

FIG·11·17 You can also add keyframes by selecting the Pen tool from the Tool palette, or pressing P and clicking on the clip at the point where you would like to add the keyframe.

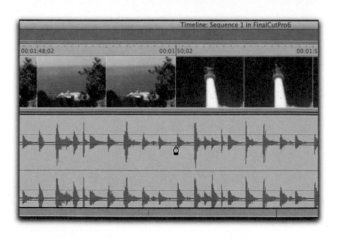

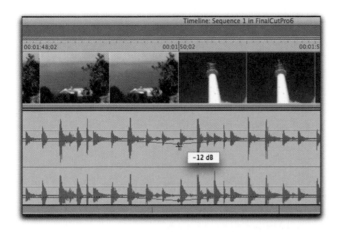

FIG-11-18 You can add additional keyframes, and then select and drag a keyframe to change the clip's audio level by dragging it up or down, or dragging it from side to side to move it forward or backward in time.

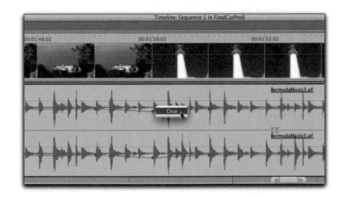

FIG-11-19 To delete a keyframe, use the Delete Point tool, or Control-click the keyframe and choose Clear from the shortcut menu.

FIG-11-20 Alternatively, you can also adjust an audio clip's levels directly in the Viewer window. Double-click the audio clip to open it in the Viewer. Then adjust the Level slider or enter a numerical value in the Level field.

FIG-11-21 You can also adjust the audio level by dragging the pink overlay line up or down, until the desired decibel level is displayed.

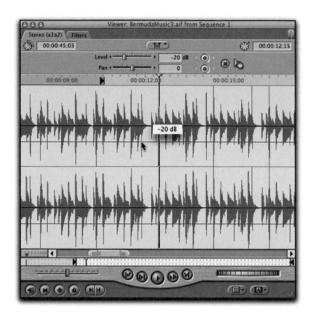

FIG-11-22 Likewise, you can adjust the Pan slider or enter a numerical value in the Pan field.

FIG-11-23 Or you can adjust the pan level by dragging the purple overlay line up or down.

FIG-11-24 You can also add level or pan keyframes in the Viewer window by positioning the playhead and clicking the Insert/Delete Keyframe button.

FIG-11-25 Position the playhead to add additional Level keyframes. Pink dots will represent the Level keyframes in the overlay.

FIG-11-26 Once the keyframes have been added, you can click the Previous Keyframe button to go back to the previous keyframe.

FIG-11-27 Or you can click the Next Keyframe button to advance to the next keyframe.

FIG-11-28 Once keyframes have been added, you can vary the audio level of the clip over time by manipulating the levels at the desired keyframes by simply dragging them up or down.

FIG-11-29 To delete a keyframe, position the playhead over the keyframe and click the Insert/Delete Keyframe button. You can also Control-click the keyframe and choose Clear from the shortcut menu. Or you can click and drag the keyframe out of the waveform display area until the cursor changes to a trashcan, then release the mouse.

Additional Audio Features

In addition to controlling audio and pan levels, Final Cut Pro also has other audio features like the Voice Over Tool to record an audio track as you watch a sequence, audio filters to clean up audio and create effects, and audio transitions to cross fade audio clips.

Voice Over Tool

The Voice Over Tool is a powerful feature because it allows you to record an audio track directly into a sequence as it plays. You can use your computer's built-in audio or a compatible audio device connected to a FireWire port, a USB port, or a PCI slot.

FIG-11-30 To activate the Voice Over Tool, select Tools > Voice Over, or press Option-0. Then choose the appropriate audio recording device from the Source pop-up menu. You can also control other desired settings, such as Rate and Gain.

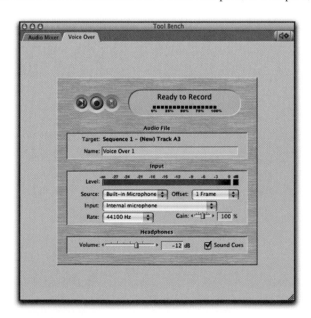

FIG-11-31 When you are ready to begin recording, press the Record button.

FIG-11-32 A countdown will prompt you when it is time to begin.

FIG-11-33 You can record the new track as the sequence plays.

FIG-11-34 Press the Stop button when you are finished.

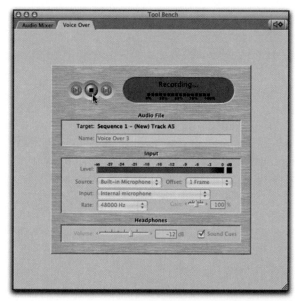

FIG-11-35 The Voice Over track will automatically be added to the Timeline.

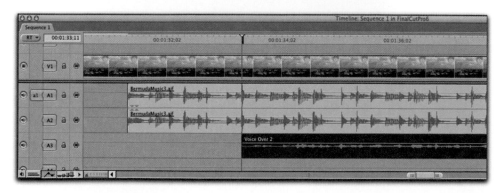

Voice Over Tips

◆ *Don't talk too closely to the microphone. Try not to "pop your P's"—the "P" sound tends to be the loudest and may cause peaks in your audio that could distort.*

◆ *Articulate clearly, and try to maintain a consistent tone, volume, and pace. Practice anything that may be difficult to pronounce beforehand.*

◆ *When working from a script, read it over a few times out loud before you begin. Time yourself and make adjustments to the script, or your pace, as needed.*

◆ *When you can't record audio in a studio, avoid unwanted sounds by placing a "Recording in Progress" sign on your closed door. Also turn off your phone's ringer, the furnace or air conditioning, and any lights that emit a hum.*

◆ *Never expect to get it right with the first take!*

Applying Audio Filters

There is an array of both Apple and Final Cut Pro audio filters included. These audio filter categories include equalization, gain and normalization, dynamics, noise reduction, and echo and reverberation. In addition, third-party filters can also be added as plug-ins.

Equalization audio filters change the frequency of a sound. **Gain and normalization filters** amplify a sound. **Dynamic filters** adjust the dynamic range (loud and quiet sounds) of an audio clip. **Noise reduction filters** remove unwanted electronic hums and reduce the intensity of "ess" and "P" sounds. **Echo and reverberation filters** create effects to simulate a particular acoustic space, such as a large hall.

➡ *Humans hear from 20 Hz to 20,000 Hz. Low frequencies range from 20 to 250 Hz. Midrange frequencies range from 250 to 4,000 Hz. High frequencies range from 4,000 to 20,000 Hz.*

TIP ✪ *Audio filters can be keyframed over time in the Viewer window.*

FIG-11-36 You can view the audio filters in the Effects tab of the Browser window. To apply an audio filter, drag it from the Effects tab to the desired audio clip in the sequence.

FIG-11-37 Double-click on the audio clip in the Timeline window, then click on the Filters tab in the Viewer window to adjust its settings.

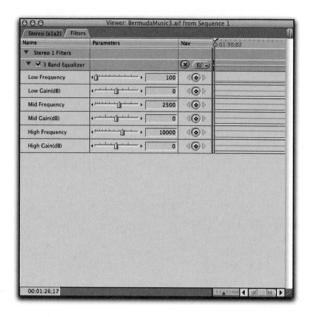

Using Audio Transitions

In addition to applying audio filters, you can also add transitions to your audio clips. Just as you would fade a video image to and from black, it is also common to fade your audio in and out. This can be accomplished by keyframing levels, or more simply by adding a Cross Fade audio transition.

FIG-11-38 Select the edit point in the sequence where you would like to place the audio transition.

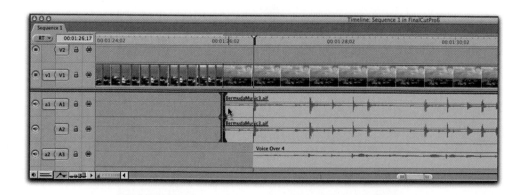

FIG-11-39 Then select Effects > Default - Cross Fade (+3dB), or press Option-Command-T.

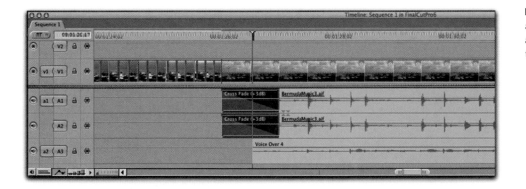

FIG-11-40 The default audio transition will appear at the edit point in the sequence.

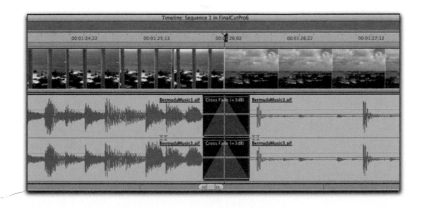

FIG-11-41 You can also add a Cross Fade between two audio clips. Keep in mind that like a video transition, enough frames need to be available to create the Cross Fade.

TIP✪ *You may want to organize your audio tracks into categories, such as dialogue, voiceover, music, ambience, and sound effects.*

TIP✪ *Refer to Final Cut Pro's User Manual, Volume III, Part I: "Exporting Audio for Mixing in Other Applications" for a detailed discussion of all of the audio export options, including exporting audio to AIFF.*

Final Steps

After you have finished adjusting the levels, adding filters and effects, and mixing the tracks, you may wish to export the audio independently of the video. You may want to take the individual audio tracks of the sequence to a post-production house for sweetening, or enhancement. Or you may choose to export the audio for DVD.

Exporting Audio

There are many options for exporting audio from Final Cut Pro. One choice is to export audio output groups as AIFF files. Final Cut Pro will export an AIFF audio file for each output channel group that is assigned to a sequence. In addition to exporting a mixed down file, you can also select to export each track grouping separately.

FIG-11-42 To export audio to AIFF, select File > Export > Audio to AIFF(s). A dialog box will open, allowing you to select the Rate, Depth, and Configuration. Stereo Mix is selected to export a single AIFF file. Click Save after you have named the file, chosen a location to save it, and selected your options.

SPOTLIGHT

In addition to all of the audio editing capabilities that are built into Final Cut Pro, you also have the option of using the standalone application Soundtrack Pro 2, which ships with Final Cut Studio. Soundtrack Pro 2 has many professional editing features, such as advanced sound design, surround and stereo mixing, and multitrack editing. Furthermore, it comes with a variety of royalty-free audio loops and sound effects to help you easily create professional soundtracks.

FIG-11-43 This is what Soundtrack Pro's interface looks like when you launch a new project.

FIG-11-44 The Browser tab allows you to easily navigate through your files. A video file is being chosen to import into this project.

FIG-11-45 You can view the video in the Video tab while you create the soundtrack.

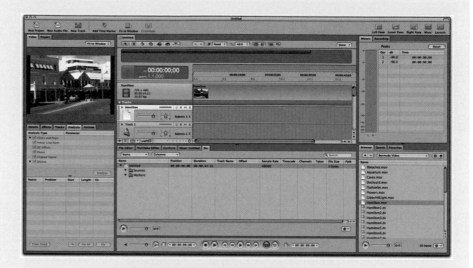

FIG-11-46 The Search tab allows you to quickly navigate through Soundtrack's loops and effects. You can even choose from a particular genre.

FIG-11-47 You can drag a loop directly from the Search tab and add it as a separate audio track. You can continue to combine loops, creating original music.

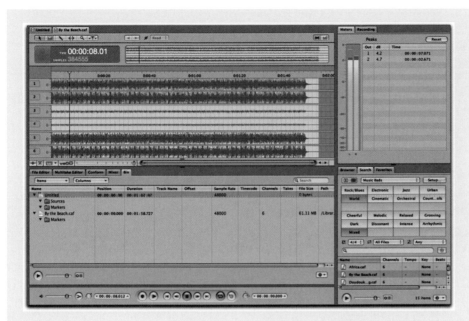

FIG-11-48 Or you can choose from Soundtrack's complete music beds and adjust the precomposed music to fit your particular project.

Summary

The audio editing capabilities in Final Cut Pro and Soundtrack Pro are vast. Even audio professionals will have plenty of tools at their disposal. But regardless of whether you are new to audio editing or an expert, the fundamental principles of good audio mixing still apply. Take advantage of Final Cut Pro's audio meters and be sure that your levels enhance your video project, rather than detract from it.

Tools > Audio Mixer	*Option-6*
Window > Audio Meters	*Option-4*
Sequence > Settings	*Command-0*
Clip Overlays button	*Option-W*
Tools > Voice Over	*Option-0*
Effects > Default - Cross Fade	*Option-Command-T*

KEYBOARD SHORTCUTS

1. Explain a sound wave and its parts.
2. Compare analog and digital audio meters.
3. What is clipped audio?
4. What is Final Cut Pro's Normalization Gain command?
5. Why use color bars and tone?
6. What does the Audio Mixer do?
7. What do the pink and purple overlay lines represent?

 REWIND

8.   What does the Voice Over Tool do?

9.   What is an audio filter? What is an audio transition?

10.   What is Soundtrack Pro?

 TAKE TWO

1.   Use the audio meters to monitor audio levels. Practice detecting audio peaks using the Normalizing Gain command and adding color bars and tone. Use the Audio Mixer to adjust levels. Also, adjust levels in the Timeline and Viewer windows. Be sure to use keyframes.

2.   Use the Voice Over Tool to record a voiceover track.

3.   Practice using audio filters and adding cross fades.

CHAPTER **12**

Rendering and Exporting

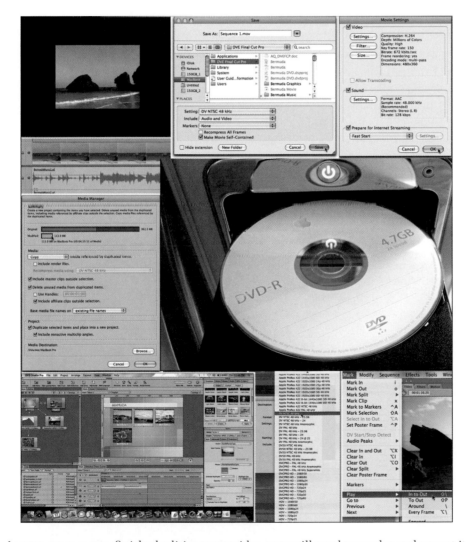

OBJECTIVES

Understand the rendering process

Learn how to prepare for export

Learn the different output methods

Understand how to export using QuickTime

Discover Compressor and DVD Studio Pro

AFTER YOU HAVE finished editing your video, you will need to render and export it. But before you can begin, you need to know how your work will be shown. Will it be broadcast on television? Burned to DVD? Or streamed over the Web? Your project's final destination will dictate which render settings and output methods you choose.

Rendering

You will need to render your final movie before you can export it. Sometimes media must be rendered before it can even be played back, depending on its codec, frame rate, and pixel dimensions. For example, MPEG-4 and H.264 are not supported by Final Cut Pro's real-time processing engine, and must first be rendered. You can determine which segments of the sequence must be rendered by looking at the **Render Status Bar** at the top of the Timeline window. Any segment with a red line requires rendering. Anything with a blue line has already been rendered. A green line signifies a real-time effect and does not require rendering for playback.

You can view and change the current render settings for a sequence at any time by selecting Final Cut Pro > User Preferences and clicking on the Render Control tab. Because rendering is time consuming, it is always prudent to review your render settings before rendering your final movie. Sometimes editors prefer to create a **test render** first, which is a quick render with lower quality or reduced settings. You can disable video filters and reduce the frame rate and size to reduce the rendering time. This can be useful if you want to check the timing of your cuts and transitions. It can also alert you to potential audio problems.

Before you render, it is a good habit to first save your project by selecting File > Save Project or pressing Command-S. Then to render a selection, select Sequence > Render Selection > Both, or press Command-R. To render everything in the sequence, select Sequence > Render All > Both, or press Option-R.

TIP ✪ *To check just the audio portion of your sequence, select Sequence > Render All > Audio. Audio renders much more quickly than video, and you can easily troubleshoot any potential problems that may necessitate an additional render.*

FIG-12-01 You can view your render settings at any time by selecting Final Cut Pro > User Preferences and clicking on the Render Control tab.

FIG·12·02 To render your entire sequence for playback, select Sequence > Render All > Both, or press Option-R.

FIG·12·03 A progress bar will appear, showing the status of the render.

Preparing to Export Video to Tape

Once you have finished rendering your final movie, you need to make preparations to export it. If you are planning to export to tape, you will first need to connect your video camera or deck to your computer. Next, you will need to choose the appropriate video and audio outputs for your equipment's configuration. Then you can select your playback settings and preferences. You will also need to confirm that you have the correct device control settings.

Connecting Equipment

If you are planning to export your project to tape, begin by connecting your video equipment. First connect your FireWire cable from the computer to your video camera or deck. Then power on the device and put it in VCR or VTR mode. Make sure a blank tape is loaded and cued up.

TIP ✪ *Some video devices use an RS-422 cable to connect to the computer, in lieu of a FireWire cable.*

FIG-12-04 Connect the FireWire cable from your computer to your video device.

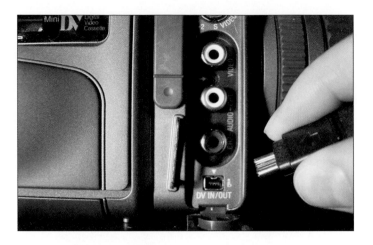

Video and Audio Outputs

After your video equipment is connected and turned on, you need to make certain that the output settings on the computer match the configuration of your video device. Select Final Cut Pro > Audio / Video Settings, and click on the A/V Devices tab. You will be able to customize your output options.

FIG-12-05 Select Final Cut Pro > Audio / Video Settings, and click on the A/V Devices tab to make certain your computer's settings match those of your video device.

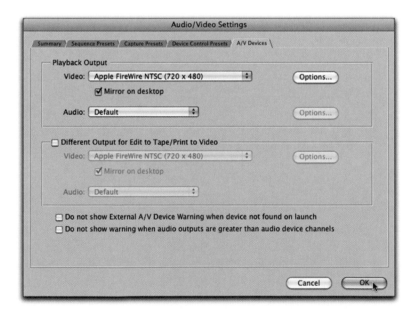

Playback Settings

In addition to controlling your output settings, you should also choose your playback settings by selecting Final Cut Pro > System Settings and clicking on the Playback Control tab. You can choose whether to record at full quality, or adjusting the playback settings and record at reduced quality.

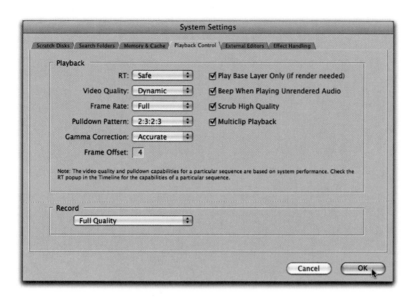

FIG-12-06 Select Final Cut Pro > System Settings and click on the Playback Control tab to control your playback settings.

Preferences

You can also control your Edit to Tape and Print to Video settings by selecting Final Cut Pro > User Preferences and clicking on the General tab. You can choose to report dropped frames that occur during playback or to abort if dropped frames should occur.

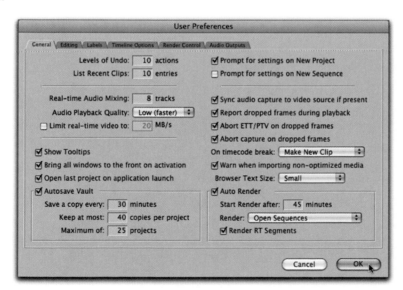

FIG-12-07 Select Final Cut Pro > User Preferences and click on the General tab to control how Final Cut Pro handles dropped frames.

Device Control

If you want Final Cut Pro to control your video device, you need to make certain the appropriate device control settings are selected. You can view your device control presets by selecting Final Cut Pro > Audio / Video Settings and clicking on the Device Control Presets tab. Or, you can modify them by selecting File > Edit to Tape and clicking on the Device Settings tab in the Edit to Tape window.

You can also use the Edit to Tape window for **blacking the tape,** which prepares a blank tape for insert editing by recording a black video signal and timecode on it.

FIG-12-08 To black the tape, select File > Edit to Tape and click on the Video tab. Then click the Black and Code button at the top of the window.

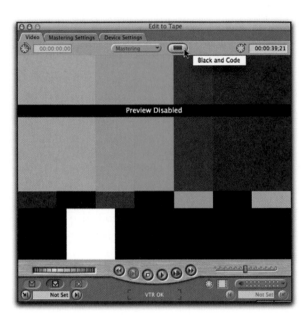

FIG-12-09 The Black and Code dialog box will open. Select the desired settings from the Settings pop-up menu and click OK.

FIG-12-10 A warning dialog box will open, cautioning you that you are about to essentially erase the tape by recording black. Click OK and the computer will automatically black the entire tape for you.

FIG-12-11 Tiffani Sherman is a producer for the Multijurisdictional Counterdrug Task Force Training Program at St. Petersburg College in Florida.

Tiffani Sherman

OCCUPATION: Video Producer, Multijurisdictional Counterdrug Task Force Training Program, St. Petersburg College, St. Petersburg, Florida
DEGREE: BA, Public Policy, Duke University
NUMBER OF YEARS IN TELEVISION AND VIDEO: Nine
NUMBER OF YEARS USING MACS: Four
NUMBER OF YEARS CREATING DV: Four
DV PROGRAMS USED: Final Cut Studio, Episode Pro, MPEG Streamclip
MACS YOU CURRENTLY USE: Mac Pro, Mac G5, Powerbook
FAVORITE DV WEBSITE: www.GeniusDV.com

1. As a video producer, what type of projects do you edit with Final Cut Pro?
I edit roll-in tapes for the broadcasts I produce and simple taped insert pieces for the broadcast. My editing skills are limited, but every time I edit a piece, I learn something new. I also work with editors on projects and it helps me to understand the editing process, so I know what can and can't be done and how difficult things can be.

2. Why did you select Final Cut Pro over other digital video applications?
While researching professional editing systems, I thought it would be easier to use and learn, and it was significantly cheaper than other professional editing systems. Before I attended a week-long Final Cut Pro editing class, I had never touched a nonlinear editor. By the end of the week, I felt comfortable with FCP, and I don't know if I could say that about other applications. I watch other people edit on other systems, and it seems a little overwhelming and not as intuitive as FCP. I also like the fact that several applications are bundled together and designed to work together. There isn't a fear the applications won't play nicely with each other like with some other editing systems.

3. What are your three favorite features or tools in Final Cut Pro and why?

I like the ease of adding transitions and filters to video. You don't have to make all sorts of changes or define parameters to create a nice transition. It's the same with filters. You can play around to find something you like and it isn't difficult to do. It's also great the system will create different clips on start/stop when digitizing HDV footage. It really speeds up the workflow because you can set up a tape, make a few mouse clicks, and walk away. When you come back, the entire tape is digitized with separate clips, and you can discard what you don't need. My favorite feature sounds silly, but it is the undo function. It's nice to know that no matter what you do, you can undo it.

4. Which other Final Cut Studio applications do you use, and what do you like about them?

I use LiveType, Soundtrack, and DVD Studio Pro. I like the fact they integrate with FCP to make using them easier and you can make nice-looking graphics without too much effort. The templates are nice places to start and are easily manipulated and customized. The royalty-free aspect of Soundtrack is a great way to create unique music that specifically fits the mood of a piece without spending hours searching online music libraries (that cost a lot to subscribe to) and CDs. You can also create the music to be as long or as short as you like. DVD Studio Pro is great for making basic DVDs of our hour-long training broadcasts with minimal effort. All you need is a QuickTime reference movie from FCP, a graphic for a menu, and a button to make it all work. Designing a basic DVD that looks good takes only minutes. I don't use Motion, but use the master templates that are in FCP, and that's a great feature because you don't really have to know how to use Motion to make them work.

5. What other digital video programs do you use and why?

I use MPEG Streamclip and Episode Pro. MPEG Streamclip is a great way to transfer footage people send us on a DVD into a QuickTime movie for use in FCP. Episode Pro is simply the best way to convert anything to anything for anyone.

6. If you could change three things about Final Cut Pro, what would they be and why?

This isn't actually my suggestion, but working with editors who use multiple professional editing systems, they like the fact effects on the Avid can become their own layer that can be manipulated independently from the clip. Also, I wish the User Preferences and System Settings had different and more descriptive names so I don't always open the wrong one. In all honesty, I really can't think of another thing to change.

7. What advice would you give an editor who is new to FCP?

I would say, accept the fact there are many different ways of doing the same thing within FCP and eventually, you'll find the one that works the best for you. People will try to say, "this is how it should be done" when you might have already found a way that works.

Exporting Methods

Once you have connected your equipment and verified your settings, you are ready to choose an export method. You can choose to output directly to videotape, or export your project using QuickTime. The method you select depends on how your project will be viewed.

Outputting to Tape

There are three primary methods for outputting to tape: Edit to Tape, Print to Video, and Record from Timeline. Outputting to tape is still the most common way to export your final movie. Popular output formats include DV formats, like DVCAM, professional analog formats, like Betacam SP, uncompressed digital formats, like Digital Betacam, and consumer analog formats, like VHS.

Edit to Tape

*The **Edit to Tape** output method is the most precise because it supports both assemble and insert editing, terms that originated in linear, tape-to-tape editing. Videotape uses a **control track,** a series of electronic pulses, to maintain consistent playback. **Assemble editing** replaces all the video, audio, control track, and timecode information beginning from the in point of the edit; however, it breaks the control track at the out point. Therefore, you cannot replace a shot in the middle of the tape. **Insert editing** never breaks the control track, and allows you to individually replace the audio, video, and timecode tracks. You need to use a blacked tape for insert editing, or a tape with an unbroken control track. Not all video devices support insert editing. The track is not wide enough in the standard DV format; however, DVCAM and DVCPRO do support insert editing. To perform assemble or insert editing, select File > Edit to Tape and use the Edit to Tape window.*

Print to Video

After the Edit to Tape method, the **Print to Video** method gives you the most control over the output process. You can record color bars and tone, black, a countdown, and a slate onto your tape. You can also choose to loop your footage multiple times. While you cannot set in and out points directly on the tape, like you can with insert editing, you can output a portion of your project by setting in and out points in your sequence. The Print to Video output method even works if your video equipment doesn't support device control. There are two ways to Print to Video: manually or automatically. The manual way to use Print to Video is to physically press the record button on your video device. This is known as **hard recording,** or **crash recording.** Or you can elect to have your computer trigger the recording process on your video device, if your video camera or deck supports device control.

TIP ✪ *Check the Black Leader box and enter a value to have black play before your project. Click the Black Trailer box and enter a value to have black play after your project.*

FIG-12-12 To manually Print to Video, first select the sequence you wish to output and set in and out points, if necessary.

FIG-12-13 Then select File > Print to Video, or press Control-M. The Print to Video dialog box will open. Customize your settings, such as Color Bars and Black. Leave the Automatically Start Recording box unchecked. Then click OK.

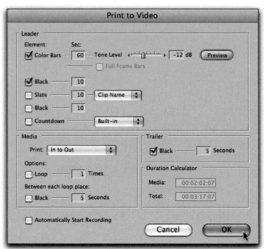

FIG-12-14 Another dialog box will open, prompting you to press record on your video device before clicking OK.

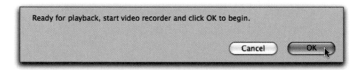

FIG-12-15 After clicking OK, the sequence will begin playing. If you opted to output bars and tone, they will play.

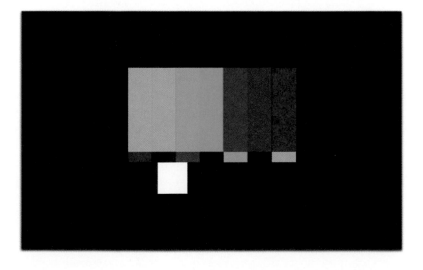

FIG-12-16 Press stop on your video camera or deck after your project finishes playing.

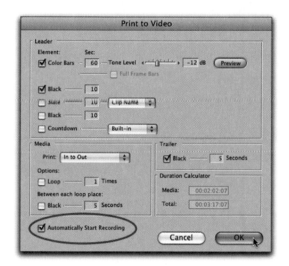

FIG-12-17 If you have device control and you want the computer to activate your recording device, check the Automatically Start Recording box.

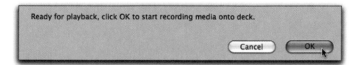

FIG-12-18 A dialog box will open, notifying you that it will start recording to tape when you press OK.

TIP ✪ *If you would like to add black before or after your project with the Record from Timeline method, you must manually build it into your sequence by using the Slug video generator.*

Record from Timeline

Alternatively, you can also use the **Record from Timeline** output method, which is the easiest. With external video output enabled, you simply press record on your video device and play your sequence from the Timeline window. This option gives you the least control.

FIG-12-19 To use the Record from Timeline method, press record on your video device and select the sequence in the Timeline. Then select Mark > Play > In to Out, or press Shift-\.

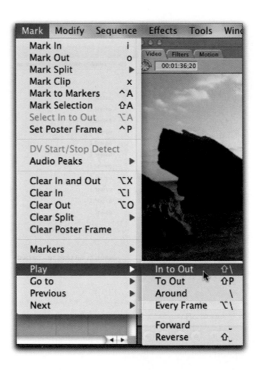

FIG-12-20 The video will play back in the Timeline window and output to your video device, as long as the Playback Output options have been properly set in the A/V Devices tab of the Audio/Video Settings.

QuickTime

In addition to outputting your project to tape, you can also export it as a QuickTime movie. You can use either the Export QuickTime Movie command or the Export Using QuickTime Conversion command.

Export QuickTime Movie

TIP *If your sequence settings match your export settings, the export process using the Export QuickTime Movie command is faster than using Export Using QuickTime Conversion, which recompresses the movie even if your settings match.*

If you select the **Export QuickTime Movie** command, you can choose audio and video settings based on Final Cut Pro's presets. You also have the option of exporting a reference movie instead of a self-contained movie. A **reference movie** points to the media in your capture and render files, rather than replicating it, and as a result saves file space. However, it is not a good method for distributing your video to other people, since they may not have access to your original stored media. A **self-contained movie**, on the other hand, stores all of the information in a single file. While it is larger, the file can easily be shared. You can also choose to export your sequence with markers for use in other applications, such as DVD Studio Pro, when you use the Export to QuickTime Movie command.

Markers

*When using the Export QuickTime Movie command, Final Cut Pro can create Chapter markers, Compression markers, Edit/Cut markers, and Scoring markers. Chapter markers are indexed points on a DVD, QuickTime Movie, or podcast. Compressor and DVD Studio Pro can recognize Chapter markers. Compression markers specify a point in time where Compressor or DVD Studio Pro should generate an MPEG I-frame, which aids in compression when there is an abrupt visual change. **Edit/Cut markers,** or **automatic compression markers,** are automatically created by Final Cut Pro at every cut and transition to alert Compressor to generate an MPEG I-frame during the compression process. Finally, Scoring markers are displayed in Soundtrack Pro to provide a visual cue for sound effects or music. You can choose which markers to export from the Markers pop-up menu: None, DVD Studio Pro Markers, Compression Markers, Chapter Markers, Audio Scoring Markers, or All Markers.*

FIG-12-21 To use the Export QuickTime Movie command, select File > Export > QuickTime Movie. The Save dialog box will open, allowing you to customize options such as creating a self-contained movie, selecting markers, and choosing a Final Cut Pro preset as the Setting. Make sure you select a hard drive with enough available free space before clicking Save.

FIG-12-22 The Writing Audio and Video dialog box will open, showing a progress bar.

Export Using QuickTime Conversion

You can also export a movie using the **Export Using QuickTime Conversion** command. This option gives you complete control over all of the settings for creating a QuickTime-compatible file. You can customize frame rate, audio and video codecs, pixel dimensions, and other options. You can export a QuickTime Movie file, an audio file, a still image or image sequence, and video for the Internet.

FIG-12-23 To use the Export Using QuickTime Conversion command, select File > Export > Using QuickTime Conversion. The Save dialog box will open, allowing you to customize your settings.

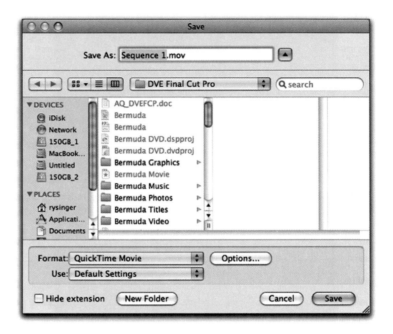

FIG-12-24 Choose a file format, such as QuickTime Movie, from the Format pop-up menu. Then click the Options button to the right.

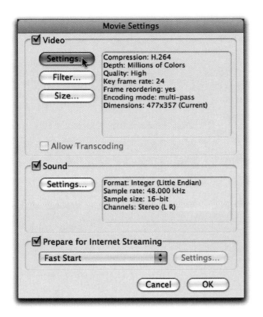

FIG-12-25 The Movie Settings dialog box will open, where you can customize the video and audio settings. Click the Settings button under Video.

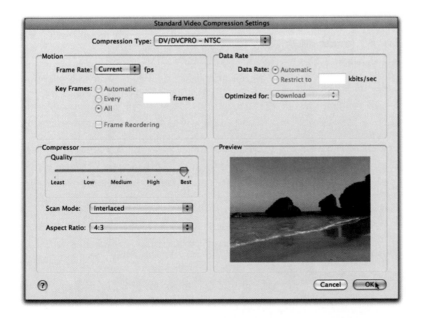

FIG-12-26 The Standard Video Compression Settings dialog box will open. Choose a setting from the Compression Type pop-up menu. You can customize Motion, Data Rate, and Compressor options. Click OK to return to the Movie Settings dialog box.

FIG-12-27 After clicking the Sound Settings button, the Sound Settings dialog box will open, where you can customize your sound options. Click OK to return to the Movie Settings dialog box.

FIG-12-28 Once you have customized your audio and video settings, click OK and a progress bar will appear.

FIG-12-29 With Export Using QuickTime Conversion, you also have the option of exporting a video frame as a still image. Position the playhead over the video frame you would like to export in either the Canvas or Timeline windows.

FIG-12-30 Then select File > Export > Using QuickTime Conversion and choose Still Image from the Format pop-up menu in the Save dialog box. Then click the Options button to the right.

FIG-12-31 The Export Image Sequence Settings dialog box will open. Choose a codec, such as TIFF, from the Format pop-up menu. Customize the options if need be and click OK to return to the Save dialog box. Name the file, designate a location to save it to, and click Save.

FIG-12-32 To export video for the Internet using the Export Using QuickTime Conversion command, select File > Export > Using QuickTime Conversion. The Save dialog box will open. With QuickTime Movie selected as the Format, choose a setting, such as Broadband-High from the Use pop-up menu. Then click the Options button to the right to view the settings.

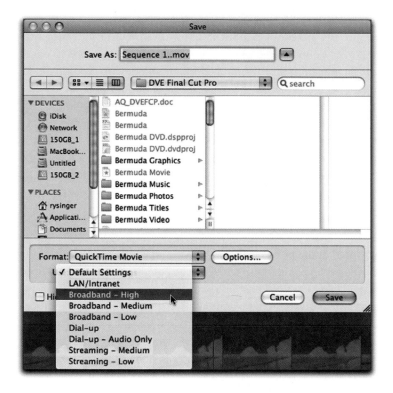

FIG-12-33 The Movie Settings dialog box will open, showing the Broadband-High settings. Click OK to return to the Save dialog box. Name the file, designate a location to save it to, and click Save.

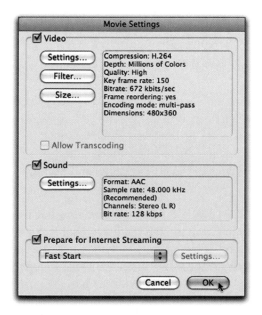

Batch Export

You may wish to render and export multiple clips and sequences at one time. Using the **Batch Export** command, you can set up an Export Queue and customize the settings for each file to be exported.

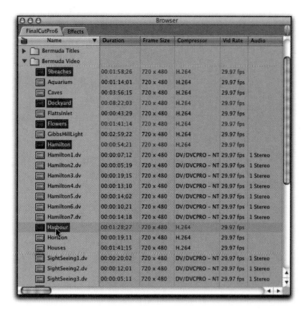

FIG-12-34 Select the items in the Browser window that you wish to export. Hold down the Command key to make multiple selections.

FIG-12-35 Then select File > Batch Export and the Export Queue window will open. With one or more items selected, click the Settings button.

FIG-12-36 The Batch 1 dialog box will open. Click the Set Destination button.

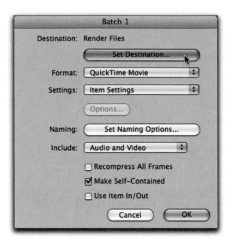

FIG-12-37 The Choose a Folder dialog box will open, prompting you to select a location to save the files. Then click the Choose button to return to the Batch 1 dialog box.

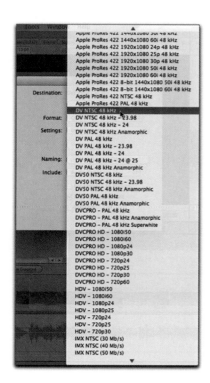

FIG-12-38 Choose a preset from the Settings pop-up menu.

FIG-12-39 When you are finished customizing your options, click OK to return to the Export Queue window.

FIG-12-40 Click the
Export button to begin the
Batch Export.

FIG-12-41 The Export
Queue dialog box will
open, displaying a
progress bar.

SPOTLIGHT

Compressor

Another option for export is to use the **Export Using Compressor** command.
Select File > Export > Using Compressor to launch Compressor. Compressor
is Final Cut Studio's standalone, professional encoding application. Compressor
allows you to assign presets for various formats—such as DVD, iPod, cell
phones, and the Internet—to multiple files for convenient conversion and
distribution.

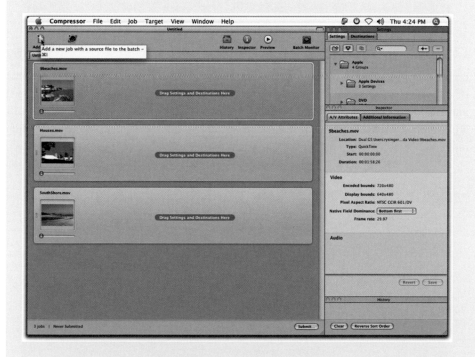

FIG-12-42 Click the
Add File button to add
a new media file to the
batch.

FIG-12-43 Then drag the desired encoding preset from the Settings tab to the media file. You can also click on the Destinations tab and drag a destination to the media file—the location where you would like the encoded file to be saved. After your files have been added and your settings and destinations have been applied, click the Submit button at the bottom of the window. Then click the Batch Monitor icon at the top of the window.

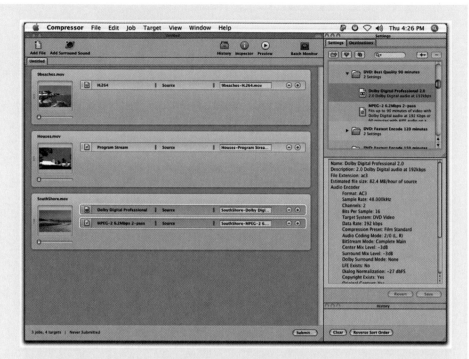

FIG-12-44 The Batch Monitor window will open, allowing you to view the progress of the encoding.

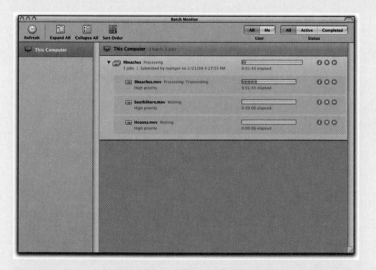

🔦 SPOTLIGHT

DVD Studio Pro

DVD Studio Pro, Final Cut Studio's professional DVD authoring program, is often used with Final Cut Pro. Chapter and Compression markers can be set in Final Cut Pro, and files can be encoded in advance using Compressor. DVDs can be played back on most standalone DVD players and on computers with DVD drives. DVD Studio Pro even supports dual-layer and high-definition DVDs.

FIG-12-45 The Advanced layout option of DVD Studio Pro is divided into four quadrants, each comprised of multiple tabs, as well as the Palette and Inspector windows, which also have tabs.

FIG-12-46 In the Templates tab of the Palette window, you can select a predesigned template to use for your project, or you can create a custom template of your own.

FIG-12-47 You can import your media files (audio, video, still images), called assets, in the Assets tab at the bottom left quadrant of the interface.

FIG-12-48 In the upper left quadrant of the interface, you can choose to view the hierarchy of your project's elements in either Graphical or Outline view.

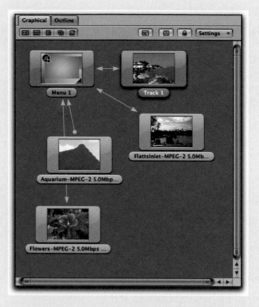

FIG-12-49 You can view and edit your video, audio, and subtitle tracks in the Track Editor in the bottom right quadrant by clicking on the Track tab.

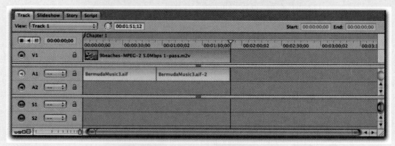

FIG-12-50 With a track selected in either the Graphical or Outline view, the Inspector will change to reveal the Track options. You can select any element in your project, such as a menu or button, and control its options in the Inspector.

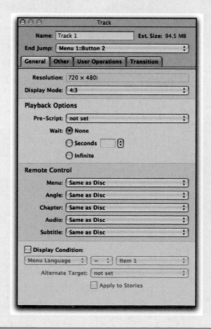

Backing Up Your Work

After you finish editing, rendering, and outputting your project, you should try to back up your work. Because digital video files are so large, it is not always feasible to keep all your project's media on hard drives. And yet, you don't want to delete all your hard work. Sometimes a client may come back years later and want to modify a project. Therefore, whenever possible, attempt to save the project file, your original timecoded video tapes, and any other digital media files, such as titles, graphics, and music. You can easily archive your project file and smaller digital media files to DVD; however, the captured video clips can be quite large. If you don't have room to back them up digitally, and your tapes have timecode, you can recapture them later, as long as you have the project file and original tapes.

FIG-12-51 Archive your project file and smaller digital media files, like titles, graphics, and music, to DVD. Also keep your original tapes with timecode.

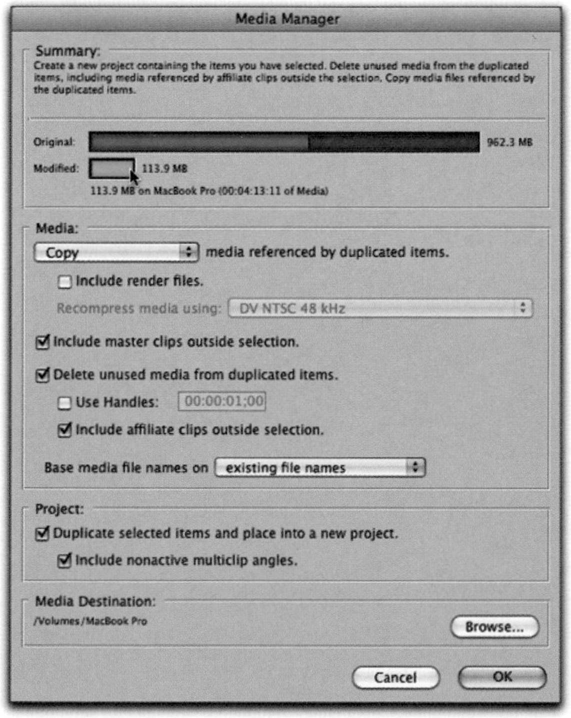

FIG-12-52 You can also use Final Cut Pro's Media Manager to help you move, copy, and delete your project's files.

Summary

Understanding how your project will be distributed will help you choose the appropriate render settings and export methods. You may choose to output your project to tape and create a QuickTime Movie. However, regardless of which method you choose for exporting your project, you may also wish to archive it, so you can return to it again at a future date. After all, editing video can be both an art form and a labor of love. When you have invested a significant amount of time and effort into a project you really enjoyed, you may find it quite difficult to delete!

KEYBOARD SHORTCUTS

Sequence > Render Selection > Both	*Command-R*
Sequence > Render All > Both	*Option-R*
File > Print to Video	*Control-M*
Mark > Play > In to Out	*Shift-*

REWIND

1. What steps should you follow for rendering?
2. What steps should you follow when preparing to export?
3. What is the Edit to Tape method of outputting video?
4. What are the steps for the Print to Video method of outputting to tape?
5. What are the steps for the Record from Timeline method of outputting to tape?
6. What is the difference between a self-contained movie and a reference movie?
7. When would you export using QuickTime Conversion?
8. What is a batch export?
9. Describe Compressor and DVD Studio Pro.
10. How and why should you back up your work?

TAKE TWO

1. Practice rendering and exporting video to tape.
2. Practice exporting QuickTime movies.
3. Explore Compressor and DVD Studio Pro.

Glossary

action safe area The outermost line of the video frame within which any action will be safely displayed in its entirety.

Add mode A transparency method where the whites, or light values, are emphasized from both images, and the blacks, or dark values, are made transparent; midrange color values that overlap are lightened.

alpha channel An extra piece of information that is written with the file, designating a portion of the image with the option of becoming transparent if later activated in another software program.

amplitude How strong, or loud, the sound wave is.

analog The traditional video signal, which is an electrical signal that fluctuates exactly like the original signal it is mimicking.

analog audio meters Audio meters that measure the signal in dB (decibels) and can range from –30 dB up to +7 dB.

Anchor Point A motion parameter used to mark the point around which the clip will move or rotate; its default is the center of the clip, but that can be changed to any other x,y coordinate.

artifact A compression anomaly that creates a distortion in an area of an image.

aspect ratio The width to height proportion of the video frame; the current NTSC video standard has a 4:3 aspect ratio.

assemble editing An editing method that replaces all the video, audio, control track, and timecode information beginning from the in point of the edit; because it breaks the control track at the out point, a shot in the middle cannot be replaced.

audio meters A feature that monitors the audio's decibel level.

audio peak marker A marker showing where audio is digitally clipping and the level should be reduced.

Audio/Video Settings Five tabs allowing you to customize Final Cut Pro to work with specific video formats and equipment.

batch capture A style of video capture in which all of the in and out points of the video clips are designated first, then the computer goes back and captures the entire list.

Batch Export A feature that sets up an Export Queue and allows you to customize the settings for each file to be exported.

batch list A special text file that contains information about all the captured clips in a project.

Bézier curve   A line with handles used to create a curve between two points.

Bézier handle   The control that is used to modify the curve of a line, which increases the bend of the line as the handle is dragged farther away from its vertex point.

bin   An individual folder in Final Cut Pro where media files are organized and stored.

bit depth   Binary numbers, or bits, that represent the audio sample; the higher the bit depth, the better the representation.

blacking the tape   Preparing a blank tape for insert editing by recording a black video signal and timecode on it.

bluescreen   A video technique used to isolate a subject by filming the subject against a blue background which will later be replaced with other footage.

Blur filter   A type of video filter that adds a blur to the entire clip or just a portion of it.

Border filter   A type of video filter that adds a border to the edges of your clips.

broadcast safe colors   A filter in most digital video editing programs, and some graphic design programs like Adobe Photoshop, that you can apply to ensure that the image's colors are safe for television broadcast.

Browser window   A Final Cut Pro window where you organize your media and determine information, such as file type, duration, frame size, and more.

Canvas window   A Final Cut Pro window that lets you view the editing sequence in the timeline.

Cartesian coordinate system or **analytical geometry**   An x,y coordinate-based system, where x is the horizontal axis and y is the vertical axis; the center of the frame is always 0,0.

CCD (charge-coupled device)   A computer chip in a video camera that converts optical images into electrical impulses.

Center   A motion parameter that marks the clip's position in the frame, using the x,y coordinate system.

Channel filter   A type of video filter that manipulates the individual red, green, blue, and alpha channels of your clips.

chapter marker   A marker that can be exported as a DVD chapter marker to DVD Studio Pro, allowing a movie to be viewed in segments called chapters on a DVD.

choker filter   A filter used to eliminate the colored fringing that occurs around the edges of the foreground subject.

chroma keying   A postproduction technique during which a specified color is selected to be keyed out, or made transparent.

chrominance   The color portion of the video signal.

Cinema Tools   Apple's software that tracks the relationship between the original film footage and its respective digital files, allowing frame-accurate, 24-fps editing for projects shot on 16mm or 35mm film, or HD.

clip   An audio, video, or graphic file in a digital video program.

clip duration   The amount of time between a clip's in and out points.

clip length   The total time of the captured clip (from the Media Start to the Media End points).

clipped audio   Any audio above 0 dBFS where the original shape of the waveform cannot be recovered.

clipping indicator   A warning that lights up during playback, alerting you to audio peaks above 0 dBFS in the floating audio meter or the Master audio meter.

CMYK   The colors used in print media to reproduce an image: cyan, magenta, yellow, and black.

codec (Compression/Decompression)   A mathematical algorithm used to decrease the file size of a video image.

Color Apple's professional color grading and finishing application that creates primary and secondary color grade adjustments for SD, HD, and 2K projects.

color bars A video clip placed at the beginning of the sequence, which serves as a reference for calibrating color at another facility.

Color Correction filter A type of video filter that allows you to control the color balance of your clips by manipulating the blacks, whites, and midtones.

color depth The number of colors represented in a video image measured in bits: 1 bit represents two colors, black and white; 8 bits is 256 colors; 16 bits is 4,000 colors; 24 bits is 16.7 million colors; and 32 bits is 16.7 million colors with 256 levels of transparency.

color matte Any single color, such as black, that fills a video frame.

component A professional video signal, in which the red, green, blue, and luminance portions are kept separate.

composite A consumer video signal, in which the chrominance and luminance portions are blended together.

composite mode A feature that uses the chrominance and luminance values of two clips to determine how those clips are blended together.

compositing, or **layering** The technique of combining multiple video layers into a single layer to achieve a special effect; the layers can be still titles, graphics, and/or video.

compression marker A marker that tells either Compressor or DVD Studio Pro where to create an MPEG I-frame during compression, reducing the possibility of artifacts.

Compressor Apple's professional encoding program for distributing media on DVD, iPod, Apple TV, mobile phones, or for streaming it over the Internet.

constant speed Speed changes that are applied to a clip will change the clip's duration, but the speed will remain constant for the duration; a slow-motion clip will have a longer duration than the original clip, whereas a sped-up clip will have a shorter duration than the original clip.

control track A series of electronic pulses used to maintain consistent videotape playback.

Crawl A text generator that creates a single line of text that moves horizontally across the frame.

credits A list of names of the people who worked on a video or film project and what their individual roles were.

crop To remove the unwanted portions of a clip by changing the clip's original in and out points.

Crop attribute A motion attribute that allows you to crop or remove the outside portion of a clip and soften the edges by feathering.

cross dissolve A common transition where one clip is superimposed over another, with the first clip fading out as the second clip fades in.

cut The simplest video transition, where one video clip ends and another begins.

Darken mode A transparency method where the darkest parts of each overlapping image are emphasized, and the whites in both images allow the overlapping areas to become transparent. Lighter midrange values are more translucent, while darker midrange values are less so.

decibel (dB) A numerical expression (dB), based on voltage or power, that represents how loud a sound is.

default transition A predetermined transition of a specified length.

desktop video A term used in the 1990s to refer to consumer digital video editing on the computer.

device control A software interface that allows your video camera or video deck to be controlled remotely from within a video editing program.

Difference mode A transparency method similar to Subtract mode; however, the darkened areas are less so.

digital filmmaking A cost-effective way for independent filmmakers to make movies by shooting digital video, editing it, and having it transferred from the computer to film.

digital full scale audio meters Audio meters that measure the signal in dBFS (decibels full scale) and can range from −60 dBFS up to 0 dBFS.

digital television (DTV) The digital video broadcast standard set forth by the FCC, which encompasses digital standard-definition television (SDTV) and high-definition television (HDTV).

digital video (DV) An analog signal converted into binary form, which is represented by a series of zeros and ones; in a broader sense, the term can encompass all digital video technology, including digital video recorders (DVRs), digital video discs (DVDs), digital cable and satellite service, as well as digital video cameras and digital video editing.

digital video card A card for a computer that converts analog video signals into digital video signals.

digital video recorder (DVR) A computerized device that records hours of television programming digitally without videotape.

Distort attribute A motion attribute that can change the shape and/or proportions of a clip.

Distort filter A type of video filter that is artistic in style and allows you to create the illusion of texture.

downloadable video A method of transmitting an entire digital video movie over the Internet to a user's computer; the copy of that movie remains on that computer until the user deletes it.

drag-to-timeline editing An editing approach where you drag a clip from the Browser window to the sequence in the Timeline window.

drop out White streaks that occur when video information is missing due to a defect in the videotape.

Drop Shadow attribute A motion attribute that creates a drop shadow behind the clip.

drop-frame timecode A format for timecode using 29.97 frames per second; the hours, minutes, seconds, and frames are separated with semicolons (00;00;00;00).

dropped frames Missing video frames that cause playback to appear stuttered, which occur when a hard drive can't keep up with the amount of information that is coming through at any given moment.

DVD (digital video disc) A new storage medium that will hold gigabytes of information on a single disc; also called digital versatile disc.

DVD Studio Pro Apple's affordable and professional DVD authoring program.

DV-NTSC The type of video compression used by FireWire (IEEE 1394).

dynamic filter A type of audio filter that adjusts the dynamic range (loud and quiet sounds) of an audio clip.

Dynamic RT Apple's technology that automatically analyzes your system and adjusts your video's quality and frame rate as it plays.

Easy Setup A preconfigured group of settings that allows Final Cut Pro to work with a specific video format.

echo and reverberation filter A type of audio filter that creates an effect to simulate a particular acoustic space, such as a large hall.

Edit Selection tool A type of Selection tool that lets you select an edit point between clips.

Edit to Tape The most precise output method that supports both assemble and insert editing.

Edit/Cut markers, or **automatic compression markers** Markers automatically created by Final Cut Pro at every cut and transition to alert Compressor to generate an MPEG I-frame during the compression process.

EDL, or **Edit Decision List** A special file that contains basic information about how the project has been edited, primarily so that it can be moved from one editing system to another.

equalization audio filter   A type of audio filter that changes the frequency of a sound.

Export QuickTime Movie   A method of QuickTime export that chooses audio and video settings based on Final Cut Pro's presets; you can choose to export a reference movie instead of a self-contained movie.

Export Using Compressor   An export option that sends the file directly to Compressor for professional encoding in a variety of formats.

Export Using QuickTime Conversion   A QuickTime export method that gives you complete control over all of the settings for creating a QuickTime-compatible file, including frame rate, audio and video codecs, pixel dimensions, and other options.

fade in from black   A cross dissolve that transitions from black to an image.

fade out to black   A cross dissolve that transitions from an image to black.

fast-start or **progressive download**   Downloadable video that can be configured to start playing while the actual download is still taking place.

Federal Communications Commission (FCC)   The government body responsible for making the laws regarding television broadcasts.

field   One of two passes during which horizontal lines of resolution are scanned to reproduce a video image on the television screen; the odd lines are scanned first, forming the first field, and the even lines are scanned second, forming the second field.

filter   A type of postproduction effect that alters an image's chrominance, luminance, or its look by manipulating its pixels.

Final Cut Express HD   Apple's midrange version of its popular professional editing application, Final Cut Pro.

Final Cut Pro   Apple's award-winning professional DV editing application.

Final Cut Studio   Apple's professional editing suite of applications that includes Final Cut Pro 6, Soundtrack

Pro 2, Compressor 3, DVD Studio Pro 4, Motion 3, and Color.

FireWire or **IEEE 1394**   A communications protocol invented by Apple Computer that allows digital video cameras and computers to transmit a digital video signal back and forth.

fit to fill edit   An edit where the speed of the clip is altered so that the clip fills, or takes up, a specified duration.

floating audio meter   A type of audio meter that shows the output levels of the Viewer or Canvas and Timeline windows.

FontMaker   Apple's utility that allows users to create their own fonts; included with LiveType.

frame   The odd and even combined video fields.

frame blending   Using two frames on either side of duplicate frames to create new frames that are a blending, or a composite, of both; used to combat strobing.

frame rate   The number of frames that are displayed in one second of video, which is measured in frames per second (fps).

frames per second (fps)   The number of frames, or still images, generated in one second to produce motion; video is 30 (29.97) fps, and film is 24 fps.

freeze frame   A video clip that freezes, or holds, a particular frame for a specified duration.

frequency   The pitch of a sound wave, measured in hertz (Hz), or cycles per second.

full-motion video   Video that runs at the 30 (29.97) fps standard.

full-screen video   The standard video resolution measured in pixels filling the entire television screen; analog video is 640 x 480 pixels, and digital video is 720 x 480 pixels.

FxPlug   Apple's new technology standard that allows third-party developers to create hundreds of real-time, hardware accelerated plug-ins.

FxPlug filters   Effects that are hardware-accelerated using Apple's OpenGL, CoreGraphics, and CoreImage technologies.

gain and normalization filter   A type of audio filter that amplifies a sound.

gap   A blank space left on the timeline after deleting a clip.

garbage matte filter   A filter that is used to help crop out the foreground subject by manipulating defined points, typically four or eight.

generation loss   The degradation of image quality caused by the duplication of an analog videotape.

Glow filter   A type of video filter that is artistic in style and allows you to create glow effects.

graphics   Computer-generated imagery that may or may not also include type.

greenscreen   A video technique used to isolate a subject by filming the subject against a green background, which will later be replaced with other footage.

Group Selection tool   A type of Selection tool that lets you select entire multiple contiguous items.

handles   Extra footage, usually one or two seconds, set at the beginning and end of each clip that can be used later in editing; typically needed when adding transitions or effects.

Hard Light mode   A transparency method where the whites and blacks in the background image interact with the overlapping midrange values, while the whites and blacks in the foreground image do not interact with the overlapping midrange values. The lighter midrange values of the background clip are screened, and the darker midrange values are multiplied.

hard recording, or **crash recording**   The manual way to use the Print to Video method by physically pressing the record button on the video device.

high-definition television (HDTV)   A television standard which uses a high resolution of either 1280 x 720 pixels (progressive) or 1920 x 1080 pixels (interlaced) and a 16:9 aspect ratio.

high-definition video (HDV)   A prosumer format that uses MPEG-2 encoding to record 16:9 high-definition video onto a standard Mini-DV tape and to stream it across standard FireWire interfaces; dubbed "HD for the masses."

iDVD   Apple's consumer DVD authoring program that allows users to easily create professional-looking DVDs that will play in most DVD players.

IEEE   The Institute of Electrical and Electronics Engineers.

Image Control filter   A type of video filter that allows you to adjust the chrominance and luminance values of your clips.

Image Mask   A type of mask filter that uses either the luma or alpha channel in one clip to create an alpha channel in another.

iMovie HD   Apple's consumer, plug-and-play digital video editing application.

in point   The numerical timecode address that marks the exact video frame where capture is to begin.

input audio meters   A feature that allows you to monitor the audio levels in the Log and Capture window.

insert edit   A type of edit that will not replace any existing media, but rather move that media to the right, farther down the timeline and out of the way.

insert editing   An editing method that never breaks the control track, and allows you to individually replace the audio, video, and timecode tracks; requires either a blackened tape or an unbroken control track.

interlaced   The method of combining two fields to form a frame; the television set is interlaced.

Key filter   A type of video filter that allows you to adjust the chrominance and luminance values of your clips.

keyframe   A video frame that marks the place in time where a particular change occurs, such as a change in size or position; keyframes are used in digital video and 3D animation.

keying A technique in which chrominance or luminance is used to make part of a video clip transparent.

Lighten mode A transparency method where the lightest parts of each overlapping image are emphasized; the lightest pixels from each clip are preserved in the composited image.

linear editing A traditional style of video editing where the program is edited consecutively from beginning to end.

LiveFonts Apple's 32-bit animated fonts that make use of color and motion.

LiveType Apple's application that makes professional titles and graphics.

long-frame marker A marker showing an abnormally long frame created during capture that can cause potential playback and output problems.

Lower 3rd A text generator, commonly used to identify a person or place, which automatically positions the text in the lower third of the frame.

luma keying A postproduction technique that uses the luminance, or brightness and darkness values, to create the transparency.

luminance The black-and-white portion of the video signal, or its lightness and darkness values.

markers Visual points of reference on clips or sequences that are used for synchronization, editing, or creating DVD chapter markers or compression markers.

mask A clip created specifically to define transparent areas in another clip.

Mask Feather A type of mask filter that allows you to feather, or soften, the edges of the clip's alpha channel by blurring them.

Mask Shape A type of mask filter that allows you to use a simple shape, such as a circle or square, as an alpha channel.

Master audio meters Individual audio meters for each audio output channel in the sequence found in the Audio Mixer window.

matte (also called a **holdout matte**) A created effect that uses information in one layer of video to reveal part of another layer of video.

Matte filter A type of video filter that allows you to mask out areas of a clip for compositing.

media The video, audio, photographs, still graphics, or motion graphics files in a digital video program.

Media Manager A Final Cut Pro feature that allows you to quickly do time-consuming tasks regarding your project and its media files.

merged clip Multiple items linked together in the timeline to create a new clip.

motion A postproduction effect that can make a video clip zoom in or out, move across the screen, rotate, or pause in place for a specified period of time.

Motion Apple's professional, real-time 3D motion graphics design program.

motion blur An effect that blurs a clip with motion that has been keyframed.

Motion Blur attribute A motion attribute that applies blurring to motion in any clip, regardless of whether the motion is part of the original clip or an effect you created.

motion path A line defined by two or more points, which illustrates movement.

Multiply mode A transparency method where the darkest parts of each overlapping image are emphasized; lighter areas in both images become more transparent, with white showing through completely, while the blacks from both images are preserved.

noise reduction filter A type of audio filter that removes unwanted electronic hums and reduces the intensity of "ess" and "P" sounds.

nondrop-frame timecode A format for timecode using 30 frames per second; the hours, minutes, seconds, and frames are separated with colons (00:00:00:00).

noninterlaced or **progressive** The method of forming a video frame by drawing all the lines of resolution in a single pass, going blank for a fraction of a second, and drawing the next frame; the computer monitor is noninterlaced.

nonlinear editing   A style of video editing which is nonconsecutive in nature; nonlinear editing is often used synonymously with professional-quality digital video.

note marker   The default marker that is added to a clip or sequence.

NTSC (National Television Standards Committee)   1. The organization responsible for the video standard used in North America and other countries; and 2. the video standard at which the signal is broadcast at 525 horizontal lines of resolution and 30 (29.97) frames per second, with a 4:3 aspect ratio.

opacity   How transparent a clip is.

Opacity attribute   A motion attribute that adjusts the degree of transparency of the clip.

out point   A numerical timecode address that marks the exact video frame where capture is to end.

Outline Text   A text generator that creates an outline around text that does not move.

out-of-synch indicator   A display that shows how many frames the audio and video portions of a clip are offset by.

Overlay mode   A transparency method where whites and blacks in the foreground image become translucent, while whites and blacks in the background image replace the overlapping areas in the foreground image. Overlapping lighter midrange values are screened, while overlapping darker midrange values are multiplied.

overwrite edit   A type of edit that places a clip at a specified point in the timeline, overwriting or replacing any media that is in the way on the track.

PAL (Phase Alternate Line)   The video standard used in the United Kingdom, Western Europe, and Africa.

Pen Delete tool or **Delete Point tool**   A tool that allows you to delete a keyframe by clicking it.

Pen tool   A tool that allows you to add keyframes by simply clicking in the keyframe graph area.

Perspective filter   A type of video filter that allows you to move a clip in space within its frame.

phase   The timing between two sound waves, measured in degrees.

pixels   Small blocks used to draw a video image.

premultiplied alpha channel   A type of alpha channel where the transparency information is kept in a separate channel, but it is also kept with the color information in the red, green, and blue channels; it is premultiplied with a color, usually white or black; also called a matted alpha channel.

Print to Video   An output method that, next to the Edit to Tape method, gives you the most control over the output process; you can record color bars and tone, black, a countdown, and a slate onto your tape and loop playback.

project file   A document that records which files are used, the order and duration the clips appear on the timeline, and what effects are used during editing.

ProRes 422   Apple's new video format that offers uncompressed HD quality at SD file sizes.

prosumer   A cross between professional and consumer.

QuickTime   A type of software compression created by Apple Computer that shrinks the size of digital video files.

QuickTime filters   A series of filters that are additional effects included with QuickTime Pro.

random access   The founding principle of digital video technology stating that it takes the same amount of time to access any file.

Range Selection tool   A type of Selection tool that lets you select multiple contiguous items, or parts thereof.

Razor Blade All tool   A tool that cuts all the media in each track along a specified point in the timeline.

Razor Blade tool A tool used to divide a clip into multiple sections.

real-time Special effects, such as basic transitions, motion, and transparency, that don't require rendering to be viewed.

Record from Timeline The easiest output method, which gives you the least control, by pressing record on your video device and playing your sequence from the Timeline window.

reference movie A QuickTime export option that points to the media in your capture and render files, rather than replicating it, and as a result saves file space.

render The process the CPU takes to carry out a particular set of instructions or tasks; the term render is commonly used to refer to the high-end calculations required to edit digital video or create 3D animation.

Render Status Bar A colored bar at the top of the Timeline window that indicates whether or not a segment requires rendering.

replace edit A type of overwrite edit that replaces the content of the sequence clip by aligning the frame at the playhead of the Viewer clip with the frame of the playhead of the sequence clip, even if no in and out points are set.

resolution The size of the video frame measured in pixels.

reverse speed The option to play a clip backwards.

RGB The three additive primary colors used to construct a video image: red, green, and blue.

ripple edit A type of edit in which the duration of a clip is altered, and the start and end times of the other clips on the track change respectively to move with it.

roll edit A type of edit in which the duration of the sequence stays the same, but the edit point between two clips shifts equally by subtracting frames from one clip and adding them to the other.

Rotation A motion parameter that revolves a clip around its center.

RT Extreme An Apple technology that harnesses the power of the Mac OS and its hardware to preview more than 150 effects in real-time for both SD and HD.

sample rate How often a signal is measured, or sampled, per second, measured in kHz; the higher the sample rate, the higher the quality.

sans-serif font A font without thin lines around the edges which reproduces well on video.

Scale A motion parameter that changes the overall size of a clip.

scoring marker A marker that provides Soundtrack Pro a visual cue for scoring.

scratch disk A hard drive that has been designated in advance by a particular software program to store specific files that the application will create.

Screen mode A transparency mode where the lightest parts of each overlapping image are emphasized; darker areas in both images become more transparent, with black showing through completely, while the whites from both images are preserved.

Scrolling Text A text generator that is used to create movie credits that roll vertically up or down the frame.

SECAM (Systeme Electronique Pour Couleur Avec Memoire) A video standard used in France, Russia, and Eastern Europe.

Select All Tracks Backward tool Selects all the media on all the tracks from a chosen point backward.

Select All Tracks Forward tool Selects all the media on all the tracks from a chosen point forward.

Select Track Backward tool Selects all the media on a track from a chosen point backward.

Select Track Forward tool Selects all the media on a track from a chosen point forward.

Select Track tool Selects all the media on a single track.

Selection tool   The default pointer that allows you to select, or choose, an item.

self-contained movie   A QuickTime export option that stores all of the information in a single file.

sequence   A series of edited media clips within a digital video project.

serif font   A font with thin lines on the points of the letters which usually does not reproduce well on video.

Sharpen filter   A type of video filter that brings out detail in clips by manipulating the contrast.

slide edit   A type of edit in which the duration of the selected clip stays the same, and the clips to either side of it adjust their durations to make room.

slip edit   A type of edit where the duration of the clip and its location stay the same, but both in and out points are changed at the same time.

Smooth Point tool   A tool that allows you to smooth a keyframe.

smoothing   The process of adding Bézier handles to specific keyframes.

snapping   A feature that allows the playhead to snap, or move directly, to edit points when it gets close to them.

Soft Edges   A type of mask filter that feathers only the edges of the video clip, ignoring any alpha channel information.

Soft Light mode   A transparency method where the whites and blacks in the foreground image become translucent, while lights and blacks in the background image replace the overlapping areas in the foreground image. Overlapping midrange color values are mixed together, differentiating Soft Light mode from Overlay mode.

sound wave   The vibration an object causes in the air, which is audible to the human ear, and includes amplitude, frequency, and phase.

Soundtrack Pro   Apple's standalone music creation program designed to allow editors to score their own video projects.

source files   The video, audio, and graphics files used in an editing project.

split edit   A technique that makes one of the linked audio or video portions longer than the other by setting different in or out points; often done for effect to soften edits.

standard-definition television (SDTV)   The new broadcast digital signal that will replace the traditional analog NTSC video standard and will be available in either standard 4:3 or widescreen 16:9 aspect ratio, but not high-definition.

still frame   A single frame of video exported to be used as a still image with other applications.

straight alpha channel   A type of alpha channel where the transparency information is kept in a separate channel, not with the color information in the red, green, and blue channels; also called an unmatted alpha channel.

streaming video   A method of transmitting video over the Internet in which the video is temporarily loaded in the system as it plays, but is not actually saved on the computer.

strobing   The stuttering playback of slow motion clips.

Stylize filter   A type of video filter that is artistic in style and allows you to create special effects.

Subtract mode   A transparency method where all the overlapped colors are darkened; the whites in the foreground image turn black, and the blacks in the foreground image become transparent. The blacks in the background image are preserved, while the whites in the background image invert the color values in the foreground image, like a film negative.

SuperDrive   Apple's combination CD-RW/DVD-R drive, first introduced in 2001, that could read and write both CDs and DVDs; today's 16x SuperDrive supports CD-R, CD-RW, DVD-R, DVD+R, DVD-RW, DVD+RW, and DVD+R DL discs.

superimpose edit   An edit where a clip is placed on the track above a clip that is already on the timeline, at the frame where the playhead is positioned.

S-video   A video signal in which the chrominance and luminance are kept separate.

System Settings   Six tabs where you control scratch disks, memory, and other options relating to how your computer is set up to work with Final Cut Pro.

test render   A render at a lower quality or with reduced settings, used to preview a project.

Text   A text generator that creates text in a single position in the frame.

text generator   A feature in Final Cut Pro that creates a title clip on a video track, which can be manipulated like any ordinary video clip.

Third-Party filters   Additional effects created by developers like CoreMelt and Noise Industries.

three-dimensional graphics   Computer-generated imagery that is created on three axes: the vertical, or Y-axis; the horizontal, or X-axis; and the depth, or Z-axis.

three-point editing   An editing approach that only requires three edit points; the software automatically calculates the fourth edit point.

Tiling filter   A type of video filter that is artistic in style and allows you to create geometric effects.

Time filter   A type of video filter that is artistic in style and allows you to create effects that appear over time.

Time Remap attribute   A motion attribute that allows you to change the speed of a clip using either constant speed changes or variable speed changes.

timecode   An electrical signal that assigns a numerical address to every frame of the videotape; timecode is measured in, and displayed as, Hours: Minutes: Seconds: Frames.

timeline   The window where individual clips are placed in chronological order to construct the edit by forming sequences.

title   A text file made up of a single word, multiple words, or phrases to provide supplementary information, to reinforce important concepts, or to clarify unusual terminology.

title safe area   The innermost line of the video frame within which any title will be safely displayed in its entirety.

Title Safe indicator   An area that is 20 percent smaller than the full video frame, where parts of the image run the risk of being cut off.

tone   An audio file placed at the beginning of the sequence, which serves as a reference for calibrating audio levels at another facility.

track meters   Individual audio meters for each track in the sequence found in the Audio Mixer window.

transition   A postproduction effect that acts as a bridge between two layers of video.

transparency   The technique of combining multiple layers into a single layer of video.

Travel Matte – Alpha mode   A transparency method where the optional background layer can be a single layer or multiple composited layers, and only a portion of it will be visible, if it is used. The middle layer requires an alpha channel, which provides the transparency. The foreground layer is on top of the background layer and is the clip to which the composite mode is actually applied.

Travel Matte – Luma mode   A transparency method where the luminance information from the clip below is used to create the transparency.

Trim Edit window   A window in Final Cut Pro that easily allows you to perform a two-sided edit.

trimming   Adjusting the frames at the edit points to fine-tune the edit.

two-dimensional graphics   Computer-generated images that are created along two axes: the vertical, or Y-axis, and the horizontal, or X-axis.

two-sided edit   A type of edit that allows you to adjust the edit point between two clips at the same time on the timeline.

Typewriter   A text generator that simulates the effect of typing directly on the screen by displaying one character at a time.

User Preferences Six tabs that allow you to customize how Final Cut Pro's features operate.

variable speed A type of speed effect where the overall duration doesn't change, but the clip's speed varies over time.

vectorscope A professional testing device used to measure the quality of a video signal by measuring the chrominance.

Video filter A type of filter that can be either artistic in style or functional for solving video related problems.

Viewer window A staging area for individual clips where you can work with the source material, as opposed to viewing your editing material in the Canvas window.

waveform monitor A professional testing device used to measure the quality of a video signal by measuring the luminance.

Index

Cengage Learning has provided you with this product for your review and, to the extent that you adopt the associated textbook for use in connection with your course, you and your students who purchase the textbook may use the Materials as described below.

IMPORTANT! READ CAREFULLY: This End User License Agreement ("Agreement") sets forth the conditions by which Cengage Learning will make electronic access to the Cengage Learning-owned licensed content and associated media, software, documentation, printed materials, and electronic documentation contained in this package and/or made available to you via this product (the "Licensed Content"), available to you (the "End User"). BY CLICKING THE "I ACCEPT" BUTTON AND/OR OPENING THIS PACKAGE, YOU ACKNOWLEDGE THAT YOU HAVE READ ALL OF THE TERMS AND CONDITIONS, AND THAT YOU AGREE TO BE BOUND BY ITS TERMS, CONDITIONS, AND ALL APPLICABLE LAWS AND REGULATIONS GOVERNING THE USE OF THE LICENSED CONTENT.

1.0 SCOPE OF LICENSE

1.1 Licensed Content. The Licensed Content may contain portions of modifiable content ("Modifiable Content") and content which may not be modified or otherwise altered by the End User ("Non-Modifiable Content"). For purposes of this Agreement, Modifiable Content and Non-Modifiable Content may be collectively referred to herein as the "Licensed Content." All Licensed Content shall be considered Non-Modifiable Content, unless such Licensed Content is presented to the End User in a modifiable format and it is clearly indicated that modification of the Licensed Content is permitted.

1.2 Subject to the End User's compliance with the terms and conditions of this Agreement, Cengage Learning hereby grants the End User, a nontransferable, nonexclusive, limited right to access and view a single copy of the Licensed Content on a single personal computer system for noncommercial, internal, personal use only, and, to the extent that End User adopts the associated textbook for use in connection with a course, the limited right to provide, distribute, and display the Modifiable Content to course students who purchase the textbook, for use in connection with the course only. The End User shall not (i) reproduce, copy, modify (except in the case of Modifiable Content), distribute, display, transfer, sublicense, prepare derivative work(s) based on, sell, exchange, barter or transfer, rent, lease, loan, resell, or in any other manner exploit the Licensed Content; (ii) remove, obscure, or alter any notice of Cengage Learning's intellectual property rights present on or in the Licensed Content, including, but not limited to, copyright, trademark, and/or patent notices; or (iii) disassemble, decompile, translate, reverse engineer, or otherwise reduce the Licensed Content. Cengage reserves the right to use a hardware lock device, license administration software, and/or a license authorization key to control access or password protection technology to the Licensed Content. The End User may not take any steps to avoid or defeat the purpose of such measures. Use of the Licensed Content without the relevant required lock device or authorization key is prohibited. UNDER NO CIRCUMSTANCES MAY NON-SALEABLE ITEMS PROVIDED TO YOU BY CENGAGE (INCLUDING, WITHOUT LIMITATION, ANNOTATED INSTRUCTOR'S EDITIONS, SOLUTIONS MANUALS, INSTRUCTOR'S RESOURCE MATERIALS AND/OR TEST MATERIALS) BE SOLD, AUCTIONED, LICENSED OR OTHERWISE REDISTRIBUTED BY THE END USER.

2.0 TERMINATION

2.1 Cengage Learning may at any time (without prejudice to its other rights or remedies) immediately terminate this Agreement and/or suspend access to some or all of the Licensed Content, in the event that the End User does not comply with any of the terms and conditions of this Agreement. In the event of such termination by Cengage Learning, the End User shall immediately return any and all copies of the Licensed Content to Cengage Learning.

3.0 PROPRIETARY RIGHTS

3.1 The End User acknowledges that Cengage Learning owns all rights, title and interest, including, but not limited to all copyright rights therein, in and to the Licensed Content, and that the End User shall not take any action inconsistent with such ownership. The Licensed Content is protected by U.S., Canadian and other applicable copyright laws and by international treaties, including the Berne Convention and the Universal Copyright Convention. Nothing contained in this Agreement shall be construed as granting the End User any ownership rights in or to the Licensed Content.

3.2 Cengage Learning reserves the right at any time to withdraw from the Licensed Content any item or part of an item for which it no longer retains the right to publish, or which it has reasonable grounds to believe infringes copyright or is defamatory, unlawful, or otherwise objectionable.

4.0 PROTECTION AND SECURITY

4.1 The End User shall use its best efforts and take all reasonable steps to safeguard its copy of the Licensed Content to ensure that no unauthorized reproduction, publication, disclosure, modification, or distribution of the Licensed Content, in whole or in part, is made. To the extent that the End User becomes aware of any such unauthorized use of the Licensed Content, the End User shall immediately notify Cengage Learning. Notification of such violations may be made by sending an e-mail to infringement@cengage.com.

5.0 MISUSE OF THE LICENSED PRODUCT

5.1 In the event that the End User uses the Licensed Content in violation of this Agreement, Cengage Learning shall have the option of electing liquidated damages, which shall include all profits generated by the End User's use of the Licensed Content plus interest computed at the maximum rate permitted by law and all legal fees and other expenses incurred by Cengage Learning in enforcing its rights, plus penalties.

6.0 FEDERAL GOVERNMENT CLIENTS

6.1 Except as expressly authorized by Cengage Learning, Federal Government clients obtain only the rights specified in this Agreement and no other rights. The Government acknowledges that (i) all software and related documentation incorporated in the Licensed Content is existing commercial computer software within the meaning of FAR 27.405(b)(2); and (2) all other data delivered in whatever form, is limited rights data within the meaning of FAR 27.401. The restrictions in this section are acceptable as consistent with the Government's need for software and other data under this Agreement.

7.0 DISCLAIMER OF WARRANTIES AND LIABILITIES

7.1 Although Cengage Learning believes the Licensed Content to be reliable, Cengage Learning does not guarantee or warrant (i) any information or materials contained in or produced by the Licensed Content, (ii) the accuracy, completeness or reliability of the Licensed Content, or (iii) that the Licensed Content is free from errors or other material defects. THE LICENSED PRODUCT IS PROVIDED "AS IS," WITHOUT ANY WARRANTY OF ANY KIND AND CENGAGE LEARNING DISCLAIMS ANY AND ALL WARRANTIES, EXPRESSED OR IMPLIED, INCLUDING, WITHOUT LIMITATION, WARRANTIES OF MERCHANTABILITY OR FITNESS FOR A PARTICULAR PURPOSE. IN NO EVENT SHALL CENGAGE LEARNING BE LIABLE FOR: INDIRECT, SPECIAL, PUNITIVE OR CONSEQUENTIAL DAMAGES INCLUDING FOR LOST PROFITS, LOST DATA, OR OTHERWISE. IN NO EVENT SHALL CENGAGE LEARNING'S AGGREGATE LIABILITY HEREUNDER, WHETHER ARISING IN CONTRACT, TORT, STRICT LIABILITY OR OTHERWISE, EXCEED THE AMOUNT OF FEES PAID BY THE END USER HEREUNDER FOR THE LICENSE OF THE LICENSED CONTENT.

8.0 GENERAL

8.1 Entire Agreement. This Agreement shall constitute the entire Agreement between the Parties and supercedes all prior Agreements and understandings oral or written relating to the subject matter hereof.

8.2 Enhancements/Modifications of Licensed Content. From time to time, and in Cengage Learning's sole discretion, Cengage Learning may advise the End User of updates, upgrades, enhancements and/or improvements to the Licensed Content, and may permit the End User to access and use, subject to the terms and conditions of this Agreement, such modifications, upon payment of prices as may be established by Cengage Learning.

8.3 No Export. The End User shall use the Licensed Content solely in the United States and shall not transfer or export, directly or indirectly, the Licensed Content outside the United States.

8.4 Severability. If any provision of this Agreement is invalid, illegal, or unenforceable under any applicable statute or rule of law, the provision shall be deemed omitted to the extent that it is invalid, illegal, or unenforceable. In such a case, the remainder of the Agreement shall be construed in a manner as to give greatest effect to the original intention of the parties hereto.

8.5 Waiver. The waiver of any right or failure of either party to exercise in any respect any right provided in this Agreement in any instance shall not be deemed to be a waiver of such right in the future or a waiver of any other right under this Agreement.

8.6 Choice of Law/Venue. This Agreement shall be interpreted, construed, and governed by and in accordance with the laws of the State of New York, applicable to contracts executed and to be wholly preformed therein, without regard to its principles governing conflicts of law. Each party agrees that any proceeding arising out of or relating to this Agreement or the breach or threatened breach of this Agreement may be commenced and prosecuted in a court in the State and County of New York. Each party consents and submits to the nonexclusive personal jurisdiction of any court in the State and County of New York in respect of any such proceeding.

8.7 Acknowledgment. By opening this package and/or by accessing the Licensed Content on this Web site, THE END USER ACKNOWLEDGES THAT IT HAS READ THIS AGREEMENT, UNDERSTANDS IT, AND AGREES TO BE BOUND BY ITS TERMS AND CONDITIONS. IF YOU DO NOT ACCEPT THESE TERMS AND CONDITIONS, YOU MUST NOT ACCESS THE LICENSED CONTENT AND RETURN THE LICENSED PRODUCT TO CENGAGE LEARNING (WITHIN 30 CALENDAR DAYS OF THE END USER'S PURCHASE) WITH PROOF OF PAYMENT ACCEPTABLE TO CENGAGE LEARNING, FOR A CREDIT OR A REFUND. Should the End User have any questions/comments regarding this Agreement, please contact Cengage Learning at Delmar.help@cengage.com.